HAMLET

Teacher's Guide

Copyright © 1988 Harcourt Brace Jovanovich Canada Inc.
55 Horner Avenue, Toronto, Ontario
M8Z 4X6

Canadian Cataloguing in Publication Data

Roy, Ken.
  Hamlet. Teacher's guide

(HBJ Shakespeare)
Supplement to: Shakespeare, William, 1564-1616.
Hamlet.
Includes text of the play.
Bibliography: p. T30-T31
ISBN 0-7747-1290-2

1. Shakespeare, William, 1564-1616. Hamlet.
I. Law, Harriet, 1931-   . II. Eisenstat, Marilyn.
III. Shakespeare, William, 1564-1616. Hamlet.
IV. Title. V. Series.

PR2807.R69 1988   822.3'3   C88-094129-4

Printed in Canada

89 90 91 92 5 4 3

HAMLET

Teacher's Guide

Series Editor: Ken Roy
Contributing Author: Harriet Law
Notes for Hamlet: Marilyn Eisenstat

Harcourt Brace Jovanovich, Canada

Toronto   Orlando   San Diego   London   Sydney

Table of Contents

Shakespeare's England

Approaches to *HBJ Shakespeare's Hamlet*

An Introduction to *HBJ Shakespeare*

PHILOSOPHY OF *HBJ SHAKESPEARE*

HBJ Shakespeare was developed in response to a growing need for an integrated language arts and student-centred approach to the study of Shakespeare. By providing a wide range of writing, speaking/listening, viewing, and independent project activities that allow for personal and creative response, this series assists students to recognize both the accessibility of Shakespeare's plays and the relevancy of the plays to their own experience, and gives them the opportunity to further explore Shakespeare in ways meaningful to them.

Students are encouraged to become familiar with and involved in the plays from the beginning of their reading by using these features common to all *HBJ Shakespeare* editions.

TEXT FEATURES

- Getting started – provides students with activities related to important themes in the play for discussion and/or written response.

- In this scene – gives students a brief scene description, allowing them to anticipate the issues they will encounter in the scene.

- For the next scene – offers students one or two predictive questions that draw upon their experience and provides them with a bridge to the next scene.

- Text notes – provide students with explanations for Shakespeare's text and help eliminate difficulties students may have with the language. These notes appear on pages that are facing the Shakespeare text and are aligned with the line(s) of text they explain.

- Illustrations – contribute detailed and historically accurate visual representations of characters and events. Illustrations appear at the beginning of each act and at the beginning of most scenes and help the students enter the world of the play.

- Activities — provide for personal writing, speaking, reading, viewing, and independent project responses from students at the end of scenes, following each act, and at the end of the play.

THE ACTIVITIES

The activities encourage students to further explore the issues they considered before and during their reading of the scenes. These interpretive and creative activities appear after all major scenes, after groupings of minor scenes, and at the end of acts. Activities that consider the whole text appear at the end of the play. Many of the activities are recommended for group work. (All the benefits of group work — such as accepting responsibility for learning, using expressive and receptive modes of communication in brainstorming, problem solving, and establishing a shared goal — can be derived as well from the study of Shakespeare as they can from any other areas of study.) In selecting and completing individual activities, students discover opportunities to:

- discuss the play, drawing upon their own experience;
- discuss and/or write about their feelings and responses to characters, situations, and concepts;
- make generalizations they can apply to new situations;
- complete independent learning projects;
- keep personal journals;
- create directors' logs;
- improvise, role play, or dramatize scene segments;
- make video recordings.

The activities at the end of acts and at the end of the play are generally intended to synthesize students' experiences of the scenes within the act. Many of these activities will require more time to complete than the end-of-scene activities.

Note: It is not expected that students should complete all activities at the end of a scene or complete activities for all scenes. Students and/or teachers should select activities appropriate to the students' interests and abilities.

HBJ Shakespeare allows students to join in the learning process by becoming actively involved in the play. We hope teachers and students will share in this dynamic experience of Shakespeare with both a feeling of comfort and a sense of confidence.

AN OVERVIEW OF THE TEACHER GUIDE

Section II of this guide offers strategies for presenting *HBJ Shakespeare* and for presenting a play in a condensed time period (approximately three to five weeks).

Section III offers historical and interpretive information about Shakespeare's England.

Section IV offers ideas for presenting *Hamlet* and includes

• suggestions for the *Getting Started* activities;

• a discussion of unfamiliar conventions (revenge, tragedy, ghosts in Elizabethan times);

• an overview of the types of activities;

• evaluation criteria;

• suggestions for presenting *Hamlet* in a condensed time period;

• a discussion of Hamlet's growth.

Suggested Strategies for Presenting *HBJ Shakespeare*

INTRODUCING AN HBJ SHAKESPEARE PLAY

If this is your students' first experience with Shakespeare, or their first experience with *HBJ Shakespeare*, you might wish to assist them in becoming comfortable with the text by allowing them time to discover and discuss the following features:

- the letter To the Reader that introduces students to the response-based approach they will find through the book and the Getting Started section that has them begin to consider important themes by drawing upon their own experience;

- the layout of Shakespeare text on right-hand pages and text explanatory notes on left-hand pages. Text notes are aligned as much as possible with the text they explain;

- Dramatis Personae – the list of characters in the play;

- visuals which appear at the beginning of each act and before most scenes;

- the "In this scene . . . " paragraphs which appear at the beginning of each act and scene and focus on important issues in the scene;

- the "For the next scene . . . " questions which appear on the page preceding each new scene and act so that students will draw upon their own experiences as they make the transition from one scene to another;

- activities which appear at the beginning of the play, at the end of most scenes, and at the end of the play. These activities have students explore many levels of thinking as they apply inferential, analytical, interpretive, and creative responses to the tasks they choose to complete individually and/or in group situations. The activities provide students with personal response-based opportunities to direct their own learning as they experience the play.

EXPERIENCING THE PLAY

You and your students might wish to discuss and record reasons for studying the play. After students have discussed and/or written their responses to the letter To the Reader and Getting Started questions, introduce the first scene by having students read "In this scene . . . " and read, view, or listen to the scene to get an overall impression of the plot and character development. Clarify any language or vocabulary difficulties students may have. Give students time to record individual responses to scenes and acts in their journals. Provide time for them to discover, react to, and record their individual responses to scenes and acts using the activities.

USING THE ACTIVITIES

The activities following scenes and acts have students use inferential, analytical, interpretive, and creative skills in their responses. Students should always be clear about the teacher's expectations for completing these tasks meaningfully. Note that because activities vary in scope and require varying lengths of time to complete, students will need assistance in selecting activities, and time provided for them to share or present their responses.

No one grouping of activities in an *HBJ Shakespeare* play will fit all class situations. It is extremely important, therefore, for the teacher to plan ahead, know the abilities and interests of the class, and have clearly stated objectives for the presentation of the scenes, acts, and activities to be undertaken.

Because many of the activities at the end of acts require more than the assignment portion of class time to complete, students should have the opportunity to work on them as the class study of the scenes progresses.

Care should be taken not to overload students with activity tasks. It is important to remember that although some students have developed skills in directing their own learning and are able to select and complete activities, others will need practice and support in developing these skills.

An overview of activities found in *HBJ Shakespeare* and strategies for facilitating student response to them follows.

Writing Activities
The writing activities present opportunities for students to write in a variety of modes and genres, for different purposes, and to different

audiences. These activities include writing items such as news articles, press releases, psychological reports, interviews, letters, journals, and editorials. To integrate a full writing program (including pre-writing, revising, and publishing activities) with the study of Shakespeare in a limited amount of time, you might choose a sequence of procedures such as the following:

Pre-writing

Pre-writing is often an on-going activity in which the student rehearses ideas for possible inclusion in writing assignments. The product of pre-writing could be a journal entry or notes made to prepare for a particular type of writing.

Students reading *Hamlet* might, for example, write a news report issued by the Palace Corps about Claudius's decision to send Hamlet to England. As a pre-writing activity they may wish to make notes about structures and styles of news reporting they observed when comparing the same news event written in several different newspapers.

Revising

Revising can occur at any time during the writing process. If students wish to have peer feedback before revising writing assignments, they could arrange peer group conferences. As a student reads his/her writing in progress, and points out a difficulty, other members of the group could offer ideas that may have worked for them in resolving a similar problem.

Publishing

Before students publish their written material, they may wish to apply a checklist including items such as points of grammar, punctuation, and syntax to their work. Students could publish a casebook or newspaper about the play, containing their writings during/at the end of the study of the play. They may prefer to put their news reports on the bulletin board following the revision stage.

Journal Activities

Students may wish to keep journals – a personal record of responses to issues in the text. Sometimes, these entries will be private reflections. Many entries, however, will be ones that students would enjoy sharing with a peer, in a group, with the teacher, or with the whole class. Teachers lend authenticity and demonstrate a commitment to writing by using the class writing time to create their own journal writing entries as writing models. These entries should also be shared.

The following is an extension of a journal activity. It is from the Act 1 "Consider the Whole Act" Activities for *Julius Caesar*.

Read through all of the journal entries you have made so far. Draw up a summary entry for Act 1. Use the following questions to help you:

- What have I discovered about the life and conditions of Rome in 44 B.C.?

- What have I learned about _____ ?
  (Fill in the name of several major characters.)

- What are some particularly interesting things about Scene 1, Scene 2, and Scene 3 in terms of the way they are presented to the audience?

Independent Learning Project Activities

Independent learning project activities provide students with the opportunity to direct their own learning as they explore new areas of study or develop skills to complete tasks they set for themselves. Many students show considerable aptitude for completing independent research and learning assignments while others may need practice and support in developing the necessary skills for acquiring knowledge independently. The independent learning project activities in *HBJ Shakespeare* are recognizable by their recommendations that students: 1) discuss the activity with the teacher and 2) keep their notes and rough drafts for the activity in a separate folder.

The following is an example of an independent activity. It is from the Act 1, Scene 1 Activities for *Romeo and Juliet*.

There are references to the mythological god and goddess Cupid and Diana in this scene. Find out as much as you can about each of these characters. What significance do they have for Romeo in this scene? Why have mythological characters such as Cupid and Diana remained so popular to readers, viewers, and writers, to the present day?

As you do research, discuss your work with the teacher to make sure you are on the right track. Keep all your notes and rough drafts in a folder.

Present a summary of your findings in an essay, a chart, or an audio-visual form at the end of the time specified for this independent activity.

The completed assignments may be presented to the teacher/class independently or in a group presentation such as a debate, a seminar, or a video presentation.

Scene Rehearsal Activities

These activities allow students to develop their dramatic perceptions of the play as they consider motivations for speeches and ways of choreographing actions, and requirements for settings and props.

When students consider the physical dimensions of an action, they often find that the dramatic content becomes clearer in their minds. For example, students often have difficulty following the sequential movement and seating arrangements in the banquet scene in *Macbeth*; but when they choreograph the scene, they gain a clearer sense of what happens and are better able to understand the cause of Macbeth's hallucinations. Likewise, when students act out the confused activity of the characters around the bushes in Act 3, Scene 1, of *A Midsummer Night's Dream*, they better understand the significance of the Duke's speech about imagination in Act 5, Scene 1.

Students could rehearse scene segments in small groups. While students are acting, you could move from group to group observing and highlighting problems they are experiencing rather than offering solutions. When students raise questions about their problems in interpreting lines dramatically, you could ask, "Why is that a problem for you?" You might ask questions such as "Would the character be standing or sitting when he/she says the lines?" "Why do you think so?" Then look for a group that has prepared an interesting interpretation of a scene segment and have them present it to the class.

Director's Log Activities

A director's log is a recording, either in note form or tape, of the ideas the group's scene-rehearsal leader wishes to keep for reference.

After a group rehearsing a scene segment chooses its director, he/she becomes responsible for conducting the group through problems it may have interpreting scene speeches and actions.

The director's log is the official record of decisions the group has reached with regard to the interpretations and the staging of the scene segment. It might include information such as

- how the group will create the scene segment,
- how the group will choreograph the action,
- where the group will place the action,
- what predominant mood the group will create for the action.

The log might also include the group's differences of opinion related to speeches, actions, and staging.

The log could record, as well, events that precede and follow the scene segment to give it context.

Directors who tape discussion related to scene-segment interpretations often find that their group gains helpful insights to the dynamics of idea-sharing by listening to the taped discussions.

The director's log activity is a useful strategy for having students combine some or all of the following skills: speaking, listening, writing, and problem-solving.

Improvisation Activities

Students often like to speculate about different characters' behaviour. By improvising, students often understand the behaviour of these characters better. It is easier for students to improvise a scene segment than it is for them to write a summary of the scene. When students improvise, they gain a sense of the character's motivation. Directors often use improvisation as a way of warming up actors for their roles. In improvisation activities, students use their imagination and their personal experiences to transform characters' speeches and so enlarge the life of the characters in their minds.

Listening Activities

Recordings
Recordings of selected scenes or specific speeches can be used to spark discussion about characters' motives and feelings.

Music
Students might enjoy choosing and taping music they feel would appropriately accompany a particular scene. A student (or group) preparing a reading of the scene could choose the music; or you could have one student (or group) prepare a reading while another prepares the "theme" music.

Viewing Activities

Film
To provide students with a sense of the whole play, you might set aside two or three periods for this viewing activity. Watching a film of the play before class study allows students to:

- acquire a sense of the plot, character relations, and shape of the play in one experience;
- appreciate the historical aspect of the play by seeing the costumes;

- gain a sense of the setting;
- become familiar with the language; and
- see the integration of language with character and actions.

Make a Video

This activity is time-consuming and requires careful planning and close monitoring. The time needed, from script to show-time, is approximately three weeks. Even the camera-shy student can become involved in the activity in some capacity. This activity stresses process as much as product and while it is a video activity, it is also a writing-process activity: it teaches concepts about narrative construction, characterization, setting, theme, and symbols, point of view; and the importance of proofreading, editing, and revising. Perhaps most important, it teaches co-operation and team work.

Although students are eager to grab a camera and begin shooting at the mere mention of the word "video," the camera shoot should always be preceded by a written or sketched series of visuals, or a "shot" list.

WHAT TO SHOOT

Establish time limits. Teachers and students should be aware that it can take from three to five classroom hours to shoot about ten minutes of finished video material. It is very important to select segments from the text that are not too long or complicated, that don't involve too many characters, that are neither too static nor too frenetic, and that are not dialogue-dominated. Have students shoot a sequence that does not go beyond fifteen minutes finished viewing time because it is simply too difficult to sustain evenness of quality in a longer shoot. Once students have decided on three or four possible scene segments, through rehearsed readings, have them test the segments.

CREATE A SHOOTING SCRIPT

This activity is the most important. It requires students to break down the text into "shooting pieces" in which the audio and the visual must support each other. The visual must highlight and support the audio (text, music, sound effects). To prepare for this part of the activity, students could divide a page in half and label one side audio and the other side video. This page will act as their storyboard. *Note: a bad storyboard is a bad video.*

When they edit their shooting script, have students consider the following:

A. Video

- Is each shot completely described? Do the visuals follow logically?
- Do the visuals maintain unity of impression? Is there an indication of what shot to use?
- Is the angle of the shots clearly indicated and is the mood consistent?
- Is the lighting effective and logical?
- Are the directions to the camera director included for each shot?
- Are the shots requiring action carefully blocked and well-rehearsed?

B. Audio

- Does the audio script support and reinforce the video portion? Will the audio fit the time allowed in the visual shot?
- Is the dialogue clear and logical? Is the audio script clear and coherent?
- Does the audio script support and balance the visual script?
- Is the audio script free from embarrassing mechanical errors?

THE FINISHED PRODUCT

- Have the videos transferred to one tape for a class video day. The class could be arranged as if students were viewing an important film screening; members of the audience could prepare and present reviews.
- The videos could be presented to a school assembly.
- The videos could provide the basis for a workshop given by the producers to students from another class who would like to undertake a similar project.
- Students might give a brief oral presentation about the importance of the writing process to the visual media.
- Finally, students could write papers on the process and difficulties of scripting a scene segment for video.

Video activities can be either group or entire class endeavours, depending on the class size. All class members can be involved with some aspect of the project. The following are some suggestions:

- technical personnel – camera operators, sound consultants, set-up staff, director, lighting consultant, set designer, prop designer, music co-ordinators

- on-camera personnel – actors, narrators, commentators
- advertising personnel – poster designers, radio ad creators, publicity personnel

EVALUATION OF THE ACTIVITIES

Evaluation is an integral part of the teaching/learning process. Handled wisely and sensitively, it can enhance the learning process provided that *objectives are clear, those objectives are communicated to the students,* and *those objectives form the basis of the evaluation process.* If careful attention is given to developing effective techniques for evaluating the process and product of students' activity-based learning, the evaluation will foster student-teacher trust, aid in measuring student progress accurately, and facilitate the entire learning process.

In *HBJ Shakespeare,* students are asked to complete activities which require the use of a wide range of skills in areas such as listening, speaking, reading, writing, viewing, problem-solving, and performing. They are asked to participate in activities by using group interaction skills and independent learning skills.

In evaluating student performance, teachers could consider these criteria:

- student understanding of the task;
- student attitude toward the task;
- variety of approaches used by the student;
- acceptance of responsibility for the task.

In group activity evaluation, teachers could consider the following:

- student willingness to accept suggestions from others;
- student attitude in discussion groups;
  - how well the student encouraged others in the group;
  - how well the student responded to suggestions from the group;
  - how well the student shared leadership and responsibility with other members of the group.

This information will help the teacher to assist the students in developing sound work habits, study and research skills, and social-interaction skills.

Throughout the *HBJ Shakespeare* activities are recommendations for students to employ *peer evaluation* as well as *self-evaluation* strategies in their approach to their learning experience.

The following are some ideas to consider in evaluating the process and product of students' work.

Writing Activities

These activities, which likely form the bulk of the student product, can be evaluated in ways such as the following:

- by formal writing assignments in which checklists are presented as the evaluation criteria;
- by journal or private writing activities;
- by a variety of writing folder activities.

Writing is usually evaluated using broad headings such as content, organization, ideas, mechanics, style, diction, use of language conventions, and originality.

Speaking activities

Evaluation of speaking skills is best accomplished in small group learning situations, dramatic enactments, role-playing activities, group and/or partner discussions, debates, interviews, panel discussions, and choral reading tasks. Speaking skills could be evaluated using criteria such as, does the student contribute ideas freely? make responses respectfully? take turns willingly?

Listening activities

Evaluation of listening skills is best accomplished during a group activity. That way student performance can be assessed in a give-and-take situation involving peers in a dynamic shared-leadership, problem-solving activity. Listening activities can be evaluated best by teacher observation of group participation in problem-solving activities.

The following checklist could be applied to the listening process:

- does the student listen quietly and attentively?
- does the student offer comments such as, "I see what you mean"; "The way I see it is . . . "; "I think this will work because . . . "; "I don't think this will work because . . . "

Problem-solving activities

Problem solving underlies all learning and happens most effectively when teachers and students are equal partners in the process. In *HBJ Shakespeare*, teachers have many opportunities to observe students' problem-solving skills as they participate in role-playing, scene-rehearsing, and other drama activities, and as they complete independent learning projects and viewing activities.

The following checklist could be applied to the problem-solving process:

- does the student hypothesize, synthesize, make analogies, and recognize possibilities?
- when considering unfamiliar concepts, does the student refer to personal experience as a basis for exploring varieties of materials in order to move from the known to unknown?
- does the student discuss, read, make educated guesses, and predictions about abstract concepts?

Independent learning project activities

In keeping with the purpose and approach of this series, the independent learning projects should be evaluated both for *process* and *product*.

In evaluating any of the *HBJ Shakespeare* activities, it is important for teachers to remember that the purposes of the activities are both to allow students to become a dynamic part of their learning experience and to encourage them to reach beyond their present abilities and extend themselves further than a teacher might take them in a teacher-centred environment.

Presenting *HBJ Shakespeare* in a Condensed Time Period

Some teachers may need to present the Shakespeare play in a condensed time period (approximately three to five weeks). The following suggestions offer ways to present the play using the student-centred approach in this series.

SINGLE FOCUS APPROACH

The class could preview part or all of the play by viewing a film to establish a focus for experiencing the play, such as one of the following:

- a main theme,
- a main character,
- the plot-line itself.

Having chosen one of the above as their primary focus in reading the text, students could then select to complete the activities related to that focus.

Single character focus

Shakespeare characters who are vital and inherent parts of the play experience and whose behaviour profoundly affects the plot development are appropriate choices for understanding and responding to the whole play through the single character focus.

In *Julius Caesar*, for example, it is Brutus (whom we first encounter in Act 1, Scene 2), whose behaviour most significantly brings the plot to its climax and denouement. The main themes of the play are revealed in his decisions and actions. Through Brutus, the personal and political conflicts of the play are resolved. Brutus, then, is a vital character in this play.

After choosing Brutus as their single character focus for *Julius Caesar*, students could direct their attention to parts of important scenes that include Brutus. Scenes such as the ones in the first two acts that introduce students to Brutus's strengths and weaknesses, and to the important decisions he makes; to the assassination scene;

the funeral scene; the final farewell between Brutus and Cassius; and Brutus's death might be considered. Students could then complete activities which focus on Brutus to further explore the language of the play, the relationships between Brutus and others, and his character.

In using the single character focus, students have an opportunity to observe and respond to the play in depth within the condensed time allotment.

STORY-TELLING AND/OR VIDEO APPROACH

A detailed study of each scene is not necessary for providing a complete learning experience of the play. It is quite possible for students to experience parts of a play without reading the script itself. Students often respond enthusiastically to the integrity and vibrancy of the dramatic experience when the play is brought to life by a story-telling or video presentation.

Similarly, students can fully appreciate the drama of the play when they see it on video. Students who are encouraged to respond critically to the choices made by actors, directors, and designers as they watch Shakespeare being performed, are likely to become enthusiastic and discriminating theatre-goers and media-viewers.

KEY SCENES APPROACH

After you and your students have previewed the play to decide what aspect (characters, theme, plot-line) is of most interest, you might designate segments of the play for attention. Below is a suggested procedure for approaching the five acts in a condensed time period.

One-third of the time for Act 1
Act 1 should be given careful attention so that characters and their motivations are clearly established, the issues and themes are made clear, and the plot is clarified. You may prefer to do this by playing a recording, by showing a video or movie version of the act, by using rehearsed readings, or by group discussions. Whatever method you choose, it should be one with which the students feel comfortable.

A focussed study of the first act of the play is important. It gives students the opportunity to identify characters and their motives, themes, and essential conflicts. Once they have familiarized themselves with the first act, students will feel more comfortable completing the activities throughout the rest of the play.

At the end of students' experience with Act 1, they may find that by completing activities from "Consider the Whole Act" they gain clearer impressions and understandings of the act's key issues.

One-third of the time for Acts 2 and 3
Select important plot development and/or character interaction scenes to use as springboards for class discussion and involvement in end-of-act/scene activities related to key issues. Since it is impossible to have students explore all the play's conflicts and themes, assist students in determining topics they may choose to develop in their activity response.

Students could make journal entry responses to scenes from Acts 2 and 3 that are not focussed during class time.

One-third of the time for Acts 4 and 5
Focus on key scenes from Acts 4 and 5. The last scene of Act 5 should include discussion about the major conflicts, issues, and themes in the play, recalling discussions about them in Act 1, so that students experience a sense of completion.

A final writing, dramatic, or viewing activity could result from this discussion. The group might wish to have a "video day" viewing of the ending of a film or video version of the play. They could choose to have a discussion about the play as tragedy (comedy, history) or to present a dramatization of selected segments of student-prepared scenes. Students might wish to debate major issues in the play.

Summing up is important because it leaves the play complete in students' minds and, although not all the issues will have been covered, students will have achieved their own experience of Shakespeare.

See Presenting *Hamlet* in a Condensed Time Period, page T44.

Shakespeare's England

HBJ Shakespeare encourages students to bring their experiences to the play. Like Shakespeare's audiences, students know about love, loyalty, taboos, leadership, revenge, identity, and ambition. As Shakespeare wrote in a time very distant from and different to our own, however, students will likely better appreciate the plays if they have some context for Shakespeare's world. You might wish to use the historical information that follows as your own resource and discuss these topics with students during their study of the play. A bibliography for Shakespeare's England appears on page T30.

WHO WAS WILLIAM SHAKESPEARE?

During Shakespeare's lifetime (1564–1616), England was ruled by Elizabeth I (1558–1603) and James I (1603–1625). Because Shakespeare was a commoner and only the nobility kept formal chronicles of themselves, we have only a few facts about his life. He was baptized on April 26, 1564, at Stratford-upon-Avon. Since it was customary to baptize on the third day, we can assume he was born on April 23. We know that he was the third of John Shakespeare's and Mary Arden's eight children and that his father was a glove-maker, a grain-dealer, and a man of some importance in the town who served as alderman and mayor.

Shakespeare attended a grammar school in Stratford-upon-Avon where the chief emphasis (as in all such schools) was on Latin. How long he remained there is not certain, but in 1583, at the age of eighteen, he married Anne Hathaway. Her home, in the adjacent village of Shottery, is now known as Anne Hathaway's cottage and has long been a main tourist attraction for Stratford visitors. The couple had three children: Susannah, born in 1583, and twins, Hamnet and Judith, born in 1585. Susannah married and had a child, Elizabeth, who also married, but she had no children. Hamnet died in 1596, at the age of eleven. Judith married, but her children did not live. In three short generations, the direct lineage of Shakespeare died out.

Sometime between 1585 and 1591, Shakespeare moved to London where we assume he spent most of his adult life. How he became an actor and a playwright we don't know, but we do know that he became one of the chief stockholders in the most important theatre company of the time (the Lord Chamberlain's Men) and a part owner of the Globe theatre. We also know that he became famous enough to draw a scathing insult from another playwright, an envious one perhaps, named Robert Greene, who called him "an upstart crow, beautified with our feathers."

When the Lord Chamberlain's Men were taken under the patronage of King James I, their name was changed to the King's Men. In this company were some of London's best actors, including Richard Burbage and Will Kempe. Shakespeare both wrote and acted for this company.

In London, Shakespeare made enough money to buy a coat of arms, giving himself the official status of "gentleman." For unknown reasons, he returned to Stratford-upon-Avon in 1612 to live in one of its finest houses, New Place. He lived there until he died, at age fifty-two, on the date of his birth.

The exact dates for Shakespeare's plays are not known. The following list gives a general frame of reference:

COMEDIES	TRAGEDIES	HISTORIES
1591		Henry VI, Part I
1592 The Comedy of Errors		Henry VI, Part II
1592 Two Gentlemen of Verona		Henry VI, Part III
1593 Love's Labour's Lost	Titus Andronicus	Richard III
1594		King John
1595 A Midsummer Night's Dream	Romeo and Juliet	Richard II
1596 The Merchant of Venice		
1596 Taming of the Shrew		
1597		Henry IV, Part I
1598 Much Ado About Nothing		Henry IV, Part II
1599 As You Like It	Julius Caesar	
1599 The Merry Wives of Windsor		Henry V
1601 Twelfth Night	Hamlet	
1602 Troilus and Cressida		
1602 All's Well That Ends Well		
1604 Measure for Measure	Othello	
1605	King Lear	
1606	Macbeth	
1607	Timon of Athens	
1607	Antony and Cleopatra	
1608 Pericles		
1609	Coriolanus	
1610 Cymbeline		
1611 The Winter's Tale		
1611 The Tempest		
1613		Henry VIII

WHAT WAS LONDON LIKE IN SHAKESPEARE'S TIME?

London in the 1590s was a bustling city of about 200,000 people. One of the first things that Shakespeare might have noticed was the great number of churches in the city. London was known as the city of churches.

The city was still walled as it had been for many years, but it was growing rapidly. People flocked to the city, causing a building boom of staggering proportions. The streets were narrow, cobble-stoned in places, but always dirty and crowded. Sanitation was unknown and plagues were common.

Shakespeare lived first in St. Helen's parish near Bishopgate Street and later near Cripplegate and across the river in Southwark. It was an exciting city for a young man from the country – full of strange sights and sounds. Since it was the age of exploration, there were many exotic sights such as clothing from the Arab countries, masks and charms from Africa, goods from China, and strange fruits and vegetables such as the tomato and the potato.

Since London was a port city, many languages were heard in the streets, such as French, Italian, Dutch, and Russian. A popular pastime was learning to speak these new languages, particularly French. Londoners received their education by reading books which spread in profusion with the advent of the printing press. It is estimated that there were over fifty printing presses in operation in London during this time. There were no public libraries or newspapers but "broadsides" (one page sheets printed on both sides) that reported news happenings in the community – especially murders, fires, deaths of important people, disasters of all kinds and, occasionally, bits of history – were sold for half a penny all over London on almost all street corners.

The streets were crammed with humanity. People begged for food and cried out for alms, shopkeepers called out to passersby to purchase their wares, balladeers sang on street corners, church bells called citizens to prayer, coaches clacked over the cobblestones, and water-bearers staggered under their loads. Londoners worked a twelve-hour day.

In addition to the noisy, sprawling markets, there were shops everywhere imaginable. Clothing was sold on London Bridge. Goldsmiths, grocers, fishmongers, and ironmongers also staked out areas to sell their wares. Even the wall around London itself gave way to shops.

Londoners loved entertainment and much of it was free. There were water games on the Thames, a small zoo in the Tower of London, cock-fights, bear-baitings, public executions, and, of course, plays, including those of Shakespeare himself, that covered just about any subject a Londoner might be interested in.

Despite the roughness of the period, it was not necessarily an unkind environment. Londoners gave generously to the poor, and London merchants experimented with various methods of finding work for the poor and the unemployed. And there was Queen Elizabeth, who made frequent appearances to the delight of the citizens.

Permanent theatres were rapidly replacing the old inn-yards as places of entertainment, and great actors were emerging to form acting troupes. New playwrights were springing up to supply the theatres with new plays. Shakespeare arrived in London when the theatres were thriving. It was a wonderful and glorious time in which to be alive and working in one of the most vibrant cities in the world.

WHAT WERE THE THEATRES FOR SHAKESPEARE'S PLAYS LIKE?

Inn-yards were favourite places for play performances in Elizabethan England because they provided a ready-made audience and because their long, narrow entrances and surrounding balconies served as makeshift theatres.

Stages were probably improvised from any available materials – some must have been quite precarious. The inn's stables and out-buildings likely would have served as change rooms, and stage properties would have been at a minimum. In the early years of these productions, performers took up a collection at the end of each play. In later years, the performers contracted with the yard-keeper to have him charge admission.

As plays grew in popularity, some actors considered having a permanent facility for their work. James Burbage, a popular actor admired by Shakespeare, built one of the first permanent theatres in 1576. To pacify the Puritans, who believed that plays were sinful, Burbage built his playhouse, called the Theatre, outside the city walls in Shoreditch. In 1577, another theatre, the Curtain, was also built in Shoreditch. The problem with Shoreditch, however, was that patrons had to walk over fields and swamps to get there. For this reason, theatre builders later chose Bankside, an area across the river from the still theatre-prohibiting city, in what is now called Southwark. In 1587 the Rose was built in Southwark, and in 1595, the Swan was erected there.

When Richard, son of James Burbage, ran into difficulties with his landlord over renewing the lease for the land on which his father's playhouse stood, he decided to move. He entered into an agreement with five of his fellow actors, one of them being Shakespeare, to build a new theatre called the Globe on Bankside in 1599. The Globe had an octagonal shape with a "thrust" stage projecting into the body of the theatre so that an audience surrounded the actors on three sides. There were three levels of balconies which enclosed the stage and an open pit in the middle that accommodated the poorer patrons. Drawings of the Globe indicate that only the balconies and some of the pit and stage were covered by a thatch roof. The rest of the theatre was exposed to the elements.

The Globe's stage was primitive by our standards. It had doors on both sides for entrances and exits and a recessed area which could serve as an inner stage. There was little room for storage or props and elaborate scenery. Above the stage recess was a balcony, and the floor had a trap door. The stage could be used, therefore, to represent heaven, earth, and hell — symbolism that would have been readily understood by an Elizabethan audience.

The Elizabethan stage provided an intimacy between actor and audience not possible in modern curtained theatres. This intimacy was sometimes hazardous for the actor if the audience were unhappy with the performance. (Some audiences, disappointed with the performances, became quite violent.) Theatrical innovations, such as the soliloquy and other devices to indicate the speedy passage of time typical of Elizabethan theatre, worked well on this simple stage.

The last big Elizabethan theatre, built in 1600, and called the Fortune, was square, unlike the O-shaped theatres that had been the norm. A stage similar to the Fortune's square stage was built in Stratford, Ontario, in the Festival Theatre, during the 1960s. Today we can see plays written by Shakespeare presented in much the same way as they had been presented for the audiences of his time.

As quickly as they sprang up, the Elizabethan theatres with their thrust stages died out, in part because they were licensed to make money for the owners, who traded on a popular interest of the time, much as rock concert promoters do today. Elizabethan theatres fulfilled a need, and when that need died, so did the theatres.

The Actors

Since all Elizabethan actors were male, all female roles were played by boys or men. It was not easy for the actors to appear convincing in female roles in broad daylight to their highly critical Elizabethan audiences. Actors were also required to perform very stylized and difficult dances that often needed both superior acrobatic skills and exceptional physical stamina. The dancing requirements were likely easy in comparison to the fight scene requirements, however. Actors were expected to fight as expert swordsmen. They needed technical skills and training as well as excellent physical conditioning to re-create duels and/or battle scenes without injuring themselves or their opponents. They had to perform actions such as running a sword through another actor's head or tearing out his entrails without impairing the opponent's usefulness for the next day's performance. Audiences of the day expected to see bloody deaths and mutilations in fight scenes. When bloodshed was involved, actors used sheep's blood because it had the right consistency for "running" well and it provided the audience with "real" blood. In stabbing scenes, actors wore concealed bladders of blood under their costumes. These bladders could be ruptured by retractable knife blades. When this action was performed correctly, the bladder worn by the char-acter being stabbed was punctured, the blood spewed forth in profusion, and the audience cheered with glee. Performed badly, the actor being stabbed was injured (not an infrequent occurrence) and had to be carted off the stage, probably also to cheers from the audience. In this case another actor had to fill in. Since acting companies were small (perhaps twelve or fifteen men), actors were required to play many parts convincingly, often on short notice, and always to a demanding audience. Acting was a hazardous occu-pation in Elizabethan England!

The Audience

They were a rough group of people, usually consisting of working-men, trade apprentices from London, seamen on leave, and country visitors to the city in search of cheap entertainment. They were frequently noisy, boisterous, and given to violent outbursts of dis-approval if their expectations were not met. They loved the sound effects, including cannons, drums, and chilling screams; the ex-travagant costumes; and the props, such as guillotines, fountains, and ladders. Most of these people stood on the ground, and so acquired their name, "groundlings." Dramatists like Shakespeare disliked these lower-class individuals and often portrayed them as humorously foolish and unsuccessful imitators of the educated peo-ple in their plays.

Surrounding the theatre were vendors, prostitutes, con-men, and pickpockets. Some patrons with money sat on benches in the bal-conies, while those who wanted to display their finery could rent stools on the stage. Members of the nobility may have attended the theatre for sheer adventure, but they usually arranged to have plays performed in their own homes.

The growing middle class attended a different type of theatre, which was indoors, had artificial lighting, special effects, a sophisticated satirical style, well-trained boy actors, and a higher entrance fee. Shakespeare's company of actors eventually purchased one of these "private" theatres (The Blackfriars), and produced many of his later plays there.

In an age in which the printing press widened literacy but could not possibly affect the lifestyle of the many illiterates, the theatre offered both a ready source of information and good entertainment.

WHAT WAS IT LIKE TO LIVE IN SHAKESPEARE'S TIME?

Shakespeare grew up in a chaotic period of history called the Renaissance. It was marked by both the vigour of powerful changes and the aftermath of drastic political upheavals. The decline of feudalism gave new importance to what would eventually become a rising middle class of merchants, shopkeepers, and professionals.

There was a sense of enthusiasm for expansion encouraged by Queen Elizabeth's emphasis on trade and travel to increase the nation's wealth. There were new ideas coming from students and teachers at the universities, and a sense of vitality in London that added to the energy and excitement.

During the Renaissance in England, guidance in spiritual matters was transferred from the Pope to the monarch, establishing the importance of individual conscience. Reformers began to look to education and the study of the classic works of Greece and Rome as alternatives to a single authority for matters of spiritual guidance.

On one hand, there were feelings of vitality, optimism, and national pride during the reign of Elizabeth. On the other hand, there was financial strain resulting from the prolonged trade wars with Spain. Toward the end of Elizabeth's reign there was also an increasing anxiety resulting from her having no heir apparent, a circumstance that would later plunge the nation into a disastrous civil war over the succession.

Shakespeare's life (1564–1616) straddled this period of hopeful change and the disillusionment that resulted from the corrupt reign of James I. Plays Shakespeare wrote during James I's reign include tragedies such as *Macbeth, Othello*, and *King Lear*.

WHAT WERE PEOPLE'S BELIEFS?

Not all people shared the same moral beliefs. Mercy, sin, pride, repentance, moderation, kingship, and God's power, however, were all central issues – important topics for sermons, for private conscience, and for literary exploration. The dramatic interest in Shakespeare's plays usually centres on the ways in which characters resolve spiritual, ethical, and political choices involving these issues. In both *Romeo and Juliet* and *The Merchant of Venice*, the issue of mercy is approached through a blending of Christian and classical ethics. In these and many other plays, Shakespeare portrayed the integration and balance of moral qualities as the basis of virtue and sound action.

"Providence," "fortune," and "chance" were important concepts to the Elizabethan people. Those who believed in Providence thought that God provided for and took care of those who trusted in Him. Protestants felt that Providence intervened directly when the winds changed in England's favour during the attempted invasion by the Spanish Armada. The evidence of providence was called fortune, a concept related to a person's fate. The image of fortune was often represented by a wheel upon which a person's career rose or fell.

Events manipulated by fortune were called "chance." Chance implies a sense of the randomness of life's incidents, which undermines any security we might have in predicting cause and effect. In *Hamlet*, we see Hamlet balance his desire for revenge with his concern that he may be misinterpreting providential "signs." In *Macbeth*, we see Macbeth realize that there are both good and evil implications in "chance": it may crown him King, but it may also expose his guilt when guardian angels "blow the horrid deed in every eye."

BIBLIOGRAPHY FOR SHAKESPEARE'S ENGLAND

The following references may be helpful to teachers and students if historical reading is desired.

Baugh, Albert C., Editor. *A Literary History of England*. Appleton-Century-Crofts, 1948

Bindoff, S.T. *Tudor England*. Penguin Books, 1969

Bowers, Fredson. *Elizabethan Revenge Tragedy*. Princeton University Press, 1966

Ferguson, Margaret F. *Rewriting the Renaissance*. University of Chicago Press, 1986

Frye, Roland Muskat. *Shakespeare and Christian Doctrine*. Princeton, University Press, 1963

Harrison, G.B. *Introducing Shakespeare*. Penguin Books, 1966

Holman, C. Hugh. *A Handbook to Literature*. Bobbs-Merrill Educational Publications, 1977

Joseph, B.L. *Shakespeare's Eden: The Commonwealth of England 1558–1629*, Blanford Press, 1971

Sandler, Robert, *Northrop Frye on Shakespeare*. Fitzhenry and Whiteside, 1986

Tillyard, Eustace M. *The Elizabethan World Picture*. Random House, 1959

Wilson, J. Dover. *Life in Shakespeare's England*. Cambridge University Press, 1962.

Approaches to HBJ Shakespeare's
Hamlet

INTRODUCTION

The activities in *HBJ Hamlet* are designed to help students discover meaning in the play by bringing their own ideas, feelings, and ex-·periences to the text. This approach aims to make the text accessible and relevant and to challenge students to deepen their understanding of this long, complex play.

The text provides a wide range of activities from which teachers and students may choose. If you are working through the activities for the first time, you may find the overview and suggestions in Strategies for Introducing *Hamlet* and the activities (pages T34-T40) helpful.

CONVENTIONS IN *HAMLET:*
GHOSTS, REVENGE TRAGEDY, AND SOLILOQUIES

Ghosts

Most students will already have basic ideas about ghosts such as the following: ghosts are troubled souls who can assume forms visible to certain living humans; they cannot rest quietly in the afterlife because of a wrong committed against them that must be corrected; ghosts who were murdered often pursue their victims. On the other hand, some students may be unfamiliar with the religious element in the play concerning ghosts—that ghosts must remain in purgatory because their sins were not absolved before they died. Students should be discouraged from thinking that ghosts are purposeless, frightening creatures who wear white Halloween costumes. The Ghost in Hamlet is a serious (but not purposely frightening) personage with a serious mission.

Revenge tragedy

The Ghost who cried for revenge was a theatrical stereotype in revenge tragedies in Shakespeare's time. Typically, the hero of a revenge tragedy was prompted by the ghost of a murdered relative or loved one to avenge the murder. Because the murdered person usually held a high status in society, and because there was a belief that the universe was an interdependent moral system, all of society was thrown out of balance by the murder. Thus the hero both avenged the individual murder and set society back in order. These revenge tragedies were also known as "tragedies of blood", reflecting the on-stage violence that audiences relished.

Shakespeare's adaptation of a revenge tragedy plot in *Hamlet* gains complexity both because of Hamlet's multi-faceted personality which blocks him from sweeping to his revenge, and because of the parallel revenge motifs in the play. Students will recognize the following parallelism: Hamlet avenged his father's murder by Claudius; Laertes avenged *his* father's murder by Hamlet. In a military subplot, we have Fortinbras Senior murdered by Hamlet Senior years before, and young Fortinbras avenging that murder by gaining the Kingdom of Denmark at the end of the play. The three avengers and their attitudes to their tasks are an interesting character analysis study.

After learning about the popularity of revenge tragedy in Shakespeare's time, students could consider some questions about popular entertainment today. Is revenge a motif of popular drama today? If so, without the prompting of ghosts, what motivates people to take revenge in modern plots? Do public figures, such as police detectives, take on the role of society's avengers in today's plots? Is the "reluctant" avenger a character that is familiar to us in modern drama? Finally, are there any television dramas or films which take popular dramatic conventions, and transform them into more complex, thought-provoking drama, as Shakespeare did in *Hamlet*?

Hamlet's soliloquies

A student-centred approach to the convention of soliloquies will help students trace the development of Hamlet's soliloquies as dynamic thinking processes rather than fixed, artificial set pieces.

The study of soliloquies might be introduced using an in-class writing activity. Students could write spontaneously about a current personal problem or preoccupation for about ten minutes. They should write privately and continuously on this topic. Sometimes their thoughts might present themselves as sentences, as clusters of words, as exclamations, or images. They should not stop or censor their writing. If their thoughts run dry, they could rewrite something they have already written until a new idea arises.

After completing the ten-minute activity, students could read it over and comment on the processing of their thoughts (not on the content). They will probably offer observations such as the following: their thoughts were repetitious or circular; they began to see the problem in a different light after writing about it; they found themselves coming back to the same idea over and over; they thought

T33

of a solution that had never previously occurred to them; the writing revealed more about their personality than they intended.

Ask them how this writing activity differed from writing a letter or having a conversation with a friend. They will probably respond that their expression was "more raw", less organized, more erratic, less coherent than their communication would be with a specific audience.

Hamlet's soliloquies could then be introduced as expressions that are close in character to the writing activity that the students have just completed. Students could look at the punctuation of Hamlet's first soliloquy (Act 1, Scene 2, lines 129-159) and observe that the exclamations and frequent pauses reflect his agitated, unprocessed thought. They might wish to trace (diagram) the way Hamlet develops his thoughts in his soliloquies, using insights about the thought process from observations they made about their own writing activity.

Once students have studied a few of Hamlet's soliloquies, they could consider what conventions fulfil the function of soliloquies in modern film. How does a movie director help us gain insight into a character's thought patterns and imagery?

Students could also consider what helps them develop their own thoughts. Some students may keep diaries, while others may find that activities such as jogging or listening to music promote development of their private thoughts.

STRATEGIES FOR INTRODUCING *HAMLET*

The *Getting Started* activities in *Hamlet* are designed to serve three purposes. They
- establish the student-centred approach;
- introduce important conflicts, themes and issues in *Hamlet*;
- introduce the use of the journal.

To create coherence in your study of *Hamlet,* consider returning to these activities, especially the third one, after completing the play. Students could decide to focus on one of the seven issues mentioned. They might choose "procrastination", for example. Having read the play, they could generate questions about Hamlet's procrastination. On the basis of these brainstormed questions, the class could then develop a thesis about Hamlet's procrastination. The next step would be to complete one of a choice of writing assignments; for example, a literary essay, a personal essay about procrastination using Hamlet as an example, or a short story.

By returning to these initial questions after completing the play, students should realize how much their own ideas have developed.

THE ACTIVITIES: AN OVERVIEW

The activities enable students to approach *Hamlet* in a variety of ways—through personal reflection, group discussion, independent writing assignments, extended research, and through performance. There are opportunities for hypothesizing, for discovering contemporary issues, for role-playing, for developing viewing and listening skills, and for exploring the world of stagecraft.

Traditional concerns such as characterization, dramatic motive, language, imagery and themes are all addressed; but the activities in *HBJ Shakespeare* allow the students to develop greater insight and to strengthen expression through their personal involvement in the play's progress.

The following overview can aid you in creating a balance of activities, focussing on specific activities and/or developing independent assignments on chosen topics.

Performance-related activties
The majority of these activities do not result in performance. Rather, they encourage students to consider some components of performance, often from the point of view of a director or actor. Without the constraints of planning an actual classroom performance, students' imaginations can range more freely.

	Activity
Act, Scene	**Brief Description**
I-CWA, 2	creating suspense (the Ghost scenes)
II-i, 3	asides (Reynaldo)
II-i, 4	blocking, body language (Reynaldo, Polonius)
II-ii, 2	costume design (Hamlet)
III-i, 5	interview of director regarding scene concept
III-i, 6	choral reading, "To be, or not to be"
III-ii, 1	discussion of Hamlet's rules of good acting
III-CWA, 3	use of props/costume to express character
IV-iv, 4	considering the staging of scene
IV-v, 3	designing a production of Ophelia's "mad" scene
V-ii, 2	considering a portrayal of Osric
CWP, 5	presenting a concept of a role, as an actor, to a director

Performance activities
I-i, 1	conveying the mood of the opening scene
I-v, 1	audiotape of the Ghost's speech

II-CWA, 1	workshop performances of scene segments
II-CWA, 2	videotape interviews; perform interviews
III-CWA, 2	prepare a version of the "dumb show"
IV-iv, 2	audiotaped reading of two passages to show different states of mind
IV-v, 5	role-play dialogue
IV-v, 6	make a video to reveal emotion
V-ii, 8	make a video conveying feelings about Hamlet
CWP. 4	videotape of a talk show with actors from a *Hamlet* production

Writing folder activities

Writing folders (instead of notebooks) encourage students to become involved in the writing process. Like an artist's studio, the writing folder contains the following: raw materials, works in progress, (temporarily) abandoned works, and finished pieces. Like the artist's studio, the writing folder becomes the repository from which the writer makes selections of what is worth exhibiting (or submitting) for evaluation. As students fill their writing folders with writing activities, make choices about what is to be polished or published, seek and record feedback, they gain a sense of their accomplishment and involvement in their work.

Suggestions for organizing and evaluating writing folders can be found in the *Evaluation* section of this guide on page T18.

Writing folder activities range from brief, spontaneous, unpolished reflections to more polished pieces that can be taken through revision and editing up to publication. (See page T10.)

Most writing folder assignments require the students to manipulate writing variables. They are asked to write in a voice other than their own, to write for a designated audience, and to write in styles that range from colloquial to formal. Generally speaking, the *diary* activities and *interior monologues* are spontaneous explorations of character and motivation; the *dialogue-writing* activities require inference skills about character and motivation; the *journalistic* reports require understanding of plot developments; the *psychological* or *anthropological* reports require the presentation of a thesis about character or behaviour, supported with evidence form the text. The following are the writing folder activities in chronological order.

I-ii, 1	newspaper report/diary/letter/psychological report about the court scene
I-iii, 3	statistical report about values
I-iii, 4	anthropologist's notes on family relationships

I-iii, 5	diary, Ophelia (reflections on Laertes' departure and Polonius' advice)
I-iv, 3	dialogue, Marcellus and Horatio
I-CWA, 5	poem using famous line as opening sentence
II-i, 5	diary, Hamlet (before and after visit to Ophelia)
II-i, 6	story, gossip about Hamlet's behaviour
II-ii, 1	letter, anonymous warning to Hamlet
II-ii, 3	interview preparation and headline for tabloid story
III-i, 1	diary, Ophelia (before and after "Nunnery Scene")
III-i, 2	paragraph describing effect of Claudius' confession
III-ii, 2	essay (thesis and supporting examples) on drama as the "mirror of nature"
III-ii, 6	diary, different responses to "The Mousetrap"
III-iii, 1	news reports (different types) announcing Hamlet's departure for England
III-iv, 6	soliloquy (interior monologue), Gertrude
III-iv, 7	letter to Hamlet commenting on his behaviour
III-iv, 8	obituary for Polonius
IV-i, 1	inner thoughts (interior monologue), Gertrude and Claudius
IV-iii, 2	psychologist's report on Claudius' and Hamlet's reactions to stress
IV-iv, 1	dialogue, Hamlet and Horatio
IV-v, 1	diary, Gertrude
IV-v, 4	psychiatrist's report on Ophelia's behaviour
IV-v, 5	dialogue, Claudius and advisor
IV-vi, 2	diary, Horatio
IV-vi, 3	letter, Hamlet to Claudius
IV-vii, 2	diary, Claudius and Laertes
IV-vii, 4	news report on Ophelia's death
IV-CWA, 4	essay on contemporary attitudes to "villains" based on interviews
IV-CWA, 5	editorial on honour
IV-CWA, 7	fable on procrastination
V-i, 2	dialogue, Horatio
V-i, 3	description from different points of view (Hamlet's return)
V-ii, 3	letter from Hamlet to Gertrude
V-ii, 7	letter from Horatio to students in Wittenberg explaining Hamlet's death
CWP, 1	monologues of three dead characters
CWP, 3	script for news report on the coronation of Fortinbras

Journal activities

The journal activities, often found in the "For the Next Scene" sections, allow students to record personal reponses to issues that will be presented in the next scene of the play. These are spontaneous explorations of experiences in their own lives which may help them to relate to what is about to happen in the play. In introducing journal activities, it is important that privacy be ensured (see page 0). However, students should be encouraged to think of ways to transform some of their initial journal thoughts into more public pieces of writing to share with classmates, e.g. personal essays, poems, short stories outlines.

Getting Started, 3	starting a journal
I-i, 3	belief in omens
I-i, FNS	different reactions to family crisis
I-ii, 4	hiding feelings toward someone
I-ii, FNS	deciding whether to follow advice of an elder
I-iv, 1	being embarrassed by the behaviour of others
I-iv, FNS	personal turning points
I-v, 5	trusting someone else as leader
I-CWA, 6	older generation's respect (or lack of respect) for younger generation
I-CWA, FNS	right of parents to "check up" on children
II-i, 7	behaviour when in love
II-ii, 7	influence of plays, movies, and TV on behaviour
II-CWA, FNS	advice to a friend in despair (contemplating suicide)
III-i, FNS	admitting guilt
III-ii, FNS	being trapped by lies
III-iii, 2	response to Claudius' prayer
III-iii, FNS	expressing anger
III-CWA, FNS	responding to others' troubles
IV-i, FNS	people who are "sponges"
IV-ii, FNS	laughing in serious situations
IV-iii, FNS	taking a stand on principle
IV-iv, 3	heroism
IV-iv, FNS	understanding changes in behaviour
IV-v, FNS	behaviour under pressure
IV-vi, FNS	uses of flattery
IV-CWA, FNS	interpreting changes in behaviour
V-i, 5	response to death of someone you know
V-i, FNS	attitude to fate

Discussion of contemporary issues

The following activities allow opportunities for discussion of contemporary social issues which are linked with events or ideas in the play:

Getting Started, 3	issues for today/Hamlet's time
I-ii, 3	ideas about marriage
I-ii, FNS	advice—deciding whether or not it is good
I-iii, 2	advising a younger brother or sister about romance
I-iii, 3	values and success
I-iii, 4	role of men and women in society
I-iii, 5	gossip
I-iii, FNS	heroism
I-iv, 2	human weakness
I-v, 3	taking the law into your own hands
I-v, 5	leadership qualities
II-i, 7	behaviour affected by being in love
II-ii, 7	influence of media/art on behaviour
III-ii, 2	realism/truth in contemporary drama
III-ii, 5	ideas about marriage
III-ii, 7	qualities of a best friend or romantic partner
IV-iii, FNS	taking a stand on principle
IV-iv, 3	heroism
IV-iv, FNS	nature of mental illness
IV-vii, 3	suicide
IV-CWA, 2	attudes towards women
IV-CWA, 3	personal qualities leading to success
IV-CWA, 4	attitudes to villains in popular culture
IV-CWA, 5	taking a stand because of honour
IV-CWA, 6	personal qualities leading to success
IV-CWA, 7	procrastination
V-i, FNS	role of fate in human life
V-ii, 1	justice and revenge
CWP, 2	advice to a friend who seems disturbed
CWP, 8	role of women
CWP, 13	ideal man or woman

Exploring imagery

These activities encourage students to explore the important image patterns of the play in a variety of ways—from recognition and interpretation, to creating their own image patterns.

I-ii, 2	exploring garden imagery
I-CWA, 1	creating an image bank

II-ii, 4	representing Hamlet's negative and positive views of the world using photographic images
III-CWA, 4	creating a visual representation of Hamlet's predicament
III-CWA, 8	applying imagery in *Hamlet* to comtemporary life
IV-ii, 1	using analogies
IV-CWA, 8	disease imagery used nowadays
V-ii, 5	personification of death—creating a visual image
CWP, 7	representing Hamlet's mind as a collage
CWP, 9	interpreting the disease and garden imagery in the play in a portfolio of drawings

Exploring themes

These activities encourage students to explore three specific themes in the play: the appearance/reality theme; the generation gap theme; and the spying theme. These activities overlap the groups of activities listed above.

- Appearance/reality theme

Getting Started, 3(b), 3(d)	playing a fool; disillusionment with adults
I-i, 3	the meaning of portents
I-ii, 5	Hamlet's concealment of his feelings
I-CWA, 3	instances of characters concealing their thoughts throughout Act I
I-CWA, 4	Hamlet's personality—different facets revealed to different people
IV-i, 1	Gertrude and Claudius dissembling to each other

- Generation gap theme

1-i FNS	different reactions to a family crisis
I-ii, 4	Hamlet's response to Gertrude's remarriage
I-ii, FNS	advice from older people
I-iii, 3	Polonius' values
I-iii, 5	Ophelia's response to Polonius
I-CWA, 6	adults' lack of respect for younger people
II-i, 3	Reynaldo's response to Polonius
II-CWA, 3	Polonius—a good father?
III-iv, 1	Gertrude seeking advice on family problems

- Spying theme

I-CWA, FNS	parents spying on children
II-i, 2	Polonius' motives for spying on Laertes
II-i, FNS	spying on a friend
III-I, 1	Ophelia's feelings about being used as "bait"

EVALUATION OF THE ACTIVITIES

In a student-centered approach, teachers are encouraged to share a range of evaluation tasks with students. It is important for senior students to participate in establishing criteria for excellence, to develop their critical skills, and to generate constructive suggestions for improvement. Working with students towards the desired level of critical awareness should begin early on in the play, so that standards of excellence are established, and methods for giving feedback for improvement are in place.

Some administrative suggestions may help you in organizing this evaluation process. Because of the variety of assignments developed to different degrees of final form, and because of the variety of activities students are completing, a common method of keeping track of activities becomes necessary. The following suggestions may help you to form your own approach. (See also pages T17 to T19 on "Evaluation of the Activities," in "Suggested Strategies for Presenting *HBJ Shakespeare*.")

Journal Writing

The journal assignments could be kept separate in a bound notebook or a separate section of the English notebook. Each journal assignment should be dated and titled, with the activity number indicated. For entries which must be kept private, students could staple the page in half vertically, and label the outside. To enable students to return to their journals to add notes or amplify ideas, suggest that they insert a right-hand margin for "later thoughts".

Some suggestions for evaluating journals follow:

• Set journal "quantity" mark for completion of assigned work.

• Make an early journal check to ensure that students are developing their thoughts as required and are using the journals, much as Hamlet used soliloquies, to explore their own thoughts and experiences and reach new insights.

• If you wish to evaluate the quality of your student journals, have them select a few journal entries to which you can respond. Students could also comment on how these journal ideas could be further developed into pieces of writing for a public audience.

• At the completion of all the journal entries, have students write their own evaluation of their journal activities, with a comment about how keeping a journal might be useful to them in the future.

Writing folder

A *Hamlet* writing folder gives students an opportunity to organize their work in a variety of ways. It is up to the teacher and class to decide which methods of organization are suitable at which stages of the study of the play. In all cases, students should keep careful track of completed assignments, giving dates, titles and references to *Hamlet* text activities. The following are some suggestions for having students organize their writing assignments:

- Divide writing into "first attempts", "work under revision" and "work ready for publication or final evaluation."

- At stages in the study of the play, call for a 'package' of material for holistic evaluation, such as 2 dialogues, one journalistic report, and one diary entry. Have students make their selections within these categories.

- Suggest that students might follow a particular theme through the play, submitting all written assignments that are related to that theme (e.g. assignments related to the theme of Ophelia's relationship with Hamlet).

The following are some suggestions for teachers and students working together to create guidelines for evaluating student work. Develop with students questions to apply to pieces of writing for the purpose of evaluation. These might be similar to the following:

- What was the writer attempting to do?
- What methods did the writer use to achieve his/her purpose?
- Were the methods successful?
- What suggestions might help improve this work in progress?"

Ask for a volunteer to submit a work in progress. (This could be submitted anonymously.) The questions should be written on the chalkboard before the work in progress is read aloud. Have members of the class respond to the questions. Keep students on track in answering the questions and make sure they support their responses with evidence from the work in progress.

Students could use the same questions when they are writing with partners or in groups. Similar questions could be adapted for use in evaluating performance and performance-related activities.

As another method of class, group, or one-to-one evaluation, a student may identify a specific problem in a work in progress; for example, "I'm not sure if I'm making Laertes too evil-sounding in this diary entry." Other students could hear the piece read aloud, and respond with comments directed *only* to the problem that the student identified.

Some suggested criteria for evaluating specific assignments:

• Formal style, thesis and supporting ideas

In the activities for Act 4, Scene 5, # 4 reads as follows: *Laertes describes Ophelia's behaviour as a "document in madness (line 176)." In the role of a court psychiatrist, write a commentary about Ophelia's behaviour. Document the behaviour first before commenting on it. You may want to make some comparisons with Hamlet's "antic disposition."*

You could apply the following questions for evaluating this activity:
1. Does the report have clear organization?
2. Is the level of language formal, objective and consistent?
3. Does the writer document his/her observations with appropriate supporting details?
4. Are the observations consistent with the *Hamlet* text?
5. In there a suitable introduction and conclusion?

• Dialogue writing assignment

In the activities for Act 1, Scene 4, # 3 reads as follows: *In pairs, take the roles of Marcellus and Horatio and write a dialogue that takes place after Hamlet has gone to follow the Ghost. Discuss Hamlet's behavior and decide what your characters should do now. Role-play your dialogue for your group.*

You could apply the following suggested questions for evaluating this activity.
1. Does the dialogue reflect the different personalities and social position of the two men, as well as their relationship to Hamlet?
2. Are their impressions consistent with what is happening in the play?
4. Is their plan of action believable and consistent?

• Performance assignment

Act 3, Scene 4, # 2

In groups of three (representing Hamlet, Gertrude and an acting coach), prepare lines 6 to 23 for dramatic reading to the class. The class should decide which readings were most effective and discuss what made them effective.

Suggested questions:
1. What kind of relationship is shown at the beginning of this dialogue?
2. What is Hamlet's mood?
3. What is Gertrude's mood?
4. What blocking or body language emphasizes these impressions of relationship and mood?

PRESENTING *HAMLET* IN A CONDENSED TIME PERIOD

The frustration of studying *Hamlet* with students in a condensed time period can be reduced by acknowledging that the whole play *cannot* be dealt with *thoroughly* in a student-centred program within a period of a few weeks. Accepting this fact, it becomes necessary to establish (in advance) which parts of the play will be studied intensively, and which parts can be left to students' independent reading, or viewing of video segments with the help of the scene focus sections provided at the beginning of the scene. The following are some suggestions that may help in this planning:

- Students need to be challenged to understand the complexities of Hamlet's personality and motivations. Decide which scenes or events (and student activities) should be examined closely to follow revelations of Hamlet's personality.

- Other characters should be examined. Decide which ones should be studied only in relationship to Hamlet. Polonius? Ophelia? Gertrude? Claudius? Laertes? Fortinbras?

- Soliloquies that reveal Hamlet's character should be investigated.

- Visually dramatic scenes have the great impact if they are viewed on video before being read. Some of these scenes are as follow: the appearance of the ghost; the nunnery scene; the players' scene; the Mousetrap; the gravediggers' scene.

- Decide which scenes or subplots could be read by students independently, without needing class, discussion or activity time.

- Read through the activities and decide which ones are likely to give them significant insights into the play.

Hamlet single character focus

If you decide that Hamlet's character and motivations should be the principal focus for your condensed study of the play, the following offers suggested scene segments for intensive study:

ACT ONE
Scene One, 1-64—Horatio joins the guards who have seen the Ghost on the battlements.
Scene Two, lines 41-159—the court scene where Claudius and Gertrude ask Hamlet to remain in Denmark; Hamlet's reply to them, and his first soliloquy.
Scene Four—Hamlet's "vicious mole" speech; appearance of the Ghost
Scene Five—Hamlet's conversation with the Ghost. His antic disposition plan.

ACT TWO
Scene One, lines 76-122—Ophelia's report to Polonius of Hamlet's visit: the first evidence of Hamlet's antic disposition.
Scene Two, lines 85-314 and lines 544-603—Polonius' theory about Hamlet's madness and his plan to "loose" Ophelia; Polonius' conversation with Hamlet; Hamlet's conversation with Rosencrantz and Guildenstern; Hamlet's soliloquy in response to the player's speech: "O what a rogue"; his plan for the play.

ACT THREE
Scene One, 57-177—Hamlet's "To Be Or Not To Be" soliloquy; the nunnery scene; Claudius's reactions.
Scene Two, lines 55-390—Hamlet's praise of Horatio; the play within the play; Hamlet's conversation with Rosencrantz and Guildenstern and his summons to his mother's room.
Scene Three, lines 37-219—Claudius' attempt to pray; Hamlet's decision not to kill him at prayer.
Scene Four—Hamlet's conversation with his mother; death of Polonius.

ACT FOUR
Scene Four—Hamlet's reaction to seeing Fortinbras' soldiers in his soliloquy (lines 31-65), "How all occasions . . ."
Scene Six—Hamlet's letter to Horatio.
Scene Seven, lines 1-162—Claudius's move to involve Laertes in his plan to rid Denmark of Hamlet.

ACT FIVE
Scene One(42-293)—Hamlet and Horatio's encounter with gravediggers; Ophelia's funeral; Hamlet's confrontation with Laertes.
Scene Two—Hamlet's description of his escape at sea; Osric's delivery of the duel challenge that will end with deaths of Gertrude, Laertes, Claudius, and Hamlet.

HAMLET: A TRAGIC HERO

> "The time is out of joint, O cursed spite,
> That ever I was born to set it right!"
> > (Act 1, Scene 5, lines 190-191)

> "The readiness is all"
> > (Act 5, Scene 2, line 213)

Hamlet's two assessments of his situation, planted at the beginning and at the end of the play, serve as foretellings of the transformation that Hamlet undergoes during this play. It is interesting to consider parallels between Hamlet's movement from the "cursed spite" view of his situation to the "readiness is all" view, with that of adolescent struggles toward adulthood today.

In Act 3, Scene 1, students learn from Ophelia about the kind of person Hamlet was before his father's death: a combination of all the virtues of the ideal man of his times, clearly fitting into the idealized role assigned to him by his society. WHAT HAPPENED? To answer this question, we should encourage our students to think beyond the response, "His father died and he was ordered by his father's ghost to avenge the murder." When students are encouraged to consider Hamlet's complex character, they may recognize parallels in their own characters, and those of people they know.

What kind of world did Hamlet live in before it was shattered? We can assume that he thrived in the ideal university setting of Wittenberg, probably making few commitments except to his intellectual development. Hamlet was admired and respected as the ideal man of his times. His parents were paragons of virtue and love. His future was assured. Thus, when he first appears in the play, it is important for students to appreciate how completely his internal world has been shattered. Even before he hears about the Ghost, he is reeling between grief over his father's sudden death, and shock and disillusion at what has happened to his mother, to the royal court, and to his own plans for the future. Life, which until now has seemed to him to be like an ordered and beautiful garden, is crawling with weeds. Students will probably recall occasions where experiences that had previously made sense were no longer reliable, or occasions in which they began to see that the adult world was not always the way it appeared to be; promises about the future were broken; the world seemed unfair and very unappealing. The meeting with the Ghost at the end of Act One emphasizes Hamlet's alienation and loneliness.

Students may criticize Hamlet's behaviour in Acts 2 and 3 as indecisive and self-pitying. They could be reminded that Hamlet is learning how to live in a world that is alien to him. Possibly the reason he cannot trust the Ghost's veracity is that he cannot be sure of *anything* anymore. His uncle, who seems to be behaving so benevolently towards him, may be a murderer as well as an adulterer. The young woman he was interested in has betrayed him. His mother, whom he once considered an ideal of love and faithfulness, is behaving despicably in his eyes. The court, which once loved his father so much, is now given to drunken celebrations. His friends Rosencrantz and Guildenstern are in the employ of the King and Queen to spy on him. With his old values lost and the new order so confused, it is no wonder that his moods swing between open disgust and passive depression.

In the light of his situation, it is interesting to consider the two plans that he develops: the antic disposition and the play within the play. Aside from the hindsight we gain that neither plan moves him very far ahead, it is interesting to note that both plans are a regression to his former student life. An antic dispositon gives him a release from responsibility, a throwback to his student days. The play within the play is like a school project, which he must conceive, write, and bring to performance. He busies himself with these regressive projects because the one task which he *must* perform, that of avenging his father's murder, he is in no way equipped to perform. Throughout these developments are his soliloquies in which Hamlet gropes to make sense of the confusion surrounding him. Students themselves may remark that if Hamlet had turned to his friend Horatio, instead of brooding in the prison of his own thoughts, Horatio might have reflected to him the futility of his efforts, and helped him to make more constructive plans.

Students may respond to the idea that, not only Hamlet, but all the young people in the play, have inherited a "rotten" world from the older generation. Even Fortinbras has inherited the older generation's military problem. Polonius summarizes the values of this adult world in his advice to Laertes when he tells Laertes to cultivate the externals and expect little from others. Then, typical of Polonius, he contradicts this cynical world view with his advice for Laertes to be true to himself. Not long after he expresses this faith in Laertes, however, he sends Reynaldo to spy on Laertes. He overrules his daughter's affections for Hamlet, and rewards her obedience by using her as bait to lure Hamlet for the King's convenience. Once students observe the sham of Hamlet's world, they should better understand his difficulty in becoming a responsible adult. Perhaps at the end of play, when Hamlet asks Horatio to report his cause aright, he is hoping that Horatio will reveal all the rottenness that Hamlet has faced.

Most people would agree that at the end of the play we feel a sense of waste. A person with great potential has been destroyed. Perhaps the particular waste that students may feel is that they have been in the presence of a person who, against great odds, finally found a way to accommodate the insane world he inherited, but died before he could experience it. Something significant happened on board the ship on his way to England. Hamlet was removed from the poisoned oppressive atmosphere around him and he could no longer resort to play-acting to solve his life-threatening problem. He returns to Denmark with a new sense of his capabilities. He is ready to acknowledge that life is short. He shows that he can break out of the prison of alienation by talking to a friend rather than by talking to himself. He can remove himself from his own situation enough to sympathize with Laertes. Whether Denmark is a prison or not, he is ready to live up to his commitment; "the readiness is all."

HAMLET

H B J   S H A K E S P E A R E

HAMLET

edited by
Marilyn Eisenstat

Harcourt Brace Jovanovich, Canada

Toronto Orlando San Diego London Sydney

HBJ Shakespeare: Series Editor, Ken Roy

Canadian Cataloguing in Publication Data

Shakespeare, William, 1564–1616
  Hamlet

(HBJ Shakespeare)
For use in high schools.
ISBN 0-7747-1268-6

I. Eisenstat, Marylin. II. Title. III. Series.

PR2807.E58 1987   822.3'3   C87-093768-5

88 89 90 91 92   5 4 3 2

Editorial Director: Murray Lamb
Senior Editor: Lydia Fletcher
Project Editor: Deborah Burrett
Production Editor: Dick Hemingway
Designer: Michael van Elsen
Illustrators: Marika and Laszlo Gal
Cover Illustrators: Marika and Laszlo Gal
Typesetter: Q Composition
Printed in Canada by Friesen Printers

Acknowledgments

The editor and publisher acknowledge the consultants
listed below for their contribution to the development of this
program:

William Boswell
former English Department Head, Westmount High School,
Protestant School Board of Greater Montreal, Montreal,
Quebec

David Bouyea
English Teacher, Lorne Jenken High School, Barrhead,
Alberta

To the Reader

You are probably already familiar with some elements of *Hamlet*—the famous soliloquy that begins with the line, "To be, or not to be: that is the question," for example, or the image of Hamlet holding a skull saying, "Alas, poor Yorick! I knew him." As you begin to read the play, you will also recognize many of the plot elements, as they are often found in movies and television dramas today. For example, murder, betrayal, friendship, destroyed love, and revenge are all part of *Hamlet*. As well, when you become familiar with Hamlet's complex, multi-faceted character, you may find yourself relating parts of his personality to your own.

This text provides you with an approach to *Hamlet* that aims both to help and to challenge you. Before reading each scene, you will have the opportunity to explore ideas or personal experiences similar to those you will read about. The short scene summaries given at the beginning of each scene will assist you to understand plot developments.

After each scene there are activities that invite you to respond in several ways to ideas and problems raised in the scene. Some involve group work and others require you to work individually. There is a wide variety of activities, ranging from private journal responses to group performances, which will encourage you to respond to ideas in different ways, and deepen your understanding of the play.

Now that you have an idea how this play will be presented, you are ready to begin your exploration of *Hamlet*.

Getting Started

Hamlet is based on an old story that Shakespeare adapted. It belongs to a tradition of revenge tragedies that were familiar to Elizabethan audiences. Tales of revenge have always been popular, and Shakespeare enriched this story with many other themes and sub-plots that still have relevance today.

1

1. Four story outlines are given below. All of these stories are found in *Hamlet*. As you read through the outlines, consider whether any of these situations are familiar to you from your own experience, or from books, television or movies.

   a) *Revenge*
      The main character is a sensitive young man who is recovering from the death of his father when he learns that someone in his own family murdered his father. There is no conclusive proof, but the main character decides to take revenge on the murderer.

   b) *Rejected Love*
      The main character (male) is in love. His girlfriend's father has forbidden her to see the young man again. She rejects the main character's advances and returns his gifts. The girlfriend and the young man are both very upset, but cope with the separation differently.

   c) *Madness*
      The main character is a young man whose comfortable life has suddenly been shattered by a violent event. He reacts to the shock by isolating himself from family and friends and either goes mad or pretends to go mad. All his relationships, including a love relationship, change as a result.

   d) *Family Pressures*
      After a young man's father dies, his mother quickly remarries someone the young man hates. The young man is disgusted by the change he observes in his mother's behaviour. He would like to escape, but his stepfather wants him to remain at home and live with them.

   In groups of three or four people, choose one of the four stories. What conflicts or themes could develop in that story? Share your findings with the class.

2. Start keeping a personal journal in which you can record your reactions both to the play itself and discussions

about it. Reflect on whether any of the ideas your group discussed, or which other groups presented to the class related to activity 1 have any relevance to your own life or to movies or television shows you have seen recently.

Keeping a journal
Your journal may be used for many different kinds of reflection as you study Hamlet. *Some of your writing will be confidential, but you may want to share some parts with your classmates and/or teacher. Decide with your teacher how to set up your journal to ensure your privacy. Using the date and a heading for each entry will help you to keep track of your developing experience of the play.*

3. *Hamlet* raises many questions that you may recognize from your own life. Thinking beforehand about some of these issues will make your experience of the play more interesting and rewarding. Discuss some of the following questions in your groups. Record in your journal any ideas you find interesting or thought-provoking. When you begin to read and discuss the play, you may want to refer to these notes and keep track of any changes in your opinions, or any surprises you find.

   a) We have all procrastinated about something important that we had to do, sometimes disappointing other people and often disappointing ourselves. Why do we procrastinate?

   b) Most people have purposely "played the fool" at some time. Why do people do this? If a person for some reason plays the fool or pretends to be disturbed for a long time, do you think the person eventually can become truly disturbed?

   c) Isolation and loneliness are feelings common to most people at one time or another. Sometimes external circumstances create this situation, and sometimes people deliberately withdraw from those around them. What can friends or relatives do when someone has purposely withdrawn and chosen to be alone with his or her problems?

d) Disillusion is a common experience of growing up. We find that people in the adult world whom we once idealized are less than ideal, and that situations we considered innocent are actually corrupt. How do young people encountering the "real world" for the first time handle these discoveries?

e) In Shakespeare's time, insane people were regarded as sources of entertainment. What is our society's attitude toward mental illness?

f) What is the difference between "taking revenge" and "getting justice"?

g) Privacy is highly valued in our society. How would you feel if you found out that you were "under surveillance" at school, at your job, at home, or among friends because of some change in your behaviour?

Having thought about this wide range of topics, you are ready to explore *Hamlet*.

Dramatis Personae

(Characters in the Play)

Claudius, King of Denmark
Hamlet, son to the late and nephew to the present King
Polonius, Lord Chamberlain
Horatio, friend to Hamlet
Laertes, son to Polonius
Voltimand
Cornelius
Rosencrantz   courtiers
Guildenstern
Osric
A Gentleman
A Priest
Marcellus   officers
Bernardo
Francisco, a soldier
Reynaldo, servant to Polonius
Players
Two clowns, grave-diggers
A Captain
English Ambassadors
Fortinbras, Prince of Norway
Gertrude, Queen of Denmark and mother to Hamlet
Ophelia, daughter to Polonius
Lords, Ladies, Officers, Soldiers, Players, Sailors,
    Messengers, and other Attendants
Ghost of Hamlet's father

Scene: Elsinore

5

Act 1, Scene 1

In this scene . . .

The play begins on the outer ramparts of the King's palace in Elsinore, the capital of Old Denmark. It is midnight. Bernardo has come to take over guard duty from Francisco. As they exchange greetings, Marcellus, another guard, approaches. He has brought along Horatio, a scholar, to verify the appearance of the ghost of old King Hamlet, who died recently. The Ghost appears twice, and Horatio, who was skeptical at first, is convinced of its presence. He promises to report the Ghost's appearance to his friend, Prince Hamlet, the son of the dead king.

Stage direction

platform: the ramparts or walls, where soldiers would keep watch

2   *unfold yourself:* identify yourself

3   *Long live the king:* the watchword for the night

6   *carefully:* precisely

12   *rivals:* partners

15   *the Dane:* King of Denmark

16   *Give you good night:* May God give you a good night.

Act 1, Scene 1

*Elsinore. A platform before
the castle.*

*Francisco on his post. Enter
to him Bernardo*

Bernardo: Who's there?
Francisco: Nay, answer me: stand, and unfold yourself.
Bernardo: Long live the king!
Francisco: Bernardo?
Bernardo: He.   5
Francisco: You come most carefully upon your hour.
Bernardo: 'Tis now struck twelve; get thee to bed, Francisco.
Francisco: For this relief much thanks: 'tis bitter cold,
    And I am sick at heart.
Bernardo: Have you had quiet guard?
Francisco: Not a mouse stirring.   10
Bernardo: Well, good night.
    If you do meet Horatio and Marcellus,
    The rivals of my watch, bid them make haste.
Francisco: I think I hear them. Stand, ho! who is there?

[*Enter Horatio and Marcellus.*]

Horatio: Friends to this ground.
Marcellus: And liegemen to the Dane.   15
Francisco: Give you good night.
Marcellus: O, farewell, honest soldier:
    Who hath relieved you?
Francisco: Bernardo hath my place.
    Give you good night.   [*Exit Francisco.*]
Marcellus: Holla! Bernardo!
Bernardo: Say,
    What, is Horatio there?

19   *a piece of him:* Different interpretations of this phrase have been given. Some people think Horatio means he is present in body but not in spirit (he wishes he were somewhere else). Others think he is referring to the cold, and still others that he is offering his hand to Bernardo. At any rate, Horatio seems to be making light of the situation.

23   *fantasy:* imagination

28   *apparition:* ghost

29   *He may approve our eyes:* He may confirm with his own eyes what we have seen.

31   *assail your ears:* force you to listen

36   *the pole:* the North Star, also known as the pole star

42   *Thou art a scholar:* Being an educated man, Horatio will know how to speak to the Ghost, perhaps in Latin.

44   *harrows:* stirs. A harrow is a heavy farm implement used to turn the soil.

45   *It would . . . to:* It was believed ghosts could not speak until they were spoken to first.

48   *buried Denmark:* the dead King of Denmark

49   *sometimes:* formerly

Horatio: A piece of him.

Bernardo: Welcome, Horatio; welcome, good Marcellus. 20

Marcellus: What, has this thing appear'd again tonight?

Bernardo: I have seen nothing.

Marcellus: Horatio says 'tis but our fantasy,
And will not let belief take hold of him
Touching this dreaded sight, twice seen of us: 25
Therefore I have entreated him along
With us to watch the minutes of this night;
That if again this apparition come,
He may approve our eyes and speak to it.

Horatio: Tush! tush! 'twill not appear.

Bernardo: Sit down a while; 30
And let us once again assail your ears,
That are so fortified against our story,
What we two nights have seen.

Horatio: Well, sit we down,
And let us hear Bernardo speak of this.

Bernardo: Last night of all, 35
When yond same star that's westward from the pole
Had made his course to illume that part of heaven
Where now it burns, Marcellus and myself,
The bell then beating one,—

Marcellus: Peace! break thee off; look, where it comes again! 40

[*Enter Ghost.*]

Bernardo: In the same figure, like the king that's dead.

Marcellus: Thou art a scholar; speak to it, Horatio.

Bernardo: Looks it not like the king? mark it, Horatio.

Horatio: Most like: it harrows me with fear and wonder.

Bernardo: It would be spoke to.

Marcellus: Question it, Horatio. 45

Horatio: What art thou, that usurp'st this time of night,
Together with that fair and warlike form
In which the majesty of buried Denmark
Did sometimes march? by heaven I charge thee, speak.

Marcellus: It is offended.

Bernardo: See, it stalks away. 50

Horatio: Stay! speak! speak! I charge thee, speak!

[*Exit Ghost.*]

56-58 *I might not . . . own eyes:* I could not believe this without the undeniable evidence of my senses.

61 *Norway:* King of Norway

62 *parle:* argument

63 *sledded Polack:* The Poles travelled in sleds.

65 *jump:* exactly

66 *martial stalk:* walking like a soldier

67 *thought:* intention

68 *in the gross . . . opinion:* as far as I can understand it

69 *This bodes . . . state:* This is a sign of some upheaval in Denmark.

71-79 Marcellus is referring to intense preparations for war being carried out in Denmark.

73 *cast:* casting

74 *foreign mart:* buying from foreign countries

75 *impress:* forced service

77 *toward:* under way

83 *emulate:* jealous

86-95 The two kings staked portions of their territories on the result of the combat, and Hamlet won.

Marcellus: 'Tis gone, and will not answer.
Bernardo: How now, Horatio! you tremble, and look pale:
  Is not this something more than fantasy?
  What think you on't? 55
Horatio: Before my God, I might not this believe,
  Without the sensible and true avouch
  Of mine own eyes.
Marcellus: Is it not like the king?
Horatio: As thou art to thyself:
  Such was the very armour he had on 60
  When he the ambitious Norway combated;
  So frown'd he once, when, in an angry parle,
  He smote the sledded Polack on the ice.
  'Tis strange.
Marcellus: Thus twice before, and jump at this dead hour, 65
  With martial stalk hath he gone by our watch.
Horatio: In what particular thought to work I know not;
  But, in the gross and scope of my opinion,
  This bodes some strange eruption to our state.
Marcellus: Good now, sit down, and tell me, he that knows, 70
  Why this same strict and most observant watch
  So nightly toils the subject of the land,
  And why such daily cast of brazen cannon,
  And foreign mart for implements of war:
  Why such impress of shipwrights, whose sore task 75
  Does not divide the Sunday from the week.
  What might be toward, that this sweaty haste
  Doth make the night joint-labourer with the day:
  Who is't that can inform me?
Horatio: That can I:
  At least the whisper goes so. Our last king, 80
  Whose image even but now appear'd to us,
  Was, as you know, by Fortinbras of Norway,
  Thereto prick'd on by a most emulate pride,
  Dared to the combat; in which our valient Hamlet—
  For so this side of our known world esteem'd him— 85
  Did slay this Fortinbras; who, by a seal'd compact,
  Well ratified by law and heraldry,
  Did forfeit, with his life, all those his lands
  Which he stood seized of, to the conqueror:

90-91　　*a moiety . . . our king:* A sufficient portion was pledged by our king.

91　　*had return'd:* would have returned

96　　*Of unimproved metal:* impetuous, not yet seasoned by experience

97　　*skirts:* outlying regions (outskirts)

98　　*Shark'd up:* gathered together; *lawless resolutes:* desperadoes

99　　*For food and diet:* The soldiers' only payment was food.

99-100　*some enterprise . . . stomach in't:* an adventure requiring courage

103　　*terms compulsatory:* conditions forced on us

106　　*head:* source

107　　*romage:* disturbance, turmoil

109　　*Well may it sort:* it may be appropriate; *portentous:* fatal, ominous

112　　*mote:* speck of dust. (The military situation is like a speck of dust in the eye—very bothersome and disruptive.)

114-125　Horatio is giving a list of unnatural occurrences that happened in Rome prior to Julius Caesar's assassination.

115　　*sheeted:* wrapped in shrouds (sometimes called "winding sheets")

118　　*Disasters in the sun:* possibly eclipses, which were thought to be evil omens; *moist star:* moon, which influences the tides

121　　*precurse:* warnings

122　　*harbingers:* forerunners

123　　*omen:* dreaded event

125　　*climatures:* territories

127　　*cross:* make the sign of the cross, or cross the path of the Ghost. (If he crosses the Ghost's path, he will be under its influence); *blast:* destroy

Against the which, a moiety competent   90
Was gaged by our king; which had return'd
To the inheritance of Fortinbras,
Had he been vanquisher; as, by the same covenant
And carriage of the article design'd,
His fell to Hamlet. Now, sir, young Fortinbras,   95
Of unimproved metal, hot and full,
Hath in the skirts of Norway, here and there
Shark'd up a list of lawless resolutes,
For food and diet, to some enterprise
That hath a stomach in't: which is no other—   100
And it doth well appear unto our state—
But to recover of us, by strong hand
And terms compulsatory, those 'foresaid lands
So by his father lost: and this, I take it,
Is the main motive of our preparations,   105
The source of this our watch and the chief head
Of this post-haste and romage in the land.

Bernardo: I think it be no other, but e'en so
    Well may it sort, that this portentous figure
    Comes armed through our watch, so like the king   110
    That was and is the question of these wars.

Horatio: A mote it is to trouble the mind's eye.
    In the most high and palmy state of Rome,
    A little ere the mightiest Julius fell,
    The graves stood tenantless, and the sheeted dead   115
    Did squeak and gibber in the Roman streets:
    As stars with trains of fire and dews of blood,
    Disasters in the sun; and the moist star,
    Upon whose influence Neptune's empire stands,
    Was sick almost to doomsday with eclipse: 120
    And even the like precurse of fierce events,
    As harbingers preceding still the fates
    And prologue to the omen coming on,
    Have heaven and earth together demonstrated
    Unto our climatures and countrymen.   125

[Re-enter Ghost.]

But soft, behold! lo, where it comes again!
I'll cross it, though it blast me. Stay, illusion!

133   *art privy to:* have secret information about

134   *happily:* by luck

140   *partizan:* long-handled battle-axe

147-157 It was a common belief that when the cock crows at daybreak, wandering spirits must return to their proper places. In agricultural societies, this encouraged farmers to go to work more cheerfully.

148   *started:* was startled, jumped guiltily

152   *god of day:* Apollo

154   *extravagant and erring spirit:* wandering spirit, one that has escaped its confines

155   *confine:* proper dwelling place

156   *probation:* proof

158   *'gainst:* in preparation for

If thou hast any sound, or use of voice,
Speak to me:
If there be any good thing to be done,   130
That may to thee do ease and grace to me,
Speak to me:
If thou art privy to thy country's fate,
Which, happily, foreknowing may avoid,
O, speak!   135
Or, if thou hast uphoarded in thy life
Extorted treasure in the womb of earth,
For which, they say, you spirits oft walk in death,
                                            [*Cock crows.*]
   Speak of it: stay, and speak! Stop it, Marcellus.
Marcellus: Shall I strike at it with my partizan?   140
Horatio: Do, if it will not stand.
Bernardo: 'Tis here!
Horatio: 'Tis here!
Marcellus: 'Tis gone!   [*Exit Ghost.*]
   We do it wrong, being so majestical,
To offer it the show of violence;
For it is, as the air, invulnerable,   145
And our vain blows malicious mockery.
Bernardo: It was about to speak when the cock crew.
Horatio: And then it started like a guilty thing
Upon a fearful summons. I have heard,
The cock, that is the trumpet to the morn,   150
Doth with his lofty and shrill-sounding throat
Awake the god of day; and at his warning,
Whether in sea or fire, in earth or air,
The extravagant and erring spirit hies
To his confine: and of the truth herein   155
This present object made probation.
Marcellus: It faded on the crowing of the cock.
Some say, that ever 'gainst that season comes
Wherein our Saviour's birth is celebrated,
The bird of dawning singeth all night long: 160
And then, they say, no spirit dare stir abroad;
The nights are wholesome; then no planets strike,
No fairy takes, nor witch hath power to charm,
So hallow'd and so gracious is the time.

166-167 *the morn. . . . clad:* The dawn is cloudy or misty; *russet* could mean brown or grey in colour. Either colour suggests the beginning of daylight.

173   *loves:* these men are Hamlet's personal friends

Horatio: So have I heard, and do in part believe it.   165
    But look. the morn, in russet mantle clad,
    Walks o'er the dew of yon high eastern hill:
    Break we our watch up; and, by my advice,
    Let us impart what we have seen to-night
    Unto young Hamlet: for, upon my life,   170
    This spirit, dumb to us, will speak to him;
    Do you consent we shall acquaint him with it,
    As needful in our loves, fitting our duty?
Marcellus: Let's do't, I pray: and I this morning know
    Where we shall find him most conveniently.   175

                                   [*Exeunt.*]

Act 1, Scene 1: Activities

1. In groups of four or five, review the first 22 lines of this scene. Determine the atmosphere or mood of this opening. You should consider both the physical setting (place, time of day, weather) and the state of mind of each character. Practise reading these lines until you are satisfied that you can convey the mood through your voices. You will have to decide what tone of voice to use, how loudly or softly to speak, how quickly to say each line, and where to pause. Using a tape recorder, you could also create sound effects for these lines. Your sound effects should intensify the atmosphere without drawing attention away from the dialogue. Perform your reading for the class. Your audience can decide how well you conveyed the mood of the scene.

2. Imagine that you are an investigative journalist for a national Danish daily newspaper. Write a brief news report (three or four paragraphs) describing the country's ongoing defence preparations and explaining the reasons for them. Keep in mind the following as you write your article:
   - You have to capture your reader's attention at the beginning of your story. Therefore, your first sentence or "lead" must be interesting and lively.
   - All the relevant facts should be presented.
   - Opinions should not be presented as if they were facts.
   - Information should be easily understandable.
   - The most important information should appear at the beginning of your story.
   - Keep your paragraphs short.

In pairs, exchange stories and discuss the differences between your reports. What questions do they raise that you want to find more answers to?

3. A portent is a sign of something that is about to happen. In groups, consider the following:
   - What portents appear in this scene? What does Horatio think these signs mean?
   - Do people believe in portents today? Can you think of any books or movies in which evil omens appear? How do the characters in these stories respond to the omens?

   In your personal journal, write a paragraph explaining why you do or do not believe in portents.

4. In groups, look for suggestions in this scene as to why the ghost of the former king has appeared. List any evidence in the scene that supports one or another of these suggestions. Once all the evidence is collected, decide whether any one possibility seems more likely than the others. Report your findings to the class.

5. From what you have seen of Horatio, why do you think Marcellus has confided in him and asked him to come and watch for the Ghost? Do you think Marcellus made a good choice?

6. Why do you think Horatio wants to tell Hamlet rather than Claudius, the King, about the Ghost? What would you have done under similar circumstances? Make a note of your ideas. As you learn more about both Hamlet and Claudius, you may want to add new possibilities.

For the next scene . . .

In your personal journal, write about a time when you and your parents reacted differently to a family crisis. How well were you able to communicate your feelings? If you could relive that time, would you change anything?

Act 1, Scene 2

In this scene . . .

This court scene is a strong contrast to the bleak first scene of the play. Claudius, brother to the dead King Hamlet, is now king. Soon after old Hamlet's death, Claudius married the King's widow, Queen Gertrude, who is Hamlet's mother. Claudius, who is conducting court business for the first time, is thinking about the impression he will make. He has planned each word and action carefully. He transacts several pieces of business, which move the action of the play forward and smooth over the awkwardness of his hasty marriage and accession to the throne. Claudius takes measures to prevent war against Norway. He grants permission to Laertes, son of the Lord Chamberlain Polonius, to return to France. Finally, he urges the depressed Prince Hamlet to stay in Denmark rather than return to university in Wittenberg. In the last part of the scene, Hamlet is alone on stage in the first of several soliloquies he speaks in the play. These soliloquies, which in some ways are like a personal journal, give us an opportunity to see the workings of Hamlet's mind; we not only learn what he is thinking, but we also learn *how* he thinks. Here, he expresses his depression and anger about his mother's remarriage. After the soliloquy, Horatio, Marcellus and Bernardo arrive to tell Hamlet about his father's ghost. Hamlet promises to join them on the castle platform that night.

2   *green:* fresh

3-4   *our whole kingdom . . . woe:* for everyone in our kingdom to be united in sorrow

5   *discretion:* prudence; *nature:* feeling

8   *sometime sister:* former sister-in-law

9   *jointress:* partner

10   *defeated:* disfigured, marred

11   *With one . . . eye:* This resembles the proverbial phrase, "To laugh with one eye and cry with the other."

13   *dole:* grief

14   *barr'd:* excluded

15-16   *gone . . . along:* approved of what was happening

18   *supposal:* estimation

20   *out of frame:* out of order

21   *Colleagued:* adding to

23   *Importing:* concerning

28   *Norway:* King of Norway

Scene 2

A room of state in the castle.

*Flourish. Enter the King, Queen,
Hamlet, Polonius, Laertes,
Voltimand, Cornelius, Lords, and
Attendants.*

King: Though yet of Hamlet our dear brother's death
  The memory be green, and that it us befitted
  To bear our hearts in grief and our whole kingdom
  To be contracted in one brow of woe,
  Yet so far hath discretion fought with nature   5
  That we with wisest sorrow think on him,
  Together with remembrance of ourselves.
  Therefore our sometime sister, now our queen,
  The imperial jointress of this warlike state,
  Have we, as 'twere with a defeated joy,—   10
  With one auspicious and a dropping eye,
  With mirth in funeral and with dirge in marriage,
  In equal scale weighing delight and dole,—
  Taken to wife: nor have we herein barr'd
  Your better wisdoms, which have freely gone   15
  With this affair along. For all, our thanks.
  Now follows that you know, young Fortinbras,
  Holding a weak supposal of our worth,
  Or thinking, by our late dear brother's death
  Our state to be disjoint and out of frame,   20
  Colleagued with the dream of his advantage,
  He hath not fail'd to pester us with message,
  Importing the surrender of those lands
  Lost by his father, with all bonds of law,
  To our most valiant brother. So much for him.   25
  Now for ourself, and for this time of meeting:
  Thus much the business is: we have here writ
  To Norway, uncle of young Fortinbras,—

31   *gait:* progress

38   *delated articles:* detailed account of the situation

39   *let your haste commend your duty:* depart quickly without standing on ceremony

41   *nothing:* not at all

43   *suit:* request

44   *of reason:* of anything reasonable

45   *lose your voice:* ask in vain

47   *native:* naturally related to

47-49 Claudius is referring to his close relationship with Laertes' father, Polonius, who may have aided Claudius in becoming King after old King Hamlet's death.

51   *leave and favour:* permission

56   *leave and pardon:* permission to leave

62   *Take thy fair hour:* Feel free to leave whenever you wish.

64   *cousin:* nephew. The word "cousin" was used to refer to an uncle, aunt, niece, nephew or cousin.

Who, impotent and bed-rid, scarcely hears
Of this his nephew's purpose,—to suppress   30
His further gait herein; in that the levies,
The lists, and full proportions, are all made
Out of his subject: and we here despatch
You, good Cornelius, and you, Voltimand,
For bearing of this greeting to old Norway,   35
Giving to you no further personal power
To business with the king, more than the scope
Of these delated articles allow.
Farewell, and let your haste commend your duty.
Cornelius, Voltimand: In that and all things will we show
    our duty.   40
King: We doubt it nothing; heartily farewell.
                   [Exeunt Voltimand and Cornelius.]
And now, Laertes, what's the news with you?
You told us of some suit: what is't, Laertes?
You cannot speak of reason to the Dane,
And lose your voice: what wouldst thou beg, Laertes,   45
That shall not be my offer, not thy asking?
The head is not more native to the heart,
The hand more instrumental to the mouth,
Than is the throne of Denmark to thy father.
What wouldst thou have, Laertes?
Laertes: My dread lord,   50
Your leave and favour to return to France,
From whence though willingly I came to Denmark,
To show my duty in your coronation,
Yet now, I must confess, that duty done,
My thoughts and wishes bend again towards France   55
And bow them to your gracious leave and pardon.
King: Have you your father's leave? What says Polonius?
Polonius: He hath, my lord, wrung from me my slow leave
    By laboursome petition, and at last
    Upon his will I seal'd my hard consent;   60
    I do beseech you, give him leave to go.
King: Take thy fair hour, Laertes; time be thine,
    And thy best graces spend it at thy will!
    But now, my cousin Hamlet, and my son.
Hamlet: [Aside.] A little more than kin, and less than kind.   65

66   *clouds:* gloomy mood

67   *I am too much i' the sun:* This is a pun on the words "sun" and "son." The audience has been aware of the brooding figure of Hamlet throughout this scene. His first words, which are cryptic, ambiguous, and sarcastic, catch our attention.

68   *nighted colour:* Hamlet is dressed in black (in mourning) while everyone else is dressed in bright colours.

69   *Denmark:* King of Denmark (i.e., Claudius)

70   *vailed lids:* downcast eyes

72   *'tis common:* it's common knowledge

75   *particular:* special

76-86   In this speech, Hamlet introduces an important theme in the play: the difference between how things *appear* and how they *really are*. Much of the plot and symbolism of the play stems from this contrast.

79   *windy suspiration of forced breath:* sighs

81   *dejected haviour of the visage:* sad facial expression

85   *passeth show:* is beyond what you see

86   *trappings:* outer clothing

92   *obsequious sorrow:* the required mourning at a funeral

98-99   *what we know . . . sense:* what we know is inevitable (i.e., death) and is one of the commonest things we experience.

King: How is it that the clouds still hang on you?
Hamlet: Not so, my lord; I am too much i' the sun.
Queen: Good Hamlet, cast thy nighted colour off,
    And let thine eye look like a friend on Denmark.
    Do not for ever with thy vailed lids   70
    Seek for thy noble father in the dust:
    Thou know'st 'tis common; all that lives must die,
    Passing through nature to eternity.
Hamlet: Ay, madam, it is common.
Queen: If it be,
    Why seems it so particular with thee?   75
Hamlet: Seems, madam! nay, it is; I know not "seems."
    'Tis not alone my inky cloak, good mother,
    Nor customary suits of solemn black,
    Nor windy suspiration of forced breath,
    No, nor the fruitful river in the eye,   80
    Nor the dejected haviour of the visage,
    Together with all forms, modes, shapes of grief,
    That can denote me truly: these indeed seem,
    For they are actions that a man might play;
    But I have that within which passeth show;   85
    These, but the trappings and the suits of woe.
King: 'Tis sweet and commendable in your nature, Hamlet,
    To give these mourning duties to your father:
    But, you must know, your father lost a father,
    That father lost, lost his, and the survivor bound   90
    In filial obligation for some term
    To do obsequious sorrow: but to persever
    In obstinate condolement is a course
    Of impious stubbornness; 'tis unmanly grief:
    It shows a will most incorrect to heaven,   95
    A heart unfortified, a mind impatient,
    An understanding simple and unschool'd:
    For what we know must be and is as common
    As any the most vulgar thing to sense,
    Why should we, in our peevish opposition   100
    Take it to heart? Fie! 'tis a fault to heaven,
    A fault against the dead, a fault to nature,
    To reason most absurd, whose common theme
    Is death of fathers, and who still hath cried,

107   *unprevailing:* useless, unavailing

109   *You are . . . throne:* In Denmark at the time, a son did not necessarily succeed his father to the throne. While some attention was paid to close blood ties, the King was elected. Therefore, Hamlet had no legal right to the throne.

113   *Wittenberg:* a town in Germany. The university there was a renowned centre of learning in Shakespeare's time.

114   *retrograde:* contrary

125   *jocund:* joyful; *health:* toast; *that Denmark drinks:* that the King drinks

125-128 Claudius looks forward to a drunken celebration during which cannons will be fired to announce each toast the King drinks.

127   *rouse:* carouse; *bruit:* echo

130   *resolve:* dissolve

132   *canon:* law

134   *uses:* routines

136-137 *Things rank . . . merely:* This is the first of a chain of images in the play which suggest an unnatural invasion of some disease, which eventually poisons the whole organism.

137   *merely:* completely

140   *Hyperion:* the sun-god in Greek mythology; *satyr:* a creature part man and part goat in Greek mythology. Satyrs were lewd and promiscuous.

141   *beteem:* allow

From the first corse till he that died to-day,   105
"This must be so." We pray you, throw to earth
This unprevailing woe; and think of us
As of a father: for let the world take note,
You are the most immediate to our throne,
And, with no less nobility of love   110
Than that which dearest father bears his son,
Do I impart towards you. For your intent
In going back to school in Wittenberg,
It is most retrograde to our desire:
And, we beseech you, bend you to remain   115
Here, in the cheer and comfort of our eye,
Our chiefest courtier, cousin and our son.
Queen: Let not thy mother lose her prayers, Hamlet:
  I pray thee, stay with us; go not to Wittenberg.
Hamlet: I shall in all my best obey you, madam.   120
King: Why, 'tis a loving and a fair reply;
  Be as ourself in Denmark. Madam, come;
  This gentle and unforced accord of Hamlet
  Sits smiling to my heart: in grace whereof,
  No jocund health that Denmark drinks to-day,   125
  But the great cannon to the clouds shall tell,
  And the king's rouse the heavens shall bruit again,
  Re-speaking earthly thunder. Come away.
                          [*Exeunt all but Hamlet.*]
Hamlet: O, that this too too-solid flesh would melt,
  Thaw, and resolve itself into a dew!   130
  Or that the Everlasting had not fix'd
  His canon 'gainst self-slaughter! God! O God!
  How weary, stale, flat, and unprofitable
  Seem to me all the uses of this world!
  Fie on't! O fie! 'tis an unweeded garden,   135
  That grows to seed; things rank and gross in nature
  Possess it merely. That it should come to this!
  But two months dead! nay, not so much, not two;
  So excellent a king; that was, to this,
  Hyperion to a satyr: so loving to my mother,   140
  That he might not beteem the winds of heaven
  Visit her face too roughly. Heaven and earth!
  Must I remember? why, she would hang on him,

147   *ere:* before

149   *Niobe:* Niobe, Queen of Thebes, wept when her fourteen children were killed as a punishment for her boasting about them. Zeus eventually turned Niobe into stone.

150   *wants discourse of reason:* lacks the ability to reason

153   *Hercules:* a hero in Greek mythology renowned for his great strength

154-155 *Ere yet . . . eyes:* before the redness (from hypocritically crying over her husband's death) had left her inflamed eyes

156   *to post:* to run quickly

163   *I'll change . . . you:* I'll be your servant, you be my friend; or, I'll exchange the name of friend with you.

171   *truster:* believer

173   *affair:* business

178   *hard upon:* soon afterward

179-180 *Thrift . . . tables:* The wedding was held so quickly in order to save money by serving the food left over from the funeral observances.

As if increase of appetite had grown
By what it fed on: and yet, within a month— 145
Let me not think on't—Frailty, thy name is woman!—
A little month, or ere those shoes were old
With which she followed my poor father's body,
Like Niobe, all tears;—why she, even she,—
O God! a beast that wants discourse of reason 150
Would have mourn'd longer,—married with mine uncle,
My father's brother, but no more like my father
Than I to Hercules: within a month;
Ere yet the salt of most unrighteous tears
Had left the flushing of her galled eyes, 155
She married:—O most wicked speed, to post
With such dexterity to incestuous sheets!
It is not, nor it cannot come to, good;
But break, my heart, for I must hold my tongue!

[*Enter Horatio, Bernardo, and Marcellus.*]

Horatio: Hail to your lordship!
Hamlet: I am glad to see you well: 160
    Horatio,—or I do forget myself,
Horatio: The same, my lord, and your poor servant ever.
Hamlet: Sir, my good friend; I'll change that name with you.
    And what make you from Wittenberg, Horatio?
    Marcellus?
Marcellus: My good lord? 165
Hamlet: I am very glad to see you. Good even, sir.
    But what, in faith, make you from Wittenberg?
Horatio: A truant disposition, good my lord.
Hamlet: I would not hear your enemy say so,
    Nor shall you do mine ear that violence, 170
    To make it truster of your own report
    Against yourself: I know you are no truant.
    But what is your affair in Elsinore?
    We'll teach you to drink deep ere you depart.
Horatio: My lord, I came to see your father's funeral. 175
Hamlet: I pray thee, do not mock me, fellow-student;
    I think it was to see my mother's wedding.
Horatio: Indeed, my lord, it follow'd hard upon.
Hamlet: Thrift, thrift, Horatio! the funeral baked meats

181   *dearest:* worst

191   *Season your admiration:* restrain your astonishment
192   *attent:* attentive

199   *to point:* fully, in readiness; *cap-à-pé:* head to foot

203   *truncheon:* staff; *distill'd:* melted
204   *act:* operation

208   *deliver'd:* reported

211   *These hands . . . like:* My two hands are no more like one
        another (than are the Ghost and Hamlet's father).
212   *platform:* ramparts

Did coldly furnish forth the marriage tables.   180
Would I had met my dearest foe in heaven
Ere I had seen that day, Horatio!
My father!—methinks, I see my father.
Horatio: O, where, my lord?
Hamlet: In my mind's eye, Horatio.
Horatio: I saw him once; he was a goodly king.   185
Hamlet: He was a man, take him for all in all,
 I shall not look upon his like again.
Horatio: My lord, I think I saw him yesternight.
Hamlet: Saw! who?
Horatio: My lord, the king your father.
Hamlet: The king my father! 190
Horatio: Season your admiration for a while
 With an attent ear, till I may deliver,
 Upon the witness of these gentlemen,
 This marvel to you.
Hamlet: For God's love, let me hear.
Horatio: Two nights together had these gentlemen,   195
 Marcellus and Bernardo, on their watch,
 In the dead waste and middle of the night,
 Been thus encounter'd. A figure like your father,
 Armed to point, exactly, cap-à-pé,
 Appears before them, and with solemn march   200
 Goes slow and stately by them: thrice he walk'd,
 By their oppress'd and fear-surprised eyes,
 Within his truncheon's length; whilst they, distill'd
 Almost to jelly with the act of fear,
 Stand dumb, and speak not to him. This to me   205
 In dreadful secrecy impart they did;
 And I with them the third night kept the watch:
 Where, as they had deliver'd, both in time,
 Form of the thing, each word made true and good,
 The apparition comes: I knew your father: 210
 These hands are not more like.
Hamlet: But where was this?
Marcellus: My lord, upon the platform where we watch'd.
Hamlet: Did you not speak to it?
Horatio: My lord, I did,
 But answer made it none: yet once methought

228   *beaver:* the part of the helmet that can be lifted up (visor)

230   *countenance:* expression

236   *tell:* count

238   *grizzled:* partly grey

240   *sable silver'd:* black streaked with silver

It lifted up its head and did address   215
Itself to motion, like as it would speak:
But even then the morning cock crew loud,
And at the sound it shrunk in haste away
And vanish'd from our sight.
Hamlet: 'Tis very strange.
Horatio: As I do live, my honour'd lord, 'tis true;   220
And we did think it writ down in our duty
To let you know of it.
Hamlet: Indeed, indeed, sirs, but this troubles me.
  Hold you the watch to-night?
All: We do, my lord.
Hamlet: Arm'd, say you?
All: Arm'd, my lord.   225
Hamlet: From top to toe?
All: My lord, from head to foot.
Hamlet: Then saw you not his face?
Horatio: O yes, my lord; he wore his beaver up.
Hamlet: What, look'd he frowningly?
Horatio: A countenance more in sorrow than in anger.   230
Hamlet: Pale, or red?
Horatio: Nay, very pale.
Hamlet: And fix'd his eyes upon you?
Horatio: Most constantly.
Hamlet: I would I had been there.
Horatio: It would have much amazed you.
Hamlet: Very like, very like. Stay'd it long?   235
Horatio: While one with moderate haste might tell a hundred.
Marcellus, Bernardo: Longer, longer.
Horatio: Not when I saw't.
Hamlet: His beard was grizzled? no?
Horatio: It was as I have seen it in his life,
  A sable silver'd.
Hamlet: I will watch to-night;   240
  Perhance 'twill walk again.
Horatio: I warrant it will.
Hamlet: If it assume my noble father's person,
  I'll speak to it, though hell itself should gape
  And bid me hold my peace. I pray you all,
  If you have hitherto conceal'd this sight,   245

246   *Let it be . . . still:* Remain silent on this subject.

249   *requite your loves:* reward you for your efforts

252   *Your love . . . you:* I would rather have your love, as you have mine.

254   *doubt:* suspect

Let it be tenable in your silence still,
And whatsoever else shall hap to-night,
Give it an understanding, but no tongue;
I will requite your loves. So fare you well:
Upon the platform, 'twixt eleven and twelve,   250
I'll visit you.
All: Our duty to your honour.
Hamlet: Your love, as mine to you: farewell.
                    [*Exeunt Horatio, Marcellus, and Bernardo.*]
My father's spirit in arms! all is not well;
I doubt some foul play: would the night were come!
Till then sit still, my soul. Foul deeds will rise,   255
Though all the earth o'erwhelm them, to men's eyes.
                                        [*Exit.*]

Act 1, Scene 2: Activities

1. Choose one of the following activities. Be prepared to read your piece to the class for their comments.

   a) In the role of a newspaper reporter for a paper you know, write a description of the court session. Give some background to Claudius' speech and provide some of your own observations on his speech. Before you begin writing, decide whether your newspaper's editorial policy supports Claudius' accession to the throne. Have your classmates comment on the bias that is revealed and explain how that bias is created.

   b) In the role of Claudius, write two entries in your private diary, one before and one after holding court. Include your innermost thoughts, your hopes and fears, and your assessment of how the court session went. Your classmates will comment on whether the diary entries are in keeping with what they have seen of Claudius to this point.

   c) In the role of Queen Gertrude's lady-in-waiting, write a letter to a close friend. Include the inside gossip of the palace, your reaction to Gertrude's hasty remarriage, and your impression of Gertrude's appearance and behaviour during the court scene. You may use background information. Your classmates will comment on how well the character you have created has observed the palace affairs and conveyed them in her letter.

   d) In the role of court psychologist, write a report on Hamlet's character. You have been present at the court session and have also overheard Hamlet's soliloquy. Give your assessment of Hamlet's state of mind and its causes. Your classmates will comment on how objective your psychological report is, and on how well you support opinions with examples of specific behaviour.

2. In his soliloquy, Hamlet uses the image of an unweeded garden (lines 135 – 136). What is Hamlet comparing to a garden? What are the weeds? Who is responsible for tending the garden? If Hamlet were the chief gardener, how do you think he would go about restoring the garden?

3. In groups, discuss Hamlet's description of his mother's marriage to Claudius. Consider the following:
   • What is Hamlet's idea of a perfect marriage? What roles would the husband and wife play? What is your definition of an ideal marriage? What roles should husband and wife play?
   • Do you think Hamlet's view of marriage is realistic? Is your definition realistic? Explain your answers.
   • Is Hamlet's reaction to his mother's remarriage fair? Why or why not?
   • What do Hamlet's comments about his father, Gertrude, and Claudius reveal about his own personality?

4. "I must hold my tongue." Why do you think Hamlet feels he must hide his thoughts? Do you think he is right? In your journal, describe an occasion when you were very upset with someone but decided to keep your thoughts to yourself. Why did you hide your feelings? Did concealing the problem change your relationship with that person?

For the next scene . . .

In your journal, write about a time when an older person gave you advice which you knew that person would not follow him or herself. What were the results? How did you feel afterwards?

Act 1, Scene 3

In this scene . . .

This scene familiarizes us with Polonius' family. Laertes is about to leave for France and is saying goodbye to his sister, Ophelia. He takes the opportunity to warn her about her romance with Hamlet. Polonius arrives and gives Laertes advice about how to behave in France. Once Laertes has departed, Polonius also warns Ophelia that Hamlet's intentions may not be honorable, and he tells her to avoid him. After attempting to defend her relationship with Hamlet to Polonius, Ophelia accepts her father's advice.

2-4   Laertes is asking his sister to write to him every day there is means to send a letter.

2   *give benefit:* are favourable

3   *convoy is assistant:* a ship is available

6   *fashion:* passing fancy, something changeable and temporary; *toy in blood:* impulsive behaviour

7   *youth of primy nature:* early spring

8   *forward:* ripening too early (and therefore likely to rot quickly)

9   *the perfume . . . minute:* brief pleasure (one that lasts only a moment)

11   *crescent:* growing

12   *thews and bulks:* muscle power and body size; *as this temple waxes:* as we grow

14   *withal:* at the same time

15-16   *now no . . . will:* Now no stain or deceit mars his good intentions.

15   *cautel:* deceit

17   *His greatness weigh'd:* when you consider his high position

19   *unvalued:* unimportant

20   *Carve for himself:* make his own (selfish) decisions

23   *yielding:* approval

25-27   *It fits . . . deed:* You would be wise to believe it only to the extent that his situation will allow him to keep his word.

Scene 3

A room in Polonius' house.

Enter Laertes and Ophelia.

Laertes: My necessities are embark'd; farewell;
  And, sister, as the winds give benefit,
  And convoy is assistant, do not sleep,
  But let me hear from you.
Ophelia: Do you doubt that?
Laertes: For Hamlet, and the trifling of his favour,   5
  Hold it a fashion, and a toy in blood,
  A violet in the youth of primy nature,
  Forward, not permanent, sweet, not lasting,
  The perfume and suppliance of a minute;
  No more.
Ophelia: No more but so?
Laertes: Think it no more: 10
  For nature crescent does not grow alone
  In thews and bulk; but, as this temple waxes,
  The inward service of the mind and soul
  Grows wide withal. Perhaps he loves you now;
  And now no soil nor cautel doth besmirch   15
  The virtue of his will; but you must fear,
  His greatness weigh'd, his will is not his own;
  For he himself is subject to his birth:
  He may not, as unvalued persons do,
  Carve for himself, for on his choice depends   20
  The safety and the health of the whole state;
  And therefore must his choice be circumscribed
  Under the voice and yielding of that body
  Whereof he is the head. Then if he says he loves you,
  It fits your wisdom so far to believe it   25
  As he in his peculiar act and place
  May give his saying deed; which is no further
  Than the main voice of Denmark goes withal.

30   *credent:* believing; *list:* listen to

31   *chaste treasure:* virginity

32   *unmaster'd importunity:* uncontrolled insistence

34   *keep within . . . affection:* Do not let emotions overpower judgment.

36-37 *The chariest maid . . . moon:* Even the most prudent girl can become reckless.

38   *Virtue itself . . . strokes:* Even virtuous people cannot escape evil gossip.

39-40 *The canker . . . disclosed:* The canker worm too often destroys early spring flowers even before they blossom.

41-42 *And in the morn . . . imminent:* And just as destructive blights occur in the morning, so violent emotions most often occur in young people.

44   *Youth . . . near:* Young people rebel against restrictions even when no one else tempts them.

47   *ungracious:* wicked

49   *puff'd:* bloated; *libertine:* loose, self-indulgent person

50   *primrose path of dalliance:* the enjoyable, easy path of pleasure

51   *recks not his own rede:* doesn't take his own advice; *fear me not:* Don't worry about me.

59   *character:* engrave (the thoughts)

60   *Nor any . . . act:* If you have an unsuitable thought, don't put it into action.

61   *Be thou . . . vulgar:* Don't socialize too much with ordinary people. (Be friendly, but don't give away too much of yourself.)

62   *their adoption tried:* their friendship tested

63   *Grapple . . . steel:* bind them to you tightly (like the metal hoops that hold a barrel together)

64-65 *But do not . . . comrade:* Do not cheapen friendship by welcoming every unproven associate.

Then weigh what loss your honour may sustain,
If with too credent ear you list his songs,   30
Or lose your heart, or your chaste treasure open
To his unmaster'd importunity.
Fear it, Ophelia, fear it, my dear sister,
And keep within the rear of your affection,
Out of the shot and danger of desire.   35
The chariest maid is prodigal enough,
If she unmask her beauty to the moon:
Virtue itself 'scapes not calumnious strokes:
The canker galls the infants of the spring
Too oft before their buttons be disclosed,   40
And in the morn and liquid dew of youth
Contagious blastments are most imminent.
Be wary then; best safety lies in fear;
Youth to itself rebels, though none else near.
Ophelia: I shall the effect of this good lesson keep,   45
As watchman to my heart. But, good my brother,
Do not, as some ungracious pastors do,
Show me the steep and thorny way to heaven,
Whilst, like a puff'd and reckless libertine,
Himself the primrose path of dalliance treads   50
And recks not his own rede.
Laertes: O fear me not.
I stay too long; but here my father comes.

[*Enter Polonius.*]

O double blessing is a double grace;
Occasion smiles upon a second leave.
Polonius: Yet here, Laertes! aboard, aboard, for shame!   55
The wind sits in the shoulder of your sail,
And you are stay'd for. There; my blessing with thee!
                [*Laying his hand on Laertes' head.*]
And these few precepts in thy memory
See thou character. Give thy thoughts no tongue,
Nor any unproportion'd thought his act.   60
Be thou familiar, but by no means vulgar.
The friends thou hast, and their adoption tried,
Grapple them to thy soul with hoops of steel,
But do not dull thy palm with entertainment

65   *new-hatch'd, unfledged:* immature

69   *censure:* opinion

70   *habit:* clothing

77   *husbandry:* thrift

81   *my blessing . . . thee:* My blessing is that this advice will bear fruit in you.

83   *tend:* wait

90   *Marry:* a mild oath; originally, "By the Virgin Mary"

94   *put on me:* told to me

97   *behoves:* suits

99   *tenders:* offers

102   *Unsifted:* lacking experience

103-109 Polonius is punning on the word "tenders." He uses it to mean "offers of love" (1.103), "credit notes," as opposed to real money (1.106), "value" (1.107) and "render" or "change into" (1.109).

Of each new-hatch'd, unfledged comrade. Beware   65
Of entrance to a quarrel; but, being in,
Bear't that the opposed may beware of thee.
Give every man thine ear, but few thy voice:
Take each man's censure, but reserve thy judgment.
Costly thy habit as thy purse can buy,   70
But not express'd in fancy; rich, not gaudy:
For the apparel oft proclaims the man;
And they in France of the best rank and station
Are most select and generous chief in that.
Neither a borrower nor a lender be: 75
For loan oft loses both itself and friend,
And borrowing dulls the edge of husbandry.
This above all: to thine own self be true,
And it must follow, as the night the day,
Thou canst not then be false to any man.   80
Farewell: my blessing season this in thee!
Laertes: Most humbly do I take my leave, my lord.
Polonius: The time invites you; go, your servants tend.
Laertes: Farewell, Ophelia; and remember well
 What I have said to you.
Ophelia: 'Tis in my memory lock'd,   85
 And you yourself shall keep the key of it.
Laertes: Farewell.   [*Exit Laertes.*]
Polonius: What is't, Ophelia, he hath said to you?
Ophelia: So please you, something touching the lord Hamlet.
Polonius: Marry, well bethought: 90
 'Tis told me, he hath very oft of late
 Given private time to you, and you yourself
 Have of your audience been most free and bounteous:
 If it be so—as so 'tis put on me,
 And that in way of caution—I must tell you,   95
 You do not understand yourself so clearly
 As it behoves my daughter and your honour.
 What is between you? give me up the truth.
Ophelia: He hath, my lord, of late, made many tenders
 Of his affection to me.   100
Polonius: Affection? pooh! you speak like a green girl,
 Unsifted in such perilous circumstance,
 Do you believe his tenders, as you call them?

108   *not to crack . . . phrase:* not to overwork the pun like a horse that's been ridden too hard

112   *go to, go to:* nonsense, don't be silly

113   *countenance:* an expression of sincerity

115   *springes to catch woodcocks:* Woodcocks were considered to be stupid birds that could be caught easily in snares.

116   *prodigal:* freely, generously

117-120 *these blazes . . . fire:* Polonius is pointing out the difference between shallow emotions, which die quickly (small blazes), and true love (fire).

121   *Be somewhat . . . presence:* Appear in public less often.

122-123 *Set . . . parley:* Make yourself more valuable by not responding to his every request.

125   *tether:* freedom, range

127-131 *Do not believe . . . beguile:* Do not believe in his promises, for they are not what they seem. They appear to be innocent, but their purpose is to trick you.

127   brokers: agents, go-betweens

128   *dye:* colour; also, quality; *investments*: priestly garments

130   *bonds:* marriage bonds

133   *slander*: misuse

Ophelia: I do not know, my lord, what I should think.

Polonius: Marry, I'll teach you: think yourself a baby, 105
    That you have ta'en these tenders for true pay,
    Which are not sterling. Tender yourself more dearly;
    Or—not to crack the wind of the poor phrase,
    Running it thus—you'll tender me a fool.

Ophelia: My lord, he hath importuned me with love 110
    In honourable fashion.

Polonius: Ay, fashion you may call it; go to, go to.

Ophelia: And hath given countenance to his speech, my
      lord,
    With almost all the holy vows of heaven.

Polonius: Ay, springes to catch woodcocks. I do know, 115
    When the blood burns, how prodigal the soul
    Gives the tongue vows: these blazes, daughter,
    Giving more light than heat, extinct in both,
    Even in their promise, as it is a making,
    You must not take for fire. From this time, daughter, 120
    Be somewhat scanter of your maiden presence;
    Set your entreatments at a higher rate
    Than a command to parley. For lord Hamlet,
    Believe so much in him, that he is young,
    And with a larger tether may he walk, 125
    Than may be given you: in few, Ophelia,
    Do not believe his vows; for they are brokers,
    Not of that dye which their investments show,
    But mere implorators of unholy suits,
    Breathing like sanctified and pious bonds, 130
    The better to beguile. This is for all:
    I would not, in plain terms, from this time forth,
    Have you so slander any moment's leisure,
    As to give words or talk with the lord Hamlet.
    Look to't, I charge you: come your ways. 135

Ophelia: I shall obey, my lord.   *[Exeunt.]*

Act 1, Scene 3: Activities

1. In pairs, summarize and role-play Laertes' advice to Ophelia (lines 5 – 44) in modern English; use either standard English or slang. If you were giving advice to a brother or sister or to a close friend, which style of language would you choose? Explain your choice.

2. What advice might an older brother give a younger sister nowadays about her first romance? What advice might an older sister give a younger brother about his first love? How does Ophelia respond to Laertes' advice? What does this suggest to you about their relationship? Discuss your ideas in groups.

3. Review Polonius' advice to Laertes (lines 58 – 81). In groups, make a list of Polonius' values concerning love, money, clothing, friendship and entertainment. Design a survey from this list to determine what students in your class (or, perhaps, in several classes) think about these values. Distribute the questionnaires, collect them when completed, and tabulate the answers. (You may want to divide these duties among the members of your group.) Summarize your findings in a report; describe your sample group (i.e., number of people surveyed, male-female ratio, grade and age levels) and give the statistical results, offering an interpretation of them. Publish your results by distributing copies of your report, or by posting it on the class bulletin board. Invite comments on your findings.

4. Suppose you are an anthropologist who is completely unfamiliar with family life in Western society. Observe the relationships in the Polonius family and make notes on your observations. Consider the relative position of men and women in the family, parent-child roles, and the hierarchy of authority. Compare your observations with those of other "anthropologists" in your group or class.

5. In the role of Ophelia, write a diary entry of your responses to your brother's departure, your feelings about palace gossip, and your reaction to your father's description of Hamlet's behaviour. Do you agree that you should stop seeing Hamlet? How do you feel about your father at this point?

For the next scene . . .

As a class, think of someone in the news lately who has attempted something dangerous, despite the warnings of others. It could be a political figure, an athlete, or a daredevil. What qualities made this person act, despite the dangers? What is your opinion of these qualities?

Act 1, Scene 4

In this scene . . .

Twenty-four hours have passed since the Ghost appeared in Scene 1. Hamlet, Horatio and Marcellus are on the platform of the castle waiting for the Ghost to reappear. In the background, the blaring of trumpets and the sound of cannons being fired announce each drink the King takes as he carouses through the night. When the Ghost appears, Hamlet questions it. The Ghost beckons Hamlet to follow. Despite his friends' warnings, Hamlet ignores the possible dangers and follows the Ghost.

1 *shrewdly:* sharply

2 *eager:* keen, sharp

6 *held his wont to walk:* was accustomed to walk

8 *The king doth wake to-night:* The King is having a celebration tonight; *rouse:* a large glass (Claudius is drinking heavily.)

9 *keeps wassail:* is drinking toasts to his guests; *up-spring:* a wild dance, originating in Germany

10 *Rhenish:* Rhine wine

15 *to the manner born:* accustomed to it from birth

16 *More honour'd . . . observance:* a custom that is better *not* practised

18 *traduced:* slandered; *tax'd:* criticized

19 *clepe:* call; *with swinish phrase:* The Danes are being called pigs.

20 *addition:* good name

22 *attribute:* reputation

24 *vicious mole of nature:* a harmful natural blemish

27 *o'ergrowth of some complexion:* In Shakespeare's time, it was believed that human nature was governed by four fluids (called "humours"): blood, black bile, yellow bile and phlegm. Too much of any one fluid would change a person's temperament (complexion), making him or her sanguine, melancholic, choleric or phlegmatic.

Scene 4

The platform.

Enter Hamlet, Horatio, and Marcellus.

Hamlet: The air bites shrewdly: it is very cold.
Horatio: It is a nipping and an eager air.
Hamlet: What hour now?
Horatio: I think it lacks of twelve.
Marcellus: No, it is struck.
Horatio: Indeed? I heard it not; then it draws near the season   5
     Wherein the spirit held his wont to walk.
        [*A flourish of trumpets, and ordnance shot off, within.*]
     What does this mean, my lord?
Hamlet: The king doth wake to-night, and takes his rouse,
     Keeps wassail, and the swaggering up-spring reels;
     And as he drains his draughts of Rhenish down,   10
     The kettle-drum and trumpet thus bray out
     The triumph of his pledge.
Horatio: Is it a custom?
Hamlet: Ay, marry, is't:
     And to my mind, though I am native here
     And to the manner born, it is a custom   15
     More honour'd in the breach than the observance.
     This heavy-headed revel east and west
     Makes us traduced and tax'd of other nations:
     They clepe us drunkards, and with swinish phrase
     Soil our addition; and, indeed, it takes   20
     From our achievements, though perform'd at height,
     The pith and marrow of our attribute.
     So, oft it chances in particular men,
     That for some vicious mole of nature in them,
     As, in their birth,—wherein they are not guilty.   25
     Since nature cannot choose his origin—
     By the o'ergrowth of some complexion,

28   *pales and forts:* defences

29   *o'er-leavens:* spoils

30   *plausive:* pleasing

31   *the stamp of one defect:* This refers to the "mole" in line 24.

32   *livery:* badge

36-38   *The dram of evil . . . scandal:* A small defect will ruin the whole personality. (This notion relates to the chain of poison/garden images that appear throughout the play.)

43   *questionable shape:* as if you want me to question you

47   *canonized:* buried according to Church ceremonies; *hearsed:* put in a coffin

48   *cerements:* shrouds

52   *complete steel:* full armour

54   *fools of nature:* mortals who do not understand the mysteries of life

55   *to shake our disposition:* to upset us, to disturb our minds

59   *As if . . . desire:* as if it wanted to talk to you; *impartment:* message

Oft breaking down the pales and forts of reason,
Or by some habit that too much o'er-leavens
The form of plausive manners, that these men—   30
Carrying, I say, the stamp of one defect,
Being nature's livery, or fortune's star,—
Their virtues else—be they as pure as grace,
As infinite as man may undergo—
Shall in the general censure take corruption   35
From that particular fault: the dram of evil
Doth all the noble substance of a doubt
To his own scandal—

[*Enter Ghost.*]

Horatio: Look, my lord, it comes!
Hamlet: Angels and ministers of grace defend us!
Be thou a spirit of health or goblin damn'd,   40
Bring with thee airs from heaven or blasts from hell,
Be thy intents wicked or charitable,
Thou com'st in such a questionable shape
That I will speak to thee: I'll call thee Hamlet,
King, father, royal Dane: O, answer me!   45
Let me not burst in ignorance, but tell
Why thy canonized bones, hearsed in death,
Have burst their cerements; why the sepulchre,
Wherein we saw thee quietly in-urn'd,
Hath oped his ponderous and marble jaws,   50
To cast thee up again. What may this mean,
That thou, dead corse, again, in complete steel,
Revisit'st thus the glimpses of the moon,
Making night hideous; and we fools of nature
So horridly to shake our disposition   55
With thoughts beyond the reaches of our souls?
Say, why is this? wherefore? what should we do?
                            [*Ghost beckons Hamlet.*]
Horatio: It beckons you to go away with it,
As if it some impartment did desire
To you alone.
Marcellus: Look, with what courteous action   60
It waves you to a more removed ground;
But do not go with it.

65   *at a pin's fee:* worth a pin

71   *beetles o'er:* overhangs

73   *Which might . . . reason:* which might rob you of your ability
to reason

75   *toys of desperation:* desperate thoughts

83   *Nemean lion:* In Greek mythology, one of the twelve labours
of Hercules was to fetch the Nemean lion's skin.

85   *lets:* hinders

Horatio: No, by no means.
Hamlet: It will not speak; then will I follow it.
Horatio: Do not, my lord.
Hamlet: Why, what should be the fear?
  I do not set my life at a pin's fee;   65
  And for my soul, what can it do to that,
  Being a thing immortal as itself?
  It waves me forth again: I'll follow it.
Horatio: What if it tempt you toward the flood, my lord,
  Or to the dreadful summit of the cliff   70
  That beetles o'er his base into the sea,
  And there assume some other horrible form,
  Which might deprive your sovereignty of reason
  And draw you into madness? think of it:
  The very place puts toys of desperation,   75
  Without more motive, into every brain
  That looks so many fathoms to the sea
  And hears it roar beneath.
Hamlet: It waves me still.
  Go on; I'll follow thee.
Marcellus: You shall not go, my lord.
Hamlet: Hold off your hands.   80
Horatio: Be ruled; you shall not go.
Hamlet: My fate cries out,
  And makes each petty artery in this body
  As hardy as the Nemean lion's nerve.—
  Still am I call'd; unhand me, gentlemen;
  By heaven, I'll make a ghost of him that lets me;   85
  I say, away! Go on; I'll follow thee.
                          [*Exeunt Ghost and Hamlet.*]
Horatio: He waxes desperate with imagination.
Marcellus: Let's follow; 'tis not fit thus to obey him.
Horatio: Have after. To what issue will this come?
Marcellus: Something is rotten in the state of Denmark.   90
Horatio: Heaven will direct it.
Marcellus: Nay, let's follow him.
                          [*Exeunt.*]

Act 1, Scene 4: Activities

1. Recall an occasion you experienced with family members or friends when someone's behaviour made you uncomfortable or embarrassed. In your journal, describe how you dealt with the situation at the time. How did this experience affect your feelings about that person? Can you relate these feelings to Hamlet's feelings at the beginning of the scene? Explain your answer.

2. In groups, discuss what you think Hamlet is saying about human nature (lines 23 – 38).
   - Summarize Hamlet's ideas.
   - Think of one or more individuals, past or present, whose lives illustrate Hamlet's theory. In each case, describe the person's character flaw and explain how it affected the course of his or her life.
   - Discuss whether or not an individual is responsible for his or her weaknesses.

3. In pairs, take the roles of Marcellus and Horatio and write a dialogue that takes place after Hamlet has gone to follow the Ghost. Discuss Hamlet's behaviour and decide what you should do now. Role-play your dialogue for your group.

For the next scene . . .

In your journal, reflect on a moment when you received some unexpected news and thought, "This news will change my life." As you think back, to what extent *did* it change your life?

Act 1, Scene 5

In this scene . . .

The Ghost tells Hamlet that he was murdered by
Claudius. He accuses Claudius and Gertrude of having
an adulterous relationship before his death, and he
describes exactly how he was poisoned. The Ghost
commands Hamlet to take revenge for these wrongs.
Hamlet is horrified by all he learns and swears to heed
the Ghost's commands. When he is joined by Horatio
and Marcellus, he does not reveal what the Ghost told
him. As his friends try to calm him, he forces them to
swear secrecy about what they have seen.

2   *Mark me:* Listen.

3   *sulphurous and tormenting flames:* a description of purgatory

13   *burnt and purged away:* Hamlet's father died without receiving
       the last rites of the Church. As a result, his soul is caught
       in purgatory, since any sins he committed in his lifetime were
       not absolved.

21   *eternal blazon:* telling of the secrets of eternity

Scene 5

A more remote part of the platform.

Enter Ghost and Hamlet.

Hamlet: Whither wilt thou lead me? speak; I'll go no further.
Ghost: Mark me.
Hamlet: I will.
Ghost: My hour is almost come,
 When I to sulphurous and tormenting flames
 Must render up myself.
Hamlet: Alas, poor ghost!
Ghost: Pity me not, but lend thy serious hearing   5
 To what I shall unfold.
Hamlet: Speak, I am bound to hear.
Ghost: So art thou to revenge, when thou shalt hear.
Hamlet: What!
Ghost: I am thy father's spirit;
 Doom'd for a certain term to walk the night,   10
 And for the day confined to fast in fires,
 Till the foul crimes done in my days of nature
 Are burnt and purged away. But that I am forbid
 To tell the secrets of my prison-house,
 I could a tale unfold whose lightest word   15
 Would harrow up thy soul; freeze thy young blood,
 Make thy two eyes, like stars, start from their spheres,
 Thy knotted and combined locks to part
 And each particular hair to stand on end,
 Like quills upon the fretful porcupine;   20
 But this eternal blazon must not be
 To ears of flesh and blood. List, list, O, list!
 If thou didst ever thy dear father love,—
Hamlet: O God!
Ghost: Revenge his foul and most unnatural murder.   25
Hamlet: Murder?

27   *in the best:* at best

33   *Lethe:* In Greek mythology, Lethe is the river of forgetfulness located in the underworld.

35   *orchard:* garden

37   *forged process:* false story

38   *abused:* misled

51   *decline:* fall to a lower level

62   *Upon my secure hour:* at a time when I was unsuspecting

63   *hebenon:* a poison plant

65   *leperous distilment:* juices as deadly as leprosy

Ghost: Murder most foul, as in the best it is,
  But this most foul, strange, and unnatural.
Hamlet: Haste me to know't; that I, with wings as swift
  As meditation or the thoughts of love,   30
  May sweep to my revenge.
Ghost: I find thee apt;
  And duller shouldst thou be than the fat weed
  That rots itself in ease on Lethe wharf,
  Wouldst thou not stir in this. Now, Hamlet, hear:
  'Tis given out that, sleeping in mine orchard,   35
  A serpent stung me; so the whole ear of Denmark
  Is by a forged process of my death
  Rankly abused: but know, thou noble youth,
  The serpent that did sting thy father's life
  Now wears his crown.   40
Hamlet: My uncle?
  O my prophetic soul!
Ghost: Ay, that incestuous, that adulterate beast,
  With witchcraft of his wit, with traitorous gifts,—
  O wicked wit and gifts, that have the power   45
  So to seduce!—won to his shameful lust
  The will of my most seeming-virtuous queen;
  O Hamlet, what a falling-off was there!
  From me, whose love was of that dignity
  That it went hand in hand even with the vow   50
  I made to her in marriage; and to decline
  Upon a wretch, whose natural gifts were poor
  To those of mine!
  But virtue, as it never will be moved,
  Though lewdness court it in a shape of heaven,   55
  So lust, though to a radiant angel link'd,
  Will sate itself in a celestial bed,
  And prey on garbage.
  But soft! methinks, I scent the morning air;
  Brief let me be. Sleeping within mine orchard,   60
  My custom always in the afternoon,
  Upon my secure hour thy uncle stole,
  With juice of cursed hebenon in a vial,
  And in the porches of mine ears did pour
  The leperous distilment; whose effect   65

69-70   *it doth posset/And curd:* it curdles and clots (the blood)

70   *eager:* acidic. The reference is to rennet, which is added to milk to curdle it.

72   *a most instant tetter bark'd about:* My skin became as rough and scaly as tree bark.

73   *lazar-like:* like leprosy

76   *despatch'd:* deprived

78   *unhousel'd, disappointed, unaneled:* without the proper religious ceremonies

82   *nature:* that which is natural to humans

84   *luxury:* lechery

90   *matin:* morning

98   *globe:* head

99   *table:* notebook (related to the word "tablet")

100   *fond:* foolish

101   *saws:* sayings; *pressures:* impressions

Holds such an enmity with blood of man
That swift as quicksilver it courses through
The natural gates and alleys of the body;
And, with a sudden vigour, it doth posset
And curd, like eager droppings into milk,   70
The thin and wholesome blood: so did it mine;
And a most instant tetter bark'd about
Most lazar-like, with vile and loathsome crust,
All my smooth body.
Thus was I, sleeping, by a brother's hand   75
Of life, of crown, of queen, at once despatch'd;
Cut off even in the blossoms of my sin,
Unhousel'd, disappointed, unaneled;
No reckoning made, but sent to my account
With all my imperfections on my head.   80
Hamlet: O, horrible! O, horrible! most horrible!
Ghost: If thou hast nature in thee, bear it not;
Let not the royal bed of Denmark be
A couch for luxury and damned incest.
But, howsoever thou pursuest this act,   85
Taint not thy mind, nor let thy soul contrive
Against thy mother aught; leave her to heaven,
And to those thorns that in her bosom lodge,
To prick and sting her. Fare thee well at once!
The glow-worm shows the matin to be near,   90
And 'gins to pale his uneffectual fire:
Adieu, adieu, adieu! remember me!   *[Exit.]*
Hamlet: O all you host of heaven! O earth! What else?
And shall I couple hell? O fie! Hold, hold, my heart;
And you, my sinews, grow not instant old,   95
But bear me stiffly up! Remember thee!
Ay, thou poor ghost, while memory holds a seat
In this distracted globe. Remember thee!
Yea, from the table of my memory
I'll wipe away all trivial fond records,   100
All saws of books, all forms, all pressures past,
That youth and observation copied there;
And thy commandment all alone shall live
Within the book and volume of my brain,
Unmix'd with baser matter: yes, by heaven!   105

116-17   *Illo, ho, ho boy!:* a falconer's cry to his bird (a signal to us that Hamlet may not be in control of his mind).

125   *an arrant knave:* complete, utter fool

128   *without . . . at all:* without more ado

O most pernicious woman!
O villain, villain, smiling, damned villain!
My tables—meet it is I set it down,
That one may smile, and smile, and be a villain;
At least I'm sure it may be so in Denmark;   110
                                    [*Writing.*]
So, uncle, there you are. Now to my word;
It is, "Adieu, adieu! remember me."
I have sworn't.
Horatio [*Without*]: My lord, my lord,—
Marcellus [*Without*]:   Lord Hamlet,—
Horatio [*Without*]:   Heaven secure him!
Marcellus [*Without*]: So be it!   115
Horatio [*Without*]: Illo, ho, ho, my lord!
Hamlet: Hillo, ho, ho, boy! come, bird, come.

   [*Enter Horatio and Marcellus.*]

Marcellus: How is't, my noble lord?
Horatio: What news, my lord?
Hamlet: O, wonderful!
Horatio: Good my lord, tell it.
Hamlet: No, you will reveal it.   120
Horatio: Not I, my lord, by heaven.
Marcellus: Nor I, my lord.
Hamlet: How say you then; would heart of man once think
      it?
   But you'll be secret?
Horatio, Marcellus: Ay, by heaven, my lord.
Hamlet: There's ne'er a villain dwelling in all Denmark
   But he's an arrant knave.   125
Horatio: There needs no ghost, my lord, come from the
      grave
To tell us this.
Hamlet: Why, right; you are i' the right:
   And so, without more circumstance at all,
   I hold it fit that we shake hands and part;
   You, as your business and desire shall point you;   130
   For every man has business and desire,
   Such as it is; and for mine own poor part,
   Look you, I'll go pray.

137   *St. Patrick:* the keeper of purgatory

149   *upon my sword:* The handle of the sword makes the form of the cross.

151   *truepenny:* honest old fellow

157   *Hic et ubique?:* (Latin) Here and everywhere?

164   *pioneer:* a soldier who dug tunnels

Horatio: These are but wild and whirling words, my lord.

Hamlet: I'm sorry they offend you, heartily;   135
   Yes, faith, heartily.

Horatio: There's no offence, my lord.

Hamlet: Yes, by St. Patrick, but there is, Horatio.
   And much offence too. Touching this vision here,
   It is an honest ghost, that let me tell you;
   For your desire to know what is between us,   140
   O'ermaster't as you may. And now, good friends,
   As you are friends, scholars, and soldiers,
   Give me one poor request.

Horatio: What is't, my lord? We will.

Hamlet: Never make known what you have seen tonight.   145

Horatio, Marcellus: My lord, we will not.

Hamlet: Nay, but swear't.

Horatio: In faith,
   My lord, not I.

Marcellus: Nor I, my lord, in faith.

Hamlet: Upon my sword.

Marcellus: We have sworn, my lord, already.

Hamlet: In deed, upon my sword, in deed.

Ghost [Beneath]: Swear!   150

Hamlet: Ah, ha, boy! say'st thou so? art thou there,
   truepenny?
   Come on: you hear this fellow in the cellarage:
   Consent to swear.

Horatio: Propose the oath, my lord,

Hamlet: Never to speak of this that you have seen,
   Swear by my sword.   155

Ghost [Beneath]: Swear!

Hamlet: Hic et ubique? then we'll shift our ground.
   Come hither, gentlemen,
   And lay your hands again upon my sword:
   Never to speak of this that you have heard,   160
   Swear by my sword.

Ghost [Beneath]: Swear!

Hamlet: Well said, old mole! canst work i' the ground so
   fast?
   A worthy pioneer! Once more remove, good friends.

Horatio: O day and night, but this is wondrous strange!   165

172   *meet:* suitable

173   *antic disposition:* strange (insane) behaviour

179   *ambiguous giving out:* vague suggestion or comment

Hamlet: And therefore as a stranger give it welcome.
　　There are more things in heaven and earth, Horatio,
　　Than are dreamt of in our philosophy.
　　But come;
　　Here, as before, never, so help you mercy,　　　　　　170
　　How strange or odd soe'er I bear myself,
　　As I perchance hereafter shall think meet
　　To put an antic disposition on,
　　That you, at such times seeing me, never shall,
　　With arms encumber'd thus, or this head-shake,　　　175
　　Or by pronouncing of some doubtful phrase,
　　As, "Well, well, we know"; or, "We could, an if we
　　　　would";
　　Or, "If we list to speak"; or, "There be, an if they
　　　　might";—
　　Or such ambiguous giving out, to note
　　That you know aught of me: this not to do,　　　　　180
　　So grace and mercy at your most need help you,
　　Swear!
Ghost [*Beneath*]: Swear!　　　　　　　　　[*They swear.*]
Hamlet: Rest, rest, perturbed spirit! So, gentlemen,
　　With all my love I do commend me to you:　　　　　185
　　And what so poor a man as Hamlet is
　　May do, to express his love and friending to you,
　　God willing, shall not lack. Let us go in together;
　　And still your fingers on your lips, I pray.
　　The time is out of joint; O cursed spite,　　　　　　190
　　That ever I was born to set it right!—
　　Nay, come, let's go together.　　　　　　[*Exeunt.*]

Act 1, Scene 5: Activities

1. In groups, prepare an audiotaped performance of the Ghost's story (lines 35 – 80). You may want to split up into three smaller groups to prepare the different elements of your tape. One person should practise reading the Ghost's lines, concentrating on tone of voice, loudness, tempo (speed and rhythm) and pauses. A second person could act as a coach, helping the reader develop the most effective delivery. Remember that the Ghost is inciting Hamlet to action. Experiment with different sound effects to accompany the speech. These sounds are meant to heighten the effect of the Ghost's words. Compose or tape music to use as the "Ghost theme," to be played each time the Ghost appears. Combine the music, sound effects and speech in a performance for your class.

2. What instructions does the Ghost give Hamlet about Gertrude? Why might the Ghost be concerned about Hamlet's reaction to Gertrude? If you were the Ghost, what suggestions would you make to Hamlet about the way he should treat his mother? Explain your answer.

3. Nowadays a person in Hamlet's situation might resort to the legal system to obtain justice. However, even today there are people who "take the law into their own hands" to avenge a wrong. With your class, cite some recent examples of this and discuss your feelings about people who do "take the law into their own hands."

4. Compare Hamlet's first response to the Ghost's call for revenge (lines 29 – 30) with his statement at the end of the scene (lines 190 – 191). How do you account for the differences between these two responses?

5. Horatio and Marcellus show their loyalty to Hamlet by swearing not to tell anyone about the appearance of the Ghost. What risks might be involved in being Hamlet's

ally? From what you know of Hamlet's character, why do you think they follow him? Would you? In your journal, explain why you would or would not trust Hamlet's leadership.

Act 1: Consider the Whole Act

1. Create an image bank using the following suggestions:
   a) In groups, list what you think are the most important images in this act. Write each image on an individual file card. Give the line reference for each image and make a note of who is speaking and what the situation is. Discuss the meaning of each image and the way it intensifies the idea.
   b) Discuss the ways in which any of the images are related to one another. Are there any headings under which these images could be grouped?
   c) Decide whether you want to arrange your file cards sequentially (following the order in which they appear in the play) or under the headings discussed in class. The file cards should be kept in a box in your class so that you all have access to them.

   You could refer to this image bank and add new images to the collection as you continue your exploration of *Hamlet*.

2. As a class, watch a film or a videotape of Scenes 1, 4 and 5. What techniques has the director used to create suspense? Consider set design, lighting, special effects, camera angle, the use of close-ups, and the length of each shot. If you were the director, what might you do differently? Talk about your ideas.

3. "I know not 'seems.' " In Scene 2 (line 76), Hamlet claims that his grief is real, not just a show. In groups, make a list of all the occasions in this act when there is a differ-

ence between the way a character seems to be and the way he or she really is. Draw up a chart with the following headings:
- The Character
- The Situation
- The Appearance
- The Reality
- The Reason for Hiding the Truth

Fill in your ideas about the characters' behaviour and compare your chart with those of other groups.

4. In this act, you have seen Hamlet in a number of very different situations. What qualities does he reveal to each of the following people: his mother, his stepfather, his friend Horatio, the Ghost, himself? How do each of these people feel about Hamlet? In the role of any one of these characters, write a diary entry about your concerns for Hamlet.

5. This act contains some lines that have become famous on their own. Some examples are "Something is rotten in the state of Denmark,"; "Frailty, thy name is woman!"; "There are more things in heaven and earth, Horatio,/Than are dreamt of in (y)our philosophy"; and, "The time is out of joint." Use one of these as the first line of a serious or humourous poem. Share your poem with members of your group.

6. In your journal, describe an occasion when an adult failed to take you seriously. Explain whether that reaction changed your own feelings about your situation in any way. In general, do you think that the older characters in this act respect the beliefs and feelings of the younger characters? With a partner, discuss the occasions that support your point of view.

For the next scene . . .

If a parent is supporting a son or daughter living away from home, do you think the parent has the right to "check up" on the child's behaviour? If so, what methods of "checking up" would you consider acceptable or not acceptable?

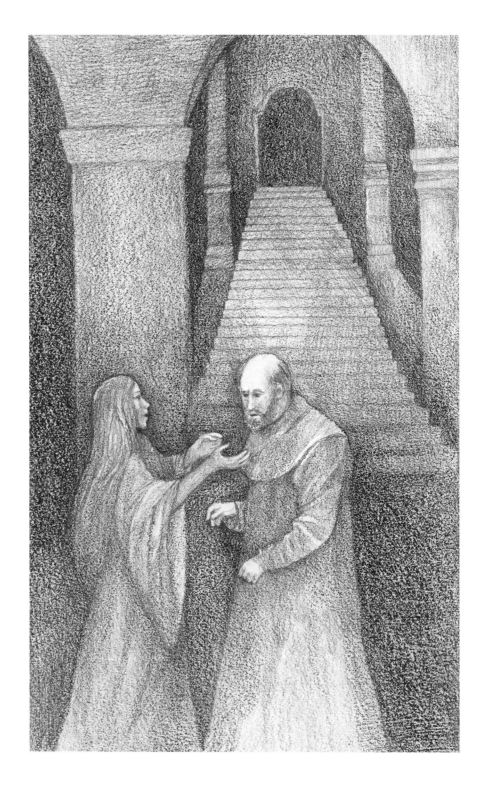

Act 2, Scene 1

In this scene . . .

Polonius dispatches his servant Reynaldo to Paris to deliver some money and also to gather information about Laertes' behaviour. Ophelia enters, upset and frightened, and tells Polonius about a disturbing visit she has just had from Hamlet. Hamlet's clothing was in disarray. He did not speak to Ophelia, but he seemed to be painfully taking his leave of her. Polonius quickly concludes that rejected love has caused Hamlet to go mad. He decides to inform the King immediately.

7   *Danskers:* Danes

8   *keep:* dwell, live

10   *By this . . . question:* by this method of indirect, casual questioning

11-12   *come you . . . touch it:* achieve your purpose better than you could by direct questioning. (Notice Polonius' personality and methods.)

19-20   *put on . . . please:* accuse him of any imagined faults you wish

20   *rank:* gross

22-24   *such wanton . . . liberty:* wild behaviour that is characteristic of young people who are on their own

24   *gaming:* gambling

26   *Drabbing:* associating with prostitutes

28   *season it in the charge:* make it sound less serious by the casual way you mention it

Act 2, Scene 1

A room in Polonius' house.

Enter Polonius and Reynaldo.

Polonius: Give him this money, and these notes, Reynaldo.
Reynaldo: I will, my lord.
Polonius: You shall do marvellous wisely, good Reynaldo,
  Before you visit him, to make inquiry
  Of his behaviour.
Reynaldo: My lord, I did intend it.   5
Polonius: Marry, well said, very well said. Look you, sir,
  Inquire me first what Danskers are in Paris,
  And how, and who, what means, and where they keep,
  What company, at what expense, and finding
  By this encompassment and drift of question   10
  That they do know my son, come you more nearer
  Than your particular demands will touch it:
  Take you, as 'twere, some distant knowledge of him,
  As thus, "I know his father, and his friends,
  And, in part, him"; do you mark this, Reynaldo?   15
Reynaldo: Ay, very well, my lord.
Polonius: "And, in part, him"; but, you may say, "not well
  But, if't be he I mean, he's very wild,
  Addicted so and so"; and there put on him
  What forgeries you please; marry, none so rank   20
  As may dishonour him; take heed of that;
  But, sir, such wanton, wild, and usual slips
  As are companions noted and most known
  To youth and liberty.
Reynaldo: As gaming, my lord.
Polonius: Ay, or drinking, fencing, swearing, quarrelling,   25
  Drabbing: you may go so far.
Reynaldo: My lord, that would dishonour him.
Polonius: Faith, no; as you may season it in the charge.
  You must not put another scandal on him,

30   *open to incontinency:* practising extreme habitual debauchery

31   *quaintly:* cleverly

32   *taints of liberty:* faults resulting from having too much freedom

35   *of general assault:* typical of young people

38   *fetch of warrant:* legitimate trick. (Obviously, Polonius believes that the end justifies the means.)

39   *sullies:* accusations of disgraceful behaviour

41   *Mark you:* pay attention

42   *Your party in converse:* the person you are talking to

43   *prenominate:* aforementioned

45   *closes . . . consequence:* agrees with you as follows

47   *addition:* title

58   *o'ertook in's rouse:* so drunk that he lost consciousness

61   *Videlicet:* (Latin) namely

63   *Your bait . . . truth:* By using lie as bait, you fish out the truth. (The carp was considered an easy fish to catch.)

64   *we . . . reach:* we who are wise and far-sighted

65   *With windlasses . . . bias:* through twists and indirect approaches

That he is open to incontinency; 30
That's not my meaning: but breathe his faults so quaintly
That they may seem the taints of liberty,
The flash and outbreak of a fiery mind,
A savageness in unreclaimed blood,
Of general assault.
Reynaldo: But, my good lord,— 35
Polonius: Wherefore should you do this?
Reynaldo: Ay, my lord,
I would know that.
Polonius: Marry, sir, here's my drift,
And I believe it is a fetch of warrant:
You laying these slight sullies on my son,
As 'twere a thing a little soil'd i' the working, 40
Mark you,
Your party in converse, him you would sound,
Having ever seen in the prenominate crimes
The youth you breathe of guilty, be assured
He closes with you in this consequence: 45
"Good sir," or so; or "friend," or "gentleman,"
According to the phrase or the addition
Of man and country.
Reynaldo: Very good, my lord.
Polonius: And then, sir, does he this—he does—
What was I about to say? By the mass, I was about to 50
say something: where did I leave?
Reynaldo: At "closes in the consequence," at "friend, or
so," and "gentleman."
Polonius: At "closes in the consequence," ay, marry;
He closes with you thus: "I know the gentleman; 55
I saw him yesterday, or t'other day,"
Or then, or then; with such or such, and, as you say,
"There was a gaming, there o'ertook in's rouse,
There falling out at tennis": or perchance,
"I saw him enter such a house of sale"; 60
Videlicet, a brothel, or so forth.
See you now;
Your bait of falsehood takes this carp of truth:
And thus do we of wisdom and of reach,
With windlasses and with assays of bias, 65

66   *By indirections find directions out:* by indirect methods find out the truth

68   *You have me:* you understand me

73   *let him ply his music:* let him carry on as he wishes (i.e., Reynaldo should only find out about Laertes' behaviour, not correct it.)

79   *his doublet all unbraced:* his jacket completely open

80   *foul'd:* loose and twisted. The image is of an anchor's ropes.

81   *down-gyved to his ancle:* fallen down to his ankle. (In Elizabethan times, a man who wanted to show that he was in love would dress negligently.)

83   *purport:* meaning

91   *perusal:* study

By indirections find directions out:
So, by my former lecture and advice,
Shall you my son. You have me, have you not?
Reynaldo: My lord, I have.
Polonius: God be wi'ye; fare ye well.
Reynaldo: Good, my lord.   70
Polonius: Observe his inclination in yourself.
Reynaldo: I shall, my lord.
Polonius: And let him ply his music.
Reynaldo: Well, my lord.
                                                   [*Exit.*]

Polonius: Farewell!

[*Enter Ophelia.*]

How now, Ophelia? what's the matter?   75
Ophelia: Alas, my lord, I have been so affrighted!
Polonius: With what, i' the name of heaven?
Ophelia: My lord, as I was sewing in my chamber,
    Lord Hamlet, with his doublet all unbraced,
    No hat upon his head, his stockings foul'd,   80
    Ungarter'd, and down-gyved to his ancle:
    Pale as his shirt, his knees knocking each other,
    And with a look so piteous in purport,
    As if he had been loosed out of hell
    To speak of horrors, he comes before me.   85
Polonius: Mad for thy love!
Ophelia: My lord, I do not know,
    But truly I do fear it.
Polonius: What said he?
Ophelia: He took me by the wrist and held me hard;
    Then goes he to the length of all his arm,
    And, with his other hand thus o'er his brow,   90
    He falls to such perusal of my face
    As he would draw it. Long stay'd he so;
    At last, a little shaking of mine arm,
    And thrice his head thus waving up and down,
    He raised a sigh so piteous and profound   95
    That it did seem to shatter all his bulk
    And end his being: that done, he lets me go:
    And with his head over his shoulder turn'd,

103   *ecstasy:* madness

104   *fordoes:* destroys

112   *access:* admittance

114   *quoted:* observed

115   *jealousy:* suspicion

116-119 *By heaven . . . discretion:* It is just as natural for old men to be overly suspicious as it is for the young to be indiscreet.

120-121 *This must . . . love:* Hamlet's love (or madness) must be reported to the King. To keep it secret might cause more harm than it would to tell about it, which might cause anger.

He seem'd to find his way without his eyes;
For out o' doors he went without their helps, 100
And to the last bended their light on me.
Polonius: Come, go with me; I will go seek the king.
This is the very ecstasy of love;
Whose violent property fordoes itself
And leads the will to desperate undertakings 105
As oft as any passion under heaven
That does afflict our natures. I am sorry.
What, have you given him any hard words of late?
Ophelia: No, my good lord; but, as you did command,
I did repel his letters and denied 110
His access to me.
Polonius: That hath made him mad.
I am sorry that with better heed and judgment
I had not quoted him: I fear'd he did but trifle
And meant to wreck thee; but beshrew my jealousy! 115
By heaven it is as proper to our age
To cast beyond ourselves in our opinions
As it is common for the younger sort
To lack discretion. Come, go we to the king:
This must be known; which, being kept close, might move 120
More grief to hide than hate to utter love.
Come. [*Exeunt.*]

Act 2, Scene 1: Activities

1. In pairs, write point-form notes that Polonius might have made before his conversation with Reynaldo.

2. As a class or in groups, make several suggestions about Polonius' motives for spying on Laertes. As you think about this, you may want to refer to the advice that Polonius gave Laertes in Act 1, Scene 3.

3. Reynaldo's replies are quite short. Suppose that he is a bright young man who sympathizes more with Laertes than with Polonius. Add some "asides" (to be heard by the audience but not by Polonius) to Reynaldo's replies, to show that Reynaldo understands Polonius' motives very well. With a partner, read the dialogue between Polonius and Reynaldo and include your asides.

4. "Blocking" is a theatre term that means deciding where each actor will be positioned on the stage and what his or her movements will be. In groups, discuss how you would block the exchange between Polonius and Reynaldo (lines 1 – 73). Some things to consider when blocking a sequence:
   - Which character(s) is closest to the audience?
   - How far apart are the characters? Does this distance change?
   - Does one character move first, followed by the other character, or do they move independently of one another?

   You should also consider what body language (posture, gestures, facial expressions) each character should use. Take turns experimenting with different movements in the roles of Polonius and Reynaldo. Perform for the class the version that best expresses the relationship between Polonius and Reynaldo, their motives and their reactions. If you wish, combine questions 3 and 4 and perform your revised version of this sequence.

5. In the role of Hamlet, write two entries in your diary—one before and one after your visit to Ophelia.

6. Imagine that you have heard the story of Hamlet's visit to Ophelia through the palace "grapevine." How might the story have been changed through several retellings? Discuss your ideas with a partner. Write your own version of this story as if you were passing it on to a friend. Include your opinion of Hamlet's behaviour.

7. Have you ever found yourself acting strangely because you were in love? If someone you loved behaved the way Ophelia says Hamlet did, how would you interpret that behaviour? How would you react to it? Record your responses in your journal or share them with your group.

For the next scene . . .

Suppose your close friend has been acting very strangely. Your friend's parents ask you to find out the reasons for the strange mood and then report back to them. Under what circumstances would you be willing to do this? How would you feel about this request? Would you tell your friend what you were doing?

Act 2, Scene 2

In this scene . . .

Two months have passed. Two old friends of Hamlet's, Rosencrantz and Guildenstern, arrive at the court and agree to spy on Hamlet for Claudius and Gertrude. Polonius enters and announces the return of the two ambassadors sent to Norway, and reports that the military threat from Norway has been resolved. He also tells Claudius and Gertrude that Hamlet's rejected love for Ophelia is the cause of Hamlet's apparent madness, and he offers to arrange an "accidental" meeting between Hamlet and Ophelia so that he and Claudius can spy on their conversation. Hamlet enters, reading a book. Polonius makes conversation with him and Hamlet replies quite irrationally, but Polonius recognizes that there is truth buried in Hamlet's mad words. Hamlet then greets Rosencrantz and Guildenstern warmly, but he soon realizes they are on a spying mission. When he tells them how depressed he is, they try to cheer him up with news about some travelling actors visiting the court. Hamlet greets the players warmly and asks the lead actor to insert an extra few lines into the play *The Murder of Gonzago*, to be performed before the King the next night. In a soliloquy, Hamlet chastises himself strongly for procrastinating in regard to his father's murder. No longer certain that the Ghost was sincere, he decides to test Claudius' guilt by watching his reaction to a play in which old King Hamlet's murder will be re-enacted.

2   *Moreover that:* over and above the fact that

3   *provoke:* cause

11   *of so young days:* from such a young age

12   *sith:* since; *neighbour'd to:* close to

13   *vouchsafe your rest:* consent to stay

18   *open'd:* if it were revealed

21   *To whom . . . adheres:* to whom he is more partial or loyal

22   *gentry:* gentlemanliness, courtesy

24   *For the supply and profit of our hope:* to help fulfill our hope
      (of finding the cause of Hamlet's disturbance)

Scene 2

A room in the castle.

Enter King, Queen, Rosencrantz,
Guildenstern, and Attendants

King: Welcome, dear Rosencrantz and Guildenstern!
  Moreover that we much did long to see you,
  The need we have to use you did provoke
  Our hasty sending. Something have you heard
  Of Hamlet's transformation; so I call it,   5
  Since not the exterior nor the inward man
  Resembles that it was. What it should be,
  More than his father's death, that thus hath put him
  So much from the understanding of himself,
  I cannot deem of: I entreat you both,   10
  That, being of so young days brought up with him
  And sith so neighbour'd to his youth and haviour,
  That you vouchsafe your rest here in our court
  Some little time: so by your companies
  To draw him on to pleasures, and to gather,   15
  So much as from occasion you may glean,
  Whether aught to us unknown afflicts him thus,
  That open'd lies within our remedy.
Queen: Good gentlemen, he hath much talk'd of you,
  And sure I am two men there are not living   20
  To whom he more adheres. If it will please you
  To show us so much gentry and good will,
  As to expend your time with us a while
  For the supply and profit of our hope,
  Your visitation shall receive such thanks   25
  As fits a king's remembrance.
Rosencrantz: Both your majesties
  Might, by the sovereign power you have of us,
  Put your dread pleasures more into command
  Than to entreaty.
Guildenstern: But we both obey,

30   *in the full bent:* to the utmost. The image is of a bow stretched
      to the limit before the arrow is loosed.

38   *practices:* actions. The word "practices" was also used to
      mean "tricks."

42   *still:* always

44-45 *I hold my duty . . . king:* I consider my duty to my king as
      important as my duty to God.

47   *Hunts not the trail of policy so sure:* doesn't follow or track
      the methods of statecraft (politics) as well

52   *fruit to that great feast:* the dessert (the sweetest, best part)

55   *distemper:* disturbed state of mind

56   *doubt: suspect; main:* chief point

58   *sift:* question closely

60   *desires:* good wishes

And here give up ourselves, in the full bent 30
To lay our service freely at your feet,
To be commanded.
King: Thanks, Rosencrantz and gentle Guildenstern.
Queen: Thanks, Guildenstern and gentle Rosencrantz:
And I beseech you instantly to visit 35
My too much changed son. Go, some of you,
And bring these gentlemen where Hamlet is.
Guildenstern: Heavens make our presence and our practices
Pleasant and helpful to him!
Queen: Ay, amen!

[*Exeunt Rosencrantz, Guildenstern, and some Attendants.*]

[*Enter Polonius.*]

Polonius: The ambassadors from Norway, my good lord, 40
Are joyfully return'd.
King: Thou still hast been the father of good news.
Polonius: Have I, my lord? Assure you my good liege,
I hold my duty as I hold my soul,
Both to my God and to my gracious king: 45
And I do think, or else this brain of mine
Hunts not the trail of policy so sure
As it hath used to do, that I have found
The very cause of Hamlet's lunacy.
King: O, speak of that; that do I long to hear. 50
Polonius: Give first admittance to the ambassadors;
My news shall be the fruit to that great feast.
King: Thyself do grace to them, and bring them in.
[*Exit Polonius.*]
He tells me, my dear Gertrude, that he hath found
The head and source of all your son's distemper. 55
Queen: I doubt it is no other but the main;
His father's death, and our o'erhasty marriage.
King: Well, we shall sift him.

[*Re-enter Polonius, with Voltimand and Cornelius.*]

Welcome, my good friends!
Say, Voltimand, what from our brother Norway?
Voltimand: Most fair return of greetings and desires. 60

61   *Upon our first:* as a result of our first conference

67   *falsely borne in hand:* deceived; *sends out arrests:* sends
       out commands (for Fortinbras) to stop his operations
69   *in fine:* in short

71   *To give . . . arms:* to test out his military strength

79-80 *On such regards . . . set down:* The document sets out the
       conditions whereby the Norwegian army will be allowed to
       pass through Denmark without posing a threat.
80   *It likes us well:* It pleases us

86-92 Polonius' speech is an example of the very thing he is criti-
       cizing. This type of humour is called satire. Shakespeare
       often pokes fun in this way at people whose speech is full of
       flourishes, but whose message is not clear.
90   *wit:* understanding
91   *outward flourishes:* display of fine clothing

Upon our first, he sent out to suppress
His nephew's levies; which to him appear'd
To be a preparation 'gainst the Polack,
But better look'd into, he truly found
It was against your highness: whereat, grieved,   65
That so his sickness, age, and impotence
Was falsely borne in hand, sends out arrests
On Fortinbras; which he, in brief, obeys,
Receives rebuke from Norway, and in fine
Makes vow before his uncle never more   70
To give the assay of arms against your majesty.
Whereon old Norway, overcome with joy,
Gives him three thousand crowns in annual fee
And his commission to employ those soldiers,
So levied as before, against the Polack: 75
With an entreaty, herein further shown,
                        [Gives a paper.]
That it might please you to give quiet pass
Through your dominions for his enterprise,
On such regards of safety and allowance
As therein are set down.

King: It likes us well,   80
And, at our more consider'd time, we'll read,
Answer, and think upon this business.
Meantime we thank you for your well-took labour:
Go to your rest; at night we'll feast together:
Most welcome home!
                [Exeunt Voltimand and Cornelius.]

Polonius: This business is well ended.   85
My liege, and madam, to expostulate
What majesty should be, what duty is,
Why day is day, night night, and time is time,
Were nothing but to waste night, day, and time.
Therefore, since brevity is the soul of wit   90
And tediousness the limbs and outward flourishes,
I will be brief. Your noble son is mad:
Mad call I it: for, to define true madness,
What is't, but to be nothing else but mad?
But let that go.

Queen: More matter, with less art.   95

98   *figure:* that is, figure of speech

105   *Perpend:* Consider (a pedantic word, unsuitable for this conversation).

110   *That's an ill phrase:* Polonius is referring to the word "beauti-fied," which he finds artificial.

112   *In her . . . bosom:* for her eyes and heart alone

119   *ill at these numbers:* untalented at writing rhyme

120   *reckon:* count

122   *machine:* body

Polonius: Madam, I swear I use no art at all.
  That he is mad 'tis true: 'tis true 'tis pity,
  And pity 'tis 'tis true: a foolish figure;
  But farewell it, for I will use no art.
  Mad let us grant him then: and now remains   100
  That we find out the cause of this effect,
  Or rather say, the cause of this defect,
  For this effect defective comes by cause:
  Thus it remains, and the remainder thus.
  Perpend.   105
  I have a daughter, have while she is mine,—
  Who in her duty and obedience, mark,
  Hath given me this: now gather, and surmise.

  [*Reads.*] To the celestial, and my soul's idol, the most
    beautified Ophelia.—

  That's an ill phrase, a vile phrase; "beautified" is a vile   110
    phrase: but you shall hear. Thus:

  In her excellent white bosom, these, etc.

Queen: Came this from Hamlet to her?
Polonius: Good madam, stay a while; I will be faithful.
                                          [*Reads.*]
    Doubt thou the stars are fire;   115
        Doubt that the sun doth move;
    Doubt truth to be a liar;
        But never doubt I love.

    O dear Ophelia, I am ill at these numbers; I have
      not art to reckon my groans; but that I love thee   120
      best, O most best, believe it. Adieu.
    Thine evermore, most dear lady, whilst this machine
      is to him. *Hamlet.*

  This in obedience hath my daughter showed me:
  And more above, hath his solicitings,
  As they fell out by time, by means and place,   125
  All given to mine ear.
King: But how hath she
  Received his love?

129   *fain:* willingly

134   *If I . . . table-book:* If I had acted as go-between, passing
        communications back and forth. (The desk or the book would
        both be places where a message could be left); *table-book:*
        memorandum book

135   *given my heart a winking:* pretended to ignore

136   *idle sight:* indifference

139   *out of thy star:* far above you. The reference is to the belief
        that every star moved within its own sphere and could not
        travel beyond it.

140   *prescripts:* orders

141   *resort:* access

143   *took the fruits:* benefited from

146   *watch:* insomnia

147   *lightness:* lightheadedness; *declension:* deterioration

157   *centre:* the centre of the earth (i.e., the most inaccessible
        place)

160   *loose:* The use of "loose" emphasizes Ophelia's passivity
        and powerlessness. It suggests a number of images such as
        letting a dog off a leash, releasing an animal as bait in a hunt,
        or even sending animals to mate.

161   *arras:* a tapestry hanging, made in Arras, France.

Polonius: What do you think of me?

King: As of a man faithful and honourable.

Polonius: I would fain prove so. But what might you think

  When I had seen this hot love on the wing,—   130

  As I perceived it, I must tell you that,

  Before my daughter told me—what might you,

  Or my dear majesty your queen here, think,

  If I had play'd the desk or table-book,

  Or given my heart a winking, mute and dumb,   135

  Or look'd upon this love with idle sight;

  What might you think? No, I went round to work,

  And my young mistress thus I did bespeak:

  "Lord Hamlet is a prince out of thy star;

  This must not be"; and then I prescripts gave her   140

  That she should lock herself from his resort,

  Admit no messengers, receive no tokens.

  Which done, she took the fruits of my advice;

  And he repulsed, a short tale to make,

  Fell into a sadness, then into a fast,   145

  Thence to a watch, thence into a weakness,

  Thence to a lightness, and by this declension

  Into the madness whereon now he raves

  And all we mourn for.

King: Do you think this?

Queen: It may be, very like.   150

Polonius: Hath there been such a time, I'd fain know that,

  That I have positively said, 'tis so,

  When it proved otherwise?

King: Not that I know.

Polonius: Take this from this, if this be otherwise:

      [*Pointing to his head and shoulder.*]

  If circumstances lead me, I will find   155

  Where truth is hid, though it were hid indeed

  Within the centre.

King: How may we try it further?

Polonius: You know, sometimes he walks four hours together

  Here in the lobby.

Queen: So he does, indeed.

Polonius: At such a time I'll loose my daughter to him: 160

  Be you and I behind an arras then;

168   *board:* accost, address

170   *God-a-mercy:* God have mercy, or thank God

172   *fishmonger:* a fishseller (also used to mean "pimp")

179   Maggots were thought to be created by the sun (probably
        because they seem to appear out of nowhere in anything out
        in the sun). The phrase also echoes the ancient idea that
        the sun can create new life.

179-180 *being a god kissing carrion:* Even the sun-god can produce
        only maggots because of the corruption (carrion) he
        encounters.

181-182 *Let her not walk i' the sun:* The sun is associated with royalty.
        Therefore, Hamlet is warning Polonius to keep Ophelia out of
        the dangerous presence of either himself or the King.

189   *extremity:* pain, pangs

192   *What is the matter?:* What is the subject?

193   *Between who?:* Hamlet is deliberately misinterpreting the
        question.

195-203 Hamlet may be pretending to read this insulting description
        of old age, thus seizing an opportunity to insult Polonius.

197   *amber:* the gummy resin of evergreen trees

Mark the encounter; if he love her not,
And be not from his reason fallen thereon,
Let me be no assistant for a state,
And keep a farm and carters.
King: We will try it.   165
Queen: But look where sadly the poor wretch comes reading.
Polonius: Away, I do beseech you, both away!
I'll board him presently.

> [*Exeunt King, Queen, and Attendants.*]

[*Enter Hamlet, reading.*]

O, give me leave, how does my good lord Hamlet?
Hamlet: Well, God-a-mercy.   170
Polonius: Do you know me, my lord?
Hamlet: Excellent well; you are a fishmonger.
Polonius: Not I, my lord.
Hamlet: Then I would you were so honest a man.
Polonius: Honest, my lord?   175
Hamlet: Ay, sir; to be honest, as this world goes, is to be
    one man picked out of ten thousand.
Polonius: That's very true, my lord.
Hamlet: For if the sun breed maggots in a dead dog, being
    a god kissing carrion—Have you a daughter?   180
Polonius: I have, my lord.
Hamlet: Let her not walk i' the sun. Conception is a blessing,
    but not as your daughter may conceive—friend look
    to't.
Polonius [*Aside*]: How say you by that? Still harping on my   185
    daughter; yet he knew me not at first; he said I was
    a fishmonger: he is far gone, far gone: and truly in my
    youth I suffered much extremity for love; very near
    this, I'll speak to him again.—What do you read, my
    lord?   190
Hamlet: Words, words, words!
Polonius: What is the matter, my lord?
Hamlet: Between who?
Polonius: I mean the matter that you read, my lord.
Hamlet: Slanders, sir; for the satirical rogue says here that   195
    old men have grey beards, that their faces are
    wrinkled, their eyes purging thick amber and plumtree

199   *hams:* thighs, buttocks

201   *honesty:* proper, fair behaviour

205   *method:* meaning, sense

207   *pregnant:* full of meaning, quick-witted

208   *happiness:* aptness of expression

211   *suddenly:* immediately

223   Notice the quick change in Hamlet's behaviour.

226   *indifferent:* average

228   *not the very button:* not the highest point (on the cap); there-
       fore, not blessed with great fortune.

233   *privates:* Hamlet is punning on the word "privates," meaning
       private parts of the body, and ordinary people (without rank).

gum, and that they have a plentiful lack of wit,
together with weak hams: all which, sir, though I most
powerfully and potently believe, yet I hold it not   200
honesty to have it thus set down; for yourself, sir, shall
grow old as I am, if, like a crab you could go
backward.

Polonius [*Aside*]: Though this be madness, yet there is
    method in't.—Will you walk out of the air, my lord?   205

Hamlet: Into my grave?

Polonius: Indeed, that's out o' the air. [*Aside.*] How pregnant
    sometimes his replies are! a happiness that often
    madness hits on, which reason and sanity could not so
    prosperously be delivered of. I will leave him, and   210
    suddenly contrive the means of meeting between him
    and my daughter.—My honourable lord, I will
    humbly take my leave of you.

Hamlet: You cannot, sir, take from me anything that I will
    more willingly part withal, except my life, except my   215
    life, except my life.

Polonius: Fare you well, my lord.

Hamlet: These tedious old fools!

   [*Enter Rosencrantz and Guildenstern.*]

Polonius: You go to seek the lord Hamlet; there he is.

Rosencrantz [*To Polonius*]: God save you, sir!   220
                           [*Exit Polonius.*]

Guildenstern: Mine honoured lord!

Rosencrantz: My most dear lord!

Hamlet: My excellent good friends! How dost thou,
    Guildenstern! Ah, Rosencrantz! Good lads, how do
    you both?   225

Rosencrantz: As the indifferent children of the earth.

Guildenstern: Happy, in that we are not over happy;
  On Fortune's cap we are not the very button.

Hamlet: Nor the soles of her shoes?

Rosencrantz: Neither, my lord.   230

Hamlet: Then you live about her waist or in the middle of
    her favours?

Guildenstern: Faith, her privates we.

Hamlet: In the secret parts of fortune? O most true; she is

235   *strumpet:* prostitute. (Fortune is a strumpet because she cannot be relied upon for continued favours; she is fickle.)

238   *doomsday:* Day of Judgment. Hamlet is cynically suggesting that if people are honest, it must be because the end of the world is near.

243   *prison:* Hamlet may be referring to the King's request that he not return to Wittenberg. Also, the feeling of being in prison was considered a symptom of melancholy.

245   *confines:* places of imprisonment

252   *ambition:* Rosencrantz is trying to establish the cause of Hamlet's strange behaviour by testing the idea that he is un-happy because his ambition to be king has been thwarted.

256   *bad dreams:* another symptom of melancholy or depression

263-264   *Then are . . . shadows:* If a king or a hero is a mere shadow because he is ambitious, then a beggar (the opposite of a king) must be the body (the opposite of a shadow) and, therefore, more substantial than a king. Hamlet has constructed a clever argument from Rosencrantz and Guil-denstern's word-play that both ridicules and puts an end to it.

265   *fay:* faith

267   *sort:* classify

269   *dreadfully attended:* poorly served

269-270   *in the beaten way of friendship:* speaking openly as one friend to another

270   *what make you:* what are you doing

a strumpet. What's the news? 235
Rosencrantz: None, my lord; but that the world's grown
honest.
Hamlet: Then is doomsday near: but your news is not true.
Let me question more in particular: what have you,
my good friends, deserved at the hands of Fortune, that 240
she sends you to prison hither?
Guildenstern: Prison, my lord!
Hamlet: Denmark's a prison.
Rosencrantz: Then is the world one.
Hamlet: A goodly one; in which there are many confines, 245
wards, and dungeons, Denmark being one o'the
worst.
Rosencrantz: We think not so, my lord.
Hamlet: Why, then, 'tis none to you: for there is nothing
either good or bad but thinking makes it so: to me it 250
is a prison.
Rosencrantz: Why, then your ambition makes it one; 'tis
too narrow for your mind.
Hamlet: O God, I could be bounded in a nut-shell, and count
myself a king of infinite space, were it not that I have 255
bad dreams.
Guildenstern: Which dreams indeed are ambition; for the
very substance of the ambitious is merely the shadow
of a dream.
Hamlet: A dream itself is but a shadow. 260
Rosencrantz: Truly, and I hold ambition of so airy and light
a quality that it is but a shadow's shadow.
Hamlet: Then are our beggars bodies, and our monarchs
and outstretched heroes the beggars' shadows. Shall we
to the court? for, by my fay, I cannot reason. 265
Rosencrantz, Guildenstern: We'll wait upon you.
Hamlet: No such matter: I will not sort you with the rest
of my servants; for, to speak to you like an honest man,
I am most dreadfully attended. But, in the beaten way
of friendship, what make you at Elsinore? 270
Rosencrantz: To visit you, my lord; no other occasion.
Hamlet: Beggar that I am, I am even poor in thanks; but I
thank you: and sure, dear friends, my thanks are too
dear a halfpenny. Were you not sent for? Is it your own

280   *colour:* disguise, camouflage

283   *conjure:* command

284   *consonancy:* good companionship

293-294 *I will tell . . . discovery:* I will tell you why you have been sent to spy on me. That way you won't be in any danger of revealing your secret.

295   *moult no feather:* remain whole

296   *foregone all custom of exercises:* given up customary exercises

297-298 *it goes so heavily with my disposition:* I am so depressed

299   *a sterile promontory:* a barren headland jutting into the sea; *canopy:* covering

300   *brave:* glorious

301   *fretted:* adorned

302-303 *foul and pestilent congregation of vapours:* oppressive, poisonous fog

303   *piece of work:* work of artistic creation

304   *faculty:* intelligence

305   *express:* fitted to the purpose

306   *apprehension:* understanding

307   *paragon:* ideal, model

308   *quintessence:* basic element that remains after other components have been removed. The image is taken from alchemy; the quintessence of a substance would be all that was left once it had been purged of earth, air, water and fire (the four elements believed to make up all matter).

inclining? Is it a free visitation? Come, deal justly with   275
me: come, come; nay, speak.

Guildenstern: What should we say, my lord?

Hamlet: Why, anything, but to the purpose. You were sent
for; and there is a kind of confession in your looks,
which your modesties have not craft enough to colour: 280
I know the good king and queen have sent for you.

Rosencrantz: To what end, my lord?

Hamlet: That you must teach me. But let me conjure you,
by the rights of our fellowship, by the consonancy
of our youth, by the obligation of our ever-preserved   285
love, and by what more dear a better proposer could
charge you withal, be even and direct with me,
whether you were sent for, or no?

Rosencrantz [Aside to Guildenstern]: What say you?

Hamlet [Aside]: Nay then, I have an eye of you: if you love   290
me, hold not off.

Guildenstern: My lord, we were sent for.

Hamlet: I will tell you why; so shall my anticipation prevent
your discovery, and your secrecy to the king and
queen moult no feather. I have of late—but wherefore   295
I know not—lost all my mirth, forgone all custom of
exercises: and indeed it goes so heavily with my
disposition that this goodly frame, the earth, seems to
me a sterile promontory; this most excellent canopy,
the air, look you, this brave o'erhanging firmament, this   300
majestical roof fretted with golden fire, why, it appears
no other thing to me than a foul and pestilent
congregation of vapours. What a piece of work is a
man! how noble in reason! how infinite in faculty! in
form and moving how express and admirable! in   305
action how like an angel! in apprehension how like a
god! the beauty of the world! the paragon of animals!
And yet, to me, what is this quintessence of dust?
man delights not me: no, nor woman neither, though
by your smiling you seem to say so.   310

Rosencrantz: My lord, there was no such stuff in my
thoughts.

Hamlet: Why did you laugh then, when I said, "man delights
not me"?

316　　*lenten:* poor, meagre. (Lent is a season of fasting.)

317　　*coted:* passed

321　　*foil and target:* sword and shield

322　　*the humorous man:* the man who is governed by humours or moods, especially those tending to violent rages

319-325 Hamlet is cataloguing the typical acting roles of Shakespeare's time. From this point until line 360, Shakespeare abandons the time and place of the play to make references to the theatre of his day.

323-324 *tickled o' the sere:* easily moved to laughter. The image is of a gun easily set off by the trigger (sere).

326　　*were wont to:* were accustomed to

326-360 These lines describe London theatre politics current in Shakespeare's time. The main features were the popularity of child actors and the war of words between companies of child actors and those of adult actors.

337　　*eyrie:* brood (of birds), group. Shakespeare is referring to a group of child actors who began performing in 1600; *eyases:* (noisy) young birds, nestlings

338　　*on the top of question:* noisily, drowning out other voices

338-339 *tyrannically clapped:* loudly applauded (so that nothing else can be heard)

340　　*berattle the common stages:* satirize, make fun of the regular theatres

341　　*many wearing . . . goose-quills:* sword-carrying noblemen are afraid of the (written) ridicule that the actors direct at them

344　　*escoted:* paid; *pursue the quality:* follow the profession

344-345 *no longer . . . sing:* until their voices crack

348-349 *exclaim . . . succession:* make fun of what they themselves will one day become (i.e., adult actors)

351　　*tarre:* incite

352-354 *there was . . . question:* The only profitable plays were those in which children's acting troupes and adult acting troupes ridiculed each other.

Rosencrantz: To think, my lord, if you delight not in man, 315
what lenten entertainment the players shall receive
from you: we coted them on the way; and hither are
they coming, to offer you service.

Hamlet: He that plays the king shall be welcome; his majesty
shall have tribute of me: the adventurous knight shall 320
use his foil and target: the lover shall not sigh gratis;
the humorous man shall end his part in peace: the clown
shall make those laugh whose lungs are tickled o' the
sere; and the lady shall say her mind freely, or the blank
verse shall halt for't. What players are they? 325

Rosencrantz: Even those you were wont to take delight in,
the tragedians of the city.

Hamlet: How chances it they travel? their residence, both
in reputation and profit, was better both ways.

Rosencrantz: I think their inhibition comes by the means of 330
the late innovation.

Hamlet: Do they hold the same estimation they did when I
was in the city? Are they so followed?

Rosencrantz: No, indeed, they are not.

Hamlet: How comes it? Do they grow rusty? 335

Rosencrantz: Nay, their endeavour keeps in the wonted pace:
but there is, sir, an eyrie of children, little eyases, that
cry out on the top of question and are most tyrannically
clapped for't: these are now the fashion, and so
berattle the common stages,—so they call them,—that 340
many wearing rapiers are afraid of goose-quills, and
dare scarce come thither.

Hamlet: What, are they children? who maintains 'em? how
are they escoted? Will they pursue the quality no
longer than they can sing? will they not say afterwards, 345
if they should grow themselves to common players,—
as it is most like, if their means are no better,—their
writers do them wrong, to make them exclaim against
their own succession?

Rosencrantz: Faith, there has been much to do on both sides, 350
and the nation holds it no sin, to tarre them to
controversy: there was for a while no money bid for
argument unless the poet and the player went to cuffs
in the question.

358   *carry it away:* win

359-360 *Hercules and his load:* The sign of the Globe Theatre showed Hercules carrying the globe. Hence, it seems that even Shakespeare's theatre suffered from the popularity of the child actors.

361-366 Hamlet compares the new admiration for the child actors to the admiration for the new king—hinting that there is little justification for either.

362   *make mowes:* make faces

364   *ducats:* gold coins; *his picture in little:* a miniature picture, usually worn on a chain; *'Sblood:* God's blood

369   *the appurtenance of welcome:* the proper behaviour that goes with a welcome

371-372 *comply . . . garb:* behave with formal politeness

372   *extent:* behaviour

376-377 *I am . . . handsaw:* Hamlet is saying that his madness depends on the weather, and that he is mad only some of the time; *I know a hawk from a handsaw:* I can distinguish one thing from another. "Handsaw" is a corruption of "hernshaw" (heron). Hawks were used to hunt herons. Thus, Hamlet is hinting that he can recognize his enemies.

381   *swathing clouts:* baby clothes

382   *Happily:* perhaps

388   *Roscius:* a famous Roman actor in Julius Caesar's time

Hamlet: Is't possible? 355

Guildenstern: O, there has been much throwing about of
brains.

Hamlet: Do the boys carry it away?

Rosencrantz: Ay, that they do, my lord; Hercules and his
load too. 360

Hamlet: It is not very strange; for mine uncle is king of
Denmark, and those that would make mowes at him
while my father lived, give twenty, forty, an hundred
ducats a-piece, for his picture in little. 'Sblood, there
is something in this more than natural, if philosophy 365
could find it out.

                       [*Flourish of trumpets without.*]

Guildenstern: There are the players.

Hamlet: Gentlemen, you are welcome to Elsinore. Your
hands, come then: the appurtenance of welcome is
fashion and ceremony: let me comply with you in the 370
garb, lest my extent to the players, which, I tell you,
must show fairly outwards, should more appear like
entertainment than yours. You are welcome: but my
uncle-father and aunt-mother are deceived.

Guildenstern: In what, my dear lord? 375

Hamlet: I am but mad north-north-west: when the wind is
southerly I know a hawk from a handsaw.

[*Enter Polonius.*]

Polonius: Well be with you, gentlemen!

Hamlet: Hark you, Guildenstern; and you too; at each ear
a hearer: that great baby you see there is not yet out of 380
his swathing clouts.

Rosencrantz: Happily he's the second time come to them;
for they say an old man is twice a child.

Hamlet: I will prophesy he comes to tell me of the players;
mark it. You say right, sir: o' Monday morning; 'twas 385
so, indeed.

Polonius: My lord, I have news to tell you.

Hamlet: My lord, I have news to tell you. When Roscius
was an actor in Rome,—

Polonius: The actors are come hither, my lord. 390

Hamlet: Buz, buz!

394-397 a catalogue of different dramatic genres of Shakespeare's time

397,398 *Seneca . . . Plautus:* two great Roman playwrights

398-399 *the law . . . liberty:* the rules of classical drama or the looser forms (such as Shakespeare's own plays)

400 *Jephthah:* Jephthah is a character in the Bible who sacrificed his daughter to fulfill an oath (Judges 11:30 – 40). Is Hamlet trying to make Polonius nervous about Ophelia?

416 *row:* stanza; *chanson:* ballad

417 *abridgment:* entertainment; also, interruption

420 *valiant:* bearded (a beard was a symbol of valour)

421-422 *my young lady:* women's roles were played by boys

424 *chopine:* an overshoe with a high-corked sole

425 *cracked within the ring:* Hamlet is comparing a boy's cracked voice to a ruined coin. (A coin that had been chipped or shaved past the ring encircling the King's head was no longer legal currency.)

Polonius: Upon mine honour,—

Hamlet: Then came each actor on his ass,—

Polonius: The best actors in the world, either for tragedy, comedy, history, pastoral, pastoral-comical, historical- 395
pastoral, tragical-historical, tragical-comical-historical-
pastoral, scene individable, or poem unlimited: Seneca
cannot be too heavy, nor Plautus too light. For the
law of writ and the liberty, these are the only men.

Hamlet: O Jephthah, judge of Israel, what a treasure hadst 400
thou!

Polonius: What a treasure had he, my lord?

Hamlet: Why—

> One fair daughter and no more,
> The which he loved passing well. 405

Polonius [*Aside*]: Still on my daughter.

Hamlet: Am I not i' the right, old Jephthah?

Polonius: If you call me Jephthah, my lord, I have a daughter
that I love passing well.

Hamlet: Nay, that follows not. 410

Polonius: What follows then, my lord?

Hamlet: Why,

> As by lot, God wot

and then you know,

> It came to pass, as most like it was. 415

The first row of the pious chanson will show you more:
for look, where my abridgment comes.

[*Enter Four or Five Players.*]

You are welcome, masters; welcome, all. I am glad to
see thee well. Welcome, good friends. O, my old
friend! Why thy face is valiant since I saw thee last; 420
comest thou to beard me in Denmark? What, my young
lady and mistress! By'r-lady, your ladyship is nearer
to heaven than when I saw you last, by the altitude of
a chopine. Pray God, your voice, like a piece of
uncurrent gold, be not cracked within the ring. Masters, 425
you are all welcome. We'll e'en to't like French

428   *straight:* right away

433-434 *'twas caviare to the general:* It was too good for average audiences.

435-436 *cried in the top of mine:* was better than mine

436   *digested:* structured

438   *sallets:* spicy comments

440   *indict . . . affectation:* cause the author to be accused of being affected

443   *Aeneas' tale to Dido:* Aeneas survived the fall of Troy and eventually founded Rome. Dido was a Carthaginian queen Aeneas made love to and then abandoned.

444   *Priam:* King of Troy

447-515 The Player's speech recounts an episode from the Trojan War, which is roughly based on the version found in Virgil's *Aeneid*. The Player describes the murder of the old Trojan king, Priam, by Pyrrhus, son of Achilles. Following this is a description of Queen Hecuba's mourning over the slaughter of her husband Priam. The speech provides an interesting counterpart to the main plot of *Hamlet*, with its elements of murder of a king and the grief-stricken reaction of the Queen.

447   *Pyrrhus:* Achilles' son. He killed Priam when Troy fell; *Hyrcanian beast:* the tiger (the embodiment of cruelty)

451   *ominous horse:* the huge wooden horse the Greeks used to steal into Troy. It was "ominous" because it brought about Troy's doom.

454   *gules:* red (a term for heraldry; here it refers to blood)

456   *the parching streets:* The streets of Troy were on fire.

459   *o'er-sized:* stiffened with its covering. (Sizing is used to stiffen cloth.)

falconers, fly at anything we see: we'll have a speech
straight: come, give us a taste of your quality; come, a
passionate speech.

First Player: What speech, my lord?   430

Hamlet: I heard thee speak me a speech once, but it was
never acted; or, if it was, not above once; for the play,
I remember, pleased not the million; 'twas caviare to
the general: but it was—as I received it, and others,
whose judgment in such matters cried in the top of   435
mine—an excellent play, well digested in the scenes,
set down with as much modesty as cunning. I remember
one said there were no sallets in the lines to make the
matter savoury, nor no matter in the phrase that might
indict the author of affectation; but called it an honest   440
method, as wholesome as sweet, and by very much more
handsome than fine. One speech in it I chiefly loved:
'twas Æneas' tale to Dido; and thereabout of it
especially, where he speaks of Priam's slaughter: if it
live in your memory, begin at this line; let me see,   445
let me see—

    The rugged Pyrrhus, like th' Hyrcanian beast.

It is not so; it begins with "Pyrrhus."
    The rugged Pyrrhus, he whose sable arms,
    Black as his purpose, did the night resemble   450
    When he lay couched in the ominous horse,
    Hath now this dread and black complexion smear'd
    With heraldry more dismal; head to foot
    Now is he total gules; horridly trick'd
    With blood of fathers, mothers, daughters, sons,   455
    Baked and impasted with the parching streets,
    That lend a tyrannous and damned light
    To their lord's murder: roasted in wrath and fire,
    And thus o'er-sized with coagulate gore,
    With eyes like carbuncles, the hellish Pyrrhus   460
    Old grandsire Priam seeks.

So, proceed you.

Polonius: 'Fore God, my lord, well spoken; with good accent
and good discretion.

First Player: Anon he finds him   465

466   *carbuncles:* red gemstones (garnets)

470   *fell:* cruel

471-473 *Then senseless . . . base:* As Priam falls, the city crashes
        down; *Ilium:* Troy

474   *Takes prisoner Pyrrhus' ear:* Pyrrhus is transfixed by the sound.

477   *painted:* motionless, as in a painting

478   *neutral:* indifferent or undecided person

480   *against:* before

481   *rack:* storm clouds

482   *orb:* the earth

486   *Cyclops:* in Roman mythology, a race of one-eyed giants who
       worked for Vulcan, the gods' blacksmith

487   *Mars:* Roman god of war; *for proof eterne:* forever able to
       withstand blows

491   *synod:* assembly

492   *fellies:* pieces of wood forming the rim of a wheel

493   *round nave:* hub

497   *Hecuba:* wife of Priam

501   *mobled:* muffled

Striking too short at Greeks; his antique sword,
Rebellious to his arm, lies where it falls,
Repugnant to command: unequal match'd,
Pyrrhus at Priam drives; in rage strikes wide;
But with the whiff and wind of his fell sword   470
The unnerved father falls. Then senseless Ilium,
Seeming to feel his blow, with flaming top
Stoops to his base, and with a hideous crash
Takes prisoner Pyrrhus' ear: for, lo! his sword,
Which was declining on the milky head   475
Of reverend Priam, seem'd i' the air to stick:
So, as a painted tyrant, Pyrrhus stood,
And like a neutral to his will and matter,
Did nothing.
But, as we often see, against some storm,   480
A silence in the heavens, the rack stand still,
The bold winds speechless and the orb below
As hush as death, anon the dreadful thunder
Doth rend the region, so after Pyrrhus' pause
Aroused vengeance sets him new awork;   485
And never did the Cyclops' hammers fall
On Mars's armours, forged for proof eterne,
With less remorse than Pyrrhus' bleeding sword
Now falls on Priam.—
Out, out, thou strumpet, Fortune! All you gods,   490
In general synod, take away her power,
Break all the spokes and fellies from her wheel,
And bowl the round nave down the hill of heaven
As low as to the fiends.

Polonius: This is too long.
Hamlet: It shall to the barber's, with your beard.   495
    Prithee, say on. He's for a jig or a tale of bawdry, or he
    sleeps. Say on; come to Hecuba.

First Player: But who, O, who hath seen the mobled
        queen,—
Hamlet: "The mobled queen"?   500
Polonius: That's good: "mobled queen" is good.
First Player: Run barefoot up and down, threat'ning the
        flames

503   *bisson rheum:* blinding tears

505   *o'erteemed:* worn out with childbearing

514-515 *Would have . . . gods:* would have made the blazing stars
        weep and roused compassion in the gods; *milch:* moist

516   *turned his colour:* turned pale

521   *abstracts and brief chronicles:* summaries and short histories

525   *Od's bodykins:* God's body

With bisson rheum; a clout about that head
Where late the diadem stood; and for a robe,
About her lank and all o'erteemed loins   505
A blanket, in the alarm of fear caught up;
Who this had seen, with tongue in venom steep'd
'Gainst Fortune's state would treason have pronounced:
But if the gods themselves did see her then,
When she saw Pyrrhus make malicious sport   510
In mincing with his sword her husband's limbs,
The instant burst of clamour that she made,
Unless things mortal move them not at all,
Would have made milch the burning eyes of heaven
And passion in the gods.   515

Polonius: Look, whether he has not turned his colour and
has tears in's eyes. Pray you, no more.
Hamlet: 'Tis well; I'll have thee speak out the rest of this
soon. Good my lord, will you see the players well
bestowed? Do you hear, let them be well used, for they   520
are the abstracts and brief chronicles of the time: after
your death you were better have a bad epitaph than
their ill report while you live.
Polonius: My lord, I will use them according to their desert.
Hamlet: Od's bodykins, man, better: use every man after   525
his desert, and who should 'scape whipping! Use them
after your own honour and dignity: the less they
deserve, the more merit is in your bounty. Take them
in.
Polonius: Come, sirs.   530
Hamlet: Follow him, friends: we'll hear a play tomorrow.
[*Exit Polonius, with all the Players but the First.*] Dost
thou hear me, old friend; can you play the Murder
of Gonzago?
First Player: Ay, my lord.   535
Hamlet: We'll have't to-morrow night. You could, for a need,
study a speech of some dozen or sixteen lines, which
I would set down, and insert in't, could you not?
First Player: Ay, my lord.
Hamlet: Very well. Follow that lord; and look you mock   540
him not. [*Exit First Player.*] My good friends, I'll leave

545   *rogue:* here, an idle vagrant

547   *dream of passion:* imaginary feeling

548   *conceit:* something conceived in the mind (not real)

549   *her working:* i.e., his soul's working; *all his visage wann'd:* his face became pale

550   *distraction in's aspect:* his appearance full of agitation

551-552 *his whole function . . . conceit:* all his actions suiting his interpretation

559   *appal the free:* frighten innocent people

560   *Confound:* confuse; *amaze:* bewilder

563   *muddy-mettled:* dull-spirited; *peak:* mope

564   *John-a-dreams:* a dull, dreamy person; *unpregnant of my cause:* without plans for revenge

566   *property:* possessions; here, the crown and his wife

567   *defeat:* destruction, ruin

568-570 Hamlet is citing actions which should provoke a strong response.

573   *'Swounds:* God's wounds (a mild oath).

574   *pigeon-liver'd:* The liver was considered the source of courage. It was thought pigeons were mild-mannered because they had no gall, a fluid secreted by the liver.

576   *kites:* birds of prey, similar to hawks

577   *offal:* guts

578   *kindless:* unnatural

you till night: you are welcome to Elsinore.
Rosencrantz: Good my lord!
Hamlet: Ay, so, God be wi' you!

> [*Exeunt Rosencrantz and Guildenstern.*]
>> Now I am alone.

O, what a rogue and peasant slave am I!   545
Is it not monstrous that this player here,
But in a fiction, in a dream of passion,
Could force his soul so to his whole conceit
That from her working all his visage wann'd;
Tears in his eyes, distraction in's aspect,   550
A broken voice, and his whole function suiting
With forms to his conceit? And all for nothing!
For Hecuba!
What's Hecuba to him, or he to Hecuba
That he should weep for her? What would he do,   555
Had he the motive and the cue for passion
That I have? He would drown the stage with tears
And cleave the general ear with horrid speech,
Make mad the guilty and appal the free,
Confound the ignorant, and amaze indeed   560
The very faculties of eyes and ears.
Yet I,
A dull and muddy-mettled rascal, peak,
Like John-a-dreams, unpregnant of my cause,
And can say nothing; no, not for a king,   565
Upon whose property and most dear life
A damn'd defeat was made. Am I a coward?
Who calls me villain? breaks my pate across?
Plucks off my beard, and blows it in my face?
Tweaks me by the nose? gives me the lie i' the throat,   570
As deep as to the lungs? Who does me this?
Ha!
'Swounds, I should take it: for it cannot be
But I am pigeon-liver'd, and lack gall
To make oppression bitter, or ere this   575
I should have fatted all the region kites
With this slave's offal. Bloody, bawdy villain!
Remorseless, treacherous, lecherous, kindless villain!
O vengeance!—

585   *scullion:* the lowest of the servants, the person who washed the dishes

586   *About, my brain!:* Get to your work, brains!

590   *malefactions:* evil deeds

595   *tent him to the quick:* probe him deeply; *blench:* flinch

596-598 In Shakespeare's time, people believed that ghosts who claimed to be the spirit of a particular person were sometimes the Devil in disguise.

599   *melancholy:* The word "melancholy" denoted two different conditions. Sometimes it meant temporary depression or low spirits. It could also mean a well-recognized disease believed to be caused by an imbalance of "humours" in the body.

601   *abuses:* deceives

602   *relative:* relevant

Why, what an ass am I! This is most brave,   580
That I, the son of the dear murder'd,
Prompted to my revenge by heaven and hell,
Must, like a whore, unpack my heart with words,
And fall a cursing, like a very drab,
A scullion!   585
Fie upon't! foh! About, my brain! Hum, I have heard,
That guilty creatures, sitting at a play,
Have by the very cunning of the scene
Been struck so to the soul that presently
They have proclaim'd their malefactions;   590
For murder, though it hath no tongue, will speak
With most miraculous organ. I'll have these players
Play something like the murder of my father
Before mine uncle: I'll observe his looks;
I'll tent him to the quick; if he but blench,   595
I know my course. The spirit that I have seen
May be the devil: and the devil hath power
To assume a pleasing shape; yea, and, perhaps
Out of my weakness and my melancholy,
As he is very potent with such spirits,   600
Abuses me to damn me. I'll have grounds
More relative than this. The play's the thing
Wherein I'll catch the conscience of the king.

                                                    [*Exit.*]

Act 2, Scene 2: Activities

1. Imagine that you are one of the attendants present throughout the first part of this scene (lines 1 – 167). Out of sympathy for Hamlet, you decide to warn him about the King's strategies. Write an anonymous letter in which you try to convince Hamlet that you are telling him the truth.

2. You are the costume designer for a contemporary production of *Hamlet*. Write a memo to the director outlining your ideas for Hamlet's costume. Would you change Hamlet's clothing in any way for this scene in order to suggest his "antic disposition"? Explain the changes you would make or give the reasons you would not alter his costume.

3. Rumours of Hamlet's "madness" have leaked out of the castle. You are a writer for a tabloid newspaper, and have gained permission to do a series of interviews. Which characters would you interview? What questions would you ask them? Write the headline for your story.

4. In lines 297 – 314, Hamlet presents two extreme views of life. Divide a page in two and list the positive statements on one side and the negative statements on the other. Underline the images Hamlet uses and make a note of which sense (or senses) each image appeals to. Carefully select two photographic images from magazines—one to create the effect of the positive view and one to create the effect of the negative view. In groups, discuss the images you have chosen. How well do the photographs create the effect of Hamlet's views? What was it about the effect(s) the photographer created through his or her technique that made you choose each image?

5. What are your first impressions of Rosencrantz and Guildenstern? Explain why you would or would not want them as friends.

6. In the soliloquy at the end of Act 2, Hamlet criticizes himself for procrastinating. If he were not being so self-critical, what other explanations could he find for the actor's passionate delivery of his speech? for the fact that two months have passed and he still has not avenged his father?

7. Hamlet says that watching a play can cause guilty people to confess their crimes (lines 594 – 598). In your group, discuss whether this could happen nowadays. In your journal, make a note of any plays, movies, or television programs that have influenced you to change something in your own life. Explain why you think they had such a strong impact on you.

Act 2: Consider the Whole Act

1. As a class, divide Act 2, Scene 2 into a number of smaller segments. Divide yourselves up into the same number of acting groups as there are scene segments. (You may decide to have more than one group working on each segment.) One person in each acting group should take the role of the director. Assume that this is the first day of rehearsals for this passage. Each actor has come to the rehearsal with some ideas about how his or her character should be portrayed. Before you begin to rehearse, discuss your ideas about your characters, and experiment with them, trying several different ways of performing the passage. The director should watch and make notes in a director's log about what works best. He or she could make suggestions and/or add new ideas as the rehearsals continue. Each group could present its scene segment to the whole class as a rehearsal. After the performance, the audience could ask the actors questions about their behaviour and motivation.

2. In groups of five or six, create a series of on-the-spot TV interviews conducted at the time of the events in Act 2. These interviews could either be acted in front of the class, or videotaped. Decide which characters should be interviewed, and what setting should be created. Your audience could comment on the quality of your questions and the consistency of the interviewed characters' answers.

3. In groups, discuss whether or not you think Polonius is a good father. In your journal, explain which of his actions were right and which were wrong. Create your own description of a good father. Write a letter to Polonius offering him advice about ways in which he could become a better parent.

For the next scene . . .

Imagine you have a friend like Hamlet who thinks deeply and reacts sensitively to events around him or her. Your friend has just written you a letter saying that human life is full of more problems and sorrow than joy and hope. Your friend goes on to say, "What's the use of living in such a 'sea of troubles'?" Write a response to your friend's letter in your journal.

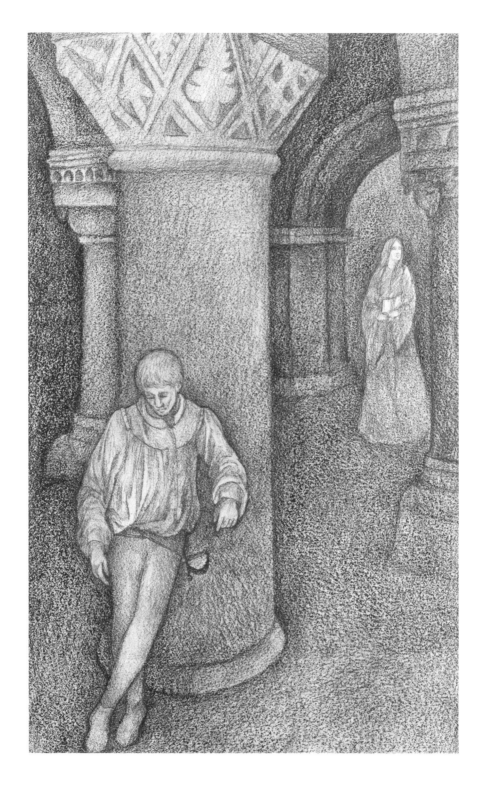

Act 3, Scene 1

In this scene . . .

Rosencrantz and Guildenstern report to the King that they have not found the cause of Hamlet's strange behaviour. Polonius and Claudius go ahead with their plan to eavesdrop on Hamlet's conversation with Ophelia. Polonius makes a comment about hypocrisy. This troubles Claudius and prompts him to reveal his guilty conscience in an aside to the audience. Hamlet enters alone, thinking aloud once again about the human condition. Then he catches sight of Ophelia praying. When Ophelia tries to return some love tokens Hamlet gave her earlier, Hamlet replies by insulting Ophelia and women in general. Claudius is not convinced by what he has overheard that Hamlet is mad, but he claims that Hamlet is dangerous. He announces his plan to send Hamlet on a mission to England. Polonius still insists that Hamlet's behaviour is caused by lovesickness, and suggests eavesdropping on a conversation between Hamlet and his mother.

1   *drift of circumstance:* roundabout conversations
2   *puts on this confusion:* pretends to be mad in this way

7   *forward to be sounded:* open to questioning

12 *with much . . . disposition:* behaving artificially
13 *Niggard of question:* hardly speaking. (Notice the distortion in Rosencrantz and Guildenstern's report to the King.)
14 *assay him:* get him involved in

17 *o'er-raught:* overtook

22 *beseech'd:* asked

26 *give him a further edge:* encourage him

Act 3, Scene 1

A room in the castle.

Enter King, Queen, Polonius,
Ophelia, Rosencrantz, and
Guildenstern.

King: And can you, by no drift of circumstance,
 Get from him why he puts on this confusion,
 Grating so harshly all his days of quiet
 With turbulent and dangerous lunacy?
Rosencrantz: He does confess he feels himself distracted,   5
 But from what cause he will by no means speak.
Guildenstern: Nor do we find him forward to be sounded;
 But, with a crafty madness, keeps aloof,
 When we would bring him on to some confession
 Of his true state.
Queen: Did he receive you well?   10
Rosencrantz: Most like a gentleman.
Guildenstern: But with much forcing of his disposition.
Rosencrantz: Niggard of question, but, of our demands,
 Most free in his reply.
Queen: Did you assay him
 To any pastime?   15
Rosencrantz: Madam, it so fell out that certain players
 We o'er-raught on the way: of these we told him,
 And there did seem in him a kind of joy
 To hear of it: they are about the court,
 And, as I think, they have already order   20
 This night to play before him.
Polonius: 'Tis most true:
 And he beseech'd me to entreat your majesties
 To hear and see the matter.
King: With all my heart; and it doth much content me
 To hear him so inclined.   25
 Good gentlemen, give him a further edge,
 And drive his purpose on to these delights.

29   *closely:* secretly

31   *Affront:* come face to face with

32   *espials:* spies

33   *bestow:* place (in this case, hide)

41   *wonted way:* accustomed behaviour

44   *this book:* probably a book of prayers

45-46   *That show . . . loneliness:* so that your being at prayer will explain why you are here alone

47-49   *with devotion's visage . . . himself:* with a display of virtuous behaviour we conceal our wickedness

51   *smart:* sharp, stinging. The image is of a wrongdoer being whipped so that he will repent.

52-54   *The harlot's . . . word:* The prostitute's makeup is just as ugly as the cheek it covers. In the same way, my hypocritical behaviour is just as ugly as the deed it is covering up.

52   *plastering art:* skill in applying makeup

57   *To be, or not to be:* The general consensus among Shakespeare scholars is that Hamlet is contemplating suicide. What other interpretations are possible?

Rosencrantz: We shall, my lord.
     [*Exeunt Rosencrantz and Guildenstern.*]
King: Sweet Gertrude, leave us too:
 For we have closely sent for Hamlet hither,
 That he, as 'twere by accident, may here   30
 Affront Ophelia.
 Her father and myself, lawful espials,
 Will so bestow ourselves that, seeing unseen,
 We may of their encounter frankly judge,
 And gather by him, as he is behaved,   35
 If't be the affliction of his love or no
 That thus he suffers for.
Queen: I shall obey you:
 And for your part, Ophelia, I do wish
 That your good beauties be the happy cause
 Of Hamlet's wildness: so shall I hope your virtues 40
 Will bring him to his wonted way again,
 To both your honours.
Ophelia: Madam, I wish it may.
       [*Exit Queen.*]
Polonius: Ophelia, walk you here. Gracious, so please you,
 We will bestow ourselves. [*To Ophelia.*] Read on this
  book;
 That show of such an exercise may colour   45
 Your loneliness. We are oft to blame in this,—
 'Tis too much proved that, with devotion's visage,
 And pious action, we do sugar o'er
 The devil himself.
King [Aside]: O, 'tis too true!   50
 How smart a lash that speech doth give my conscience!
 The harlot's cheek, beautied with plastering art,
 Is not more ugly to the thing that helps it
 Than is my deed to my most painted word:
 O heavy burden!   55
Polonius: I hear him coming; let's withdraw, my lord.
     [*Exeunt King and Polonius.*]

[*Enter Hamlet.*]

Hamlet: To be, or not to be: that is the question:
 Whether 'tis nobler in the mind to suffer

59   *The slings . . . fortune:* Fortune is described as waging war on humans.

61   *opposing:* struggling, fighting back

62   *No more:* merely this

64   *That flesh is heir to:* that are part of our human condition; *consummation:* final ending

66   *rub:* obstacle

68   *shuffled off . . . coil:* gotten rid of this life of turmoil

69-70   *there's the respect . . . life:* there's the consideration that causes us to live through a long life filled with calamity

71   *the whips and scorns of time:* the harsh experiences of life

72   *contumely:* scorn, insults

74-75   *of office:* of people in official positions; *the spurns . . . takes:* the insults that inferior people direct at quiet, worthy people

76   *quietus:* release

77   *bodkin:* dagger; *fardels:* burdens

80   *bourn:* limit, boundary

84   *conscience:* thinking

85   *the native hue of resolution:* the natural colour of courage

87   *pith and moment:* significance

88   *their currents turn awry:* The image is of a river that loses its force when its path is changed.

90-91   *Nymph . . . remember'd:* Lady, ask forgiveness for my sins while you are playing.

94   *remembrances:* gifts

The slings and arrows of outrageous fortune,
Or to take arms against a sea of troubles, 60
And by opposing end them. To die: to sleep:
No more; and by a sleep to say we end
The heart-ache, and the thousand natural shocks
That flesh is heir to, 'tis a consummation
Devoutly to be wish'd. To die, to sleep; 65
To sleep: perchance to dream: ay, there's the rub;
For in that sleep of death what dreams may come,
When we have shuffled off this mortal coil,
Must give us pause: there's the respect
That makes calamity of so long life: 70
For who would bear the whips and scorns of time,
The oppressor's wrong, the proud man's contumely,
The pang of despised love, the law's delay,
The insolence of office, and the spurns
That patient merit of the unworthy takes, 75
When he himself might his quietus make
With a bare bodkin? who would fardels bear,
To grunt and sweat under a weary life,
But that the dread of something after death,
The undiscover'd country from whose bourn 80
No traveller returns, puzzles the will,
And makes us rather bear those ills we have
Than fly to others that we know not of?
Thus conscience does make cowards of us all,
And thus the native hue of resolution 85
Is sicklied o'er with the pale cast of thought,
And enterprises of great pith and moment
With this regard their currents turn awry
And lose the name of action. Soft you now!
The fair Ophelia! Nymph, in thy orisons 90
Be all my sins remember'd.
Ophelia: Good my lord,
How does your honour for this many a day?
Hamlet: I humbly thank you: well, well, well.
Ophelia: My lord, I have remembrances of yours,
That I have longed long to re-deliver; 95
I pray you, now receive them.
Hamlet: No, not I. I never gave you aught.

100   *their perfume lost:* since they have lost the value that your affection once gave them

102   *wax:* become

104   *honest:* truthful or virtuous

108-109 *your honesty . . . beauty:* Your chastity ("honesty") should prevent contact with your beauty.

110   *commerce:* association

111-113 *for the power . . . likeness:* Beauty will corrupt chastity more readily than chastity will purify beauty.

117-118 *for virtue . . . relish of it:* A new branch cannot be grafted onto an ailing tree without also being infected. In the same way, virtue cannot take hold in human nature without being tainted by sinfulness.

118   *inoculate:* graft; *old stock:* original tree (here, a reference to the original sin of Adam); *relish of it:* taste of it (i.e., retain traces of it)

121   *nunnery:* convent; a place where Ophelia will be free of sin and temptation. The word also means "brothel."

122   *indifferent:* more or less, moderately

128   *crawling:* The image is of a worm.

129   *arrant knaves:* extreme rascals

Ophelia: My honour'd lord, I know right well you did;
    And with them words of so sweet breath composed
    As made the things more rich: their perfume lost,   100
    Take these again; for to the noble mind
    Rich gifts wax poor when givers prove unkind.
    There, my lord.
Hamlet: Ha, ha! are you honest?
Ophelia: My lord?   105
Hamlet: Are you fair?
Ophelia: What means your lordship?
Hamlet: That if you be honest and fair, your honesty should
    admit no discourse to your beauty.
Ophelia: Could beauty, my lord, have better commerce than
    with honesty?   110
Hamlet: Ay, truly; for the power of beauty will sooner
    transform honesty from what it is to a bawd than the
    force of honesty can translate beauty into his likeness:
    this was sometime a paradox, but now the time gives
    it proof. I did love you once.   115
Ophelia: Indeed, my lord, you made me believe so.
Hamlet: You should not have believed me: for virtue cannot
    so inoculate our old stock but we shall relish of it: I
    loved you not.
Ophelia: I was the more deceived.   120
Hamlet: Get thee to a nunnery: why wouldst thou be a
    breeder of sinners? I am myself indifferent honest, but
    yet I could accuse me of such things that it were better
    my mother had not borne me: I am very proud,
    revengeful, ambitious, with more offences at my beck   125
    than I have thoughts to put them in, imagination to
    give them shape, or time to act them in. What should
    such fellows as I do crawling between heaven and
    earth! We are arrant knaves, all; believe none of us. Go
    thy ways to a nunnery. Where's your father?   130
Ophelia: At home, my lord.
Hamlet: Let the doors be shut upon him, that he may play
    the fool nowhere but in's own house. Farewell.
Ophelia: O, help him, you sweet heavens!
Hamlet: If thou dost marry, I'll give thee this plague for   135
    thy dowry: be thou as chaste as ice, as pure as snow,

137   *calumny:* slander

143   *paintings:* women's makeup

145   *you jig, you amble:* These are dancing movements that suggest sexual, seductive behaviour; *lisp:* In Shakespeare's time, lisping was associated with sexually immoral behaviour.

146   *nickname God's creatures:* give offensive, immodest nicknames to things

146-147 *make your . . . ignorance:* excuse your bad behaviour by saying you didn't know any better

153-156 Ophelia is describing Hamlet as the ideal Renaissance man.

154   *expectancy:* hope. This may refer also to the expectation that Hamlet will inherit the throne; *rose:* symbol of perfection

155   *The glass . . . form:* the ideal of fashion and behaviour; *glass:* mirror; *mould:* model

158   *suck'd the honey of his music vows:* believed his sweet words

161   *blown youth:* youth in his prime (in full bloom)

162   *Blasted with ecstasy:* destroyed by madness

164   *affections:* feelings

168   *doubt:* suspect

172   *our neglected tribute:* payments owing to Denmark

173   *Haply:* perhaps

174   *variable objects:* change of environment

thou shalt not escape calumny. Get thee to a nunnery,
go; farewell. Or, if thou wilt needs marry, marry a
fool; for wise men know well enough what monsters you
make of them. To a nunnery, go; and quickly too.   140
Farewell.

Ophelia: O heavenly powers, restore him!

Hamlet: I have heard of your paintings too, well enough.
God hath given you one face, and you make
yourselves another; you jig, you amble, and you lisp,   145
and nickname God's creatures, and make your
wantonness your ignorance. Go to, I'll no more on't;
it hath made me mad. I say, we will have no more
marriages: those that are married already, all but
one, shall live; the rest shall keep as they are. To a   150
nunnery, go.   [*Exit Hamlet.*]

Ophelia: O, what a noble mind is here o'erthrown!
The courtier's, soldier's, scholar's, eye, tongue, sword;
The expectancy and rose of the fair state,
The glass of fashion and the mould of form,   155
The observed of all observers, quite, quite down!
And I, of ladies most deject and wretched,
That suck'd the honey of his music vows,
Now see that noble and most sovereign reason,
Like sweet bells jangled, out of tune and harsh;   160
That unmatch'd form and feature of blown youth
Blasted with ecstasy: O, woe is me,
To have seen what I have seen, see what I see!

[*Re-enter King and Polonius.*]

King: Love! his affections do not that way tend;
Nor what he spake, though it lack'd form a little,   165
Was not like madness. There's something in his soul
O'er which his melancholy sits on brood,
And I do doubt the hatch and the disclose
Will be some danger: which for to prevent,
I have in quick determination   170
Thus set it down: he shall with speed to England
For the demand of our neglected tribute:
Haply, the seas, and countries different
With variable objects shall expel

177   *fashion of himself:* his normal behaviour

185   *grief:* grievances; *round:* straightforward

186-187 *I'll be placed . . . conference:* I'll be hidden where I can hear everything; *find him not:* doesn't find out the truth

This something-settled matter in his heart,   175
Whereon his brains still beating puts him thus
From fashion of himself. What think you on't?
Polonius: It shall do well; but yet do I believe
    The origin and commencement of his grief
    Sprung from neglected love. How now, Ophelia!   180
    You need not tell us what Lord Hamlet said;
    We heard it all. My lord, do as you please;
    But, if you hold it fit, after the play,
    Let his queen mother all alone entreat him
    To show his grief; let her be round with him;   185
    And I'll be placed, so please you, in the ear
    Of all their conference. If she find him not,
    To England send him, or confine him where
    Your wisdom best shall think.
King: It shall be so;
    Madness in great ones must not unwatch'd go.   190

                                        [Exeunt.]

Act 3, Scene 1: Activities

1. In the role of Ophelia, write a diary entry before your encounter with Hamlet expressing your feelings about being "set up" by Claudius and Polonius. Then write a second entry expressing your feelings after Hamlet has left.

2. Claudius admits that he is suffering from his guilty conscience (lines 50 – 55). Does this confession change your opinion of Claudius in any way? Explain your answer in a paragraph.

3. In his soliloquy (lines 57 – 89), Hamlet ranges beyond his own particular situation to contemplate the problems of life in general. If Hamlet were living in the twentieth century, which of the problems listed in the soliloquy might he still include as belonging to our "sea of troubles" today? What other problems might he add?

4. Rather than criticizing Hamlet's behaviour, Ophelia describes what Hamlet used to be like. Does Ophelia's response change your feelings toward Hamlet at this point?

5. In pairs, act out the following situation. One of you is the director of a new production of *Hamlet*. The other is an eager theatre critic who, curious about the conception of the nunnery scene (lines 90 – 151), interviews the director. If the director's answers are not clear or detailed enough, the critic should follow up with further questions. You could act out or tape the following interview for the class:
   - There is no clear indication in the text as to when Hamlet realizes that Polonius and Claudius are spying on Ophelia and himself. In your production, when will he realize this, and how?
   - The scene begins with Hamlet's words, "Nymph, in thy orisons/Be all my sins remember'd." What tone will Hamlet use in saying these lines? Will Ophelia hear these words?

- The famous line, "Get thee to a nunnery" can be interpreted as "Go to a convent," or "Go to a brothel." Which interpretation will you be suggesting? How will a modern audience know this?
- Where do you think the emotional climax of this scene occurs? Why have you made this choice?
- After Hamlet's exit (line 151), would you consider having Hamlet rush back to kiss Ophelia, or make some other gesture revealing his emotions, as has been done in some other productions?

6. In your group, create a choral reading of the "To be, or not to be" soliloquy. In order to do this, first break the soliloquy up into shorter passages. Then decide how to read each passage. You should consider the following:
   - Is the passage to be read as a solo, a duet, an ensemble, or as a single voice against a group background?
   - Can you make use of alternating voices, repetition or echoes?
   - How loudly or softly should the passage be read?
   - What tone of voice should you use?
   - How quickly should you read? What rhythm is appropriate?
   - What words or phrases should be emphasized?

   Once you have decided how each passage will be read and have assigned all the parts, practise your reading a few times. Work out the best physical arrangement for the speakers. (You may also decide that you need one person to act as a conductor.) Perform your reading for the class.

For the next scene . . .

In your journal, write about an incident when you trapped someone (*or* when someone trapped you) into admitting guilt about something. How did you feel?

Act 3, Scene 2

In this scene . . .

Hamlet gives the actors some last-minute advice on how to perform the play. He then confides in Horatio, telling him of his plan to test Claudius' guilt. Horatio promises to observe Claudius' reaction to the play. When the King and Queen, Polonius, Ophelia and the rest of the court enter, Hamlet again plays the madman. The performance of *The Mousetrap* begins with a "dumb show" or pantomime of the plot. Then the play itself gets underway. At the moment when the murder of the King is enacted, Claudius walks out, putting an end to the performance. Hamlet and Horatio are both convinced of Claudius' guilt. As the scene ends, Rosencrantz and Guildenstern return to tell Hamlet that the King is angry. Polonius informs Hamlet that his mother wishes to speak to him.

1-47   Hamlet, in his instructions to the actors, is probably reflecting Shakespeare's own preferences for a natural, unexaggerated, sincere style of acting.

2   *trippingly on the tongue:* smoothly; *mouth:* say the words without showing you understand them

4   *saw the air:* use exaggerated hand gestures

7   *temperance:* self-control

9   *robustious:* violent, blustering; *periwig-pated:* wearing a wig

9-10   *tear a passion . . . rags:* use a melodramatic, exaggerated acting style

11   *groundlings:* rowdy spectators standing in the pit (i.e., in the innyard or the ground floor of the theatre)

11-12   *are capable . . . noise:* enjoy only the lowest form of entertainment (pantomime)

13,14   *Termagant, Herod:* violent, ranting stage characters

16-24   In these lines, Hamlet is reflecting the Renaissance idea that drama should present an image of real life.

19   *modesty:* moderation

20   *from:* far from

23   *scorn:* that which should be scorned

24   *pressure:* image

25   *come tardy off:* done inadequately

27   *censure:* judgment; *in your allowance:* in your opinion

Scene 2

A hall in the same.

Enter Hamlet and Players.

Hamlet: Speak the speech, I pray you, as I pronounced it
to you, trippingly on the tongue: but if you mouth it,
as many of your players do, I had as lief the town-
crier spoke my lines. Nor do not saw the air too much
with your hand, thus: but use all gently: for in the   5
very torrent, tempest, and, as I may say, whirlwind of
your passion, you must acquire and beget a temperance
that may give it smoothness. O, it offends me to the
soul, to see a robustious periwig-pated fellow tear a
passion to tatters, to very rags, to split the ears of the   10
groundlings, who, for the most part, are capable of
nothing but inexplicable dumb shows and noise: I could
have such a fellow whipped for o'erdoing Termagant;
it out-herods Herod: pray you, avoid it.

First Player: I warrant your honour.   15

Hamlet: Be not too tame neither, but let your own discretion
be your tutor: suit the action to the word, the word
to the action; with this special observance, that you
o'erstep not the modesty of nature; for anything so
overdone is from the purpose of playing, whose end,   20
both at the first and now, was and is, to hold, as 'twere,
the mirror up to nature; to show virtue her own
feature, scorn her own image, and the very age and
body of the time his form and pressure. Now this
overdone or come tardy off, though it make the   25
unskilful laugh, cannot but make the judicious grieve;
the censure of the which one must in your allowance
o'erweigh a whole theatre of others. O, there be
players that I have seen play, and heard others praise,
and that highly, not to speak it profanely, that neither   30

33   *journeymen:* unskilled workers, craftsmen who have not yet mastered their trade

36   *indifferently:* more or less

38-45 This is a criticism of comedians who ad lib among themselves on stage, drawing attention away from the main action.

41   *barren:* brainless

47   *presently:* immediately

53   *just:* well-balanced

54   *as e'er . . . coped withal:* as I have ever encountered

59   *let . . . pomp:* Let the flatterer use sugary words on those rich men who make a ridiculous display of their wealth.

60-61 *And crook . . . fawning:* kneel and fawn in order to gain some advantage (thrift); *pregnant:* ever-ready

having the accent of Christians, nor the gait of Christian,
pagan, nor man, have so strutted and bellowed, that
I have thought some of nature's journeymen had made
men, and not made them well, they imitated humanity
so abominably.   35

First Player: I hope we have reformed that indifferently with
us, sir.

Hamlet: O, reform it altogether. And let those that play
your clowns speak no more than is set down for them:
for there be of them, that will themselves laugh, to   40
set on some quantity of barren spectators to laugh too,
though in the meantime some necessary question of
the play be then to be considered: that's villainous, and
shows a most pitiful ambition in the fool that uses
it. Go, make you ready.   45

                                                        [*Exeunt Players.*]

[*Enter Polonius, Rosencrantz, and Guildenstern.*]

How now, my lord? will the king hear this piece of work?
Polonius: And the queen too, and that presently.
Hamlet: Bid the players make haste.   [*Exit Polonius.*]
Will you too help to hasten them?
Both: We will, my lord.   50

                           [*Exeunt Rosencrantz and Guildenstern.*]
Hamlet: What ho, Horatio!

[*Enter Horatio.*]

Horatio: Here, sweet lord, at your service.
Hamlet: Horatio, thou art e'en as just a man
    As e'er my conversation coped withal.
Horatio: O, my dear lord,—
Hamlet: Nay, do not think I flatter: 55
    For what advancement may I hope from thee,
    That no revenue hast but thy good spirits,
    To feed and clothe thee? Why should the poor be flatter'd?
    No, let the candied tongue lick absurd pomp,
    And crook the pregnant hinges of the knee   60
    Where thrift may follow fawning. Dost thou hear?
    Since my dear soul was mistress of her choice,

63   *election:* choice

64-67 *thou hast been . . . thanks:* You have accepted both good and bad fortune with a calm disposition.

68   *blood:* Blood represents passion. Hence, "blood" and "judgment" (reason) are opposites, which in Horatio are "well commingled" (well mixed).

78   *with . . . soul:* with your very sharpest observation

79   *occulted:* secret

80   *unkennel:* reveal

81   *damned ghost:* an evil, deceiving ghost

83   *Vulcan's stithy:* the smithy of Vulcan, god of blacksmiths. The image also suggests Hell.

86   *In censure of his seeming:* in judging his appearance

89   *idle:* unoccupied or possibly mad

91   *fares:* Claudius probably means "How are (fare) you, Hamlet?" Hamlet purposely misinterprets the question as "What do you eat?"

92   *chameleon:* According to an ancient belief, the chameleon feeds on air.

94-95 *I have . . . mine:* These words mean nothing to me.

And could of men distinguish, her election
Hath seal'd thee for herself: for thou has been
As one, in suffering all, that suffers nothing; 65
A man that fortune's buffets and rewards
Hast ta'en with equal thanks: and blessed are those
Whose blood and judgment are so well commingled
That they are not a pipe for Fortune's finger
To sound what stop she please. Give me that man 70
That is not passion's slave, and I will wear him
In my heart's core, ay, in my heart of heart,
As I do thee. Something too much of this.
There is a play to-night before the king;
One scene of it comes near the circumstance 75
Which I have told thee of my father's death:
I prithee, when thou seest that act a-foot,
Even with the very comment of thy soul
Observe mine uncle: if his occulted guilt
Do not itself unkennel in one speech, 80
It is a damned ghost that we have seen,
And my imaginations are as foul
As Vulcan's stithy. Give him heedful note;
For I mine eyes will rivet to his face,
And after we will both our judgments join 85
In censure of his seeming.
Horatio: Well, my lord:
If he steal aught the whilst this play is playing,
And 'scape detecting, I will pay the theft.
Hamlet: They are coming to the play; I must be idle:
Get you a place. 90

[Danish march. A flourish. Enter King, Queen, Polonius,
    Ophelia, Rosencrantz, Guildenstern, and other Lords
    attendant with the Guard, carrying torches.]

King: How fares our cousin Hamlet?
Hamlet: Excellent, i' faith; of the chameleon's dish: I eat
    the air, promise-crammed; you cannot feed capons so.
King: I have nothing with this answer, Hamlet; these words
    are not mine. 95
Hamlet: No, nor mine now. [To Polonius.] My lord, you
    played once in the university, you say?

107   *here's metal more attractive:* Ophelia (metal) has more magnetic (attractive) power.

109   *Lady . . . lap?:* Hamlet implies something indecent and then, in line 113, denies it.

113   *country matters:* boorish, indecent behaviour

121   *your only jig-maker:* chief comedian

127   *a suit of sables:* rich furs (not necessarily black)

130-131 *shall he . . . on:* he will be forgotten; *hobby-horse:* In earlier times, the hobby-horse (a man dressed in a horse costume) had been part of the May Day celebrations. The Puritans, however, had suppressed the May Day rituals. Hence, the hobby-horse was forgotten.

Stage directions

(following line 133): *Hautboys:* renaissance wind instrument, the forerunner of the modern oboe; *the dumb show:* this is a pantomime preview of the action of the play that will follow. There are many differing opinions among critics as to whether or not Claudius sees the dumb show, since he seems not to react to it.

Polonius: That I did, my lord, and was accounted a good
    actor.
Hamlet: What did you enact?   100
Polonius: I did enact Julius Cæsar: I was killed i' the Capitol:
    Brutus killed me.
Hamlet: It was a brute part of him to kill so capital a calf
    there. Be the players ready?
Rosencrantz: Ay, my lord; they stay upon your patience.   105
Queen: Come hither, my dear Hamlet, sit by me.
Hamlet: No, good mother, here's metal more attractive.
Polonius: O ho! do you mark that?   *[To the King.]*
Hamlet: Lady, shall I lie in your lap?
                [Lying down at Ophelia's feet.]
Ophelia: No, my lord.   110
Hamlet: I mean, my head upon your lap?
Ophelia: Ay, my lord.
Hamlet: Do you think I meant country matters?
Ophelia: I think nothing, my lord.
Hamlet: That's a fair thought to lie between maids' legs.   115
Ophelia: What is, my lord?
Hamlet: Nothing!
Ophelia: You are merry, my lord.
Hamlet: Who, I?
Ophelia: Ay, my lord.   120
Hamlet: O God, your only jig-maker. What should a man
    do, but be merry? for, look you, how cheerfully my
    mother looks, and my father died within these two
    hours.
Ophelia: Nay, 'tis twice two months, my lord.   125
Hamlet: So long? Nay, then, let the devil wear black, for
    I'll have a suit of sables. O heavens! die two months
    ago, and not forgotten yet? Then there's hope a great
    man's memory may outlive his life half a year: but,
    by'r lady, he must build churches then: or else shall   130
    he suffer not thinking on, with the hobby-horse,
    whose epitaph is, "For, O, for, O, the hobby-horse is
    forgot."

[Hautboys play. The dumb show enters.]

[Enter a King and a Queen, very lovingly; the Queen

135   *miching mallecho:* sneaking mischief

136   *imports the argument:* presents the theme

138-139 *The players . . . tell all:* Is Hamlet annoyed that the actors
       have given away too much of the story in the dumb show?

139   *keep counsel:* keep a secret

144   *naught:* naughty

148   *posy of a ring:* a short motto engraved inside a ring

151   *Phoebus' cart:* the chariot of the sun-god, Phoebus Apollo

152   *Neptune's salt wash:* the sea. (Neptune was the Roman god
       of the sea); *Tellus' orbed ground:* the earth. Tellus mater
       (mother earth) was the Roman goddess of the earth.

155   *Hymen:* god of marriage

*embracing him and he her. She kneels, and makes show
of protestation unto him. He takes her up, and declines his
head upon her neck; lays him down upon a bank of
flowers; she, seeing him asleep, leaves him. Anon comes in
a fellow, takes off his crown, kisses it, and pours poison
in the King's ears, and exit. The Queen returns; finds the
King dead, and makes passionate action. The Poisoner,
with some two or three Mutes, comes in again, seeming to
lament with her. The dead body is carried away. The
Poisoner woos the Queen with gifts; she seems loath and
unwilling awhile, but, in the end, accepts his love.]*

                                                   [Exeunt.]

Ophelia: What means this, my lord?

Hamlet: Marry, this is miching mallecho; it means mischief.   135

Ophelia: Belike this show imports the argument of the
    play.

[Enter Prologue.]

Hamlet: We shall know by this fellow: the players cannot
    keep counsel; they'll tell all.

Ophelia: Will he tell us what this show meant?   140

Hamlet: Ay, or any show that you'll show him. Be not
    ashamed to show; he'll not shame to tell you what it
    means.

Ophelia: You are naught, you are naught. I'll mark the play.

Prologue: For us, and for our tragedy,   145
          Here stooping to your clemency,
          We beg your hearing patiently.

Hamlet: Is this a prologue, or the posy of a ring?

Ophelia: 'Tis brief, my lord.

Hamlet: As woman's love.   150

[Enter two Players, King and Queen.]

Player King: Full thirty times hath Phœbus' cart gone
    round
    Neptune's salt wash, and Tellus' orbed ground;
    And thirty dozen moons with borrowed sheen
    About the world have times twelve thirties been;
    Since love our hearts, and Hymen did our hands,   155
    Unite commutual in most sacred bands.

161   *distrust:* worry about

162   *Discomfort:* upset

163-164 *For women's fear . . . extremity:* A woman either does not feel fear and love, or feels both in extreme.

170   *My operant powers . . . do:* I am losing my faculties.

173   *confound the rest:* damn the rest

177   *wormwood:* bitter words

178   *instances:* motives

179   *base respects of thrift:* motives of gain

184-187 *Purpose is but . . . be:* Our strong intentions (like unripe fruit on a tree) weaken with time and, forgotten, fall like ripened fruit from the tree.

188-189 *Most necessary . . . debt:* It is inevitable (necessary) that we don't keep (pay) our promises (debt) to ourselves.

192-193 *The violence . . . destroy:* The very intensity of grief or joy prevents us from acting upon them.

194-195 *Where joy . . . accident:* Emotional people experience extreme mood changes, triggered by small things.

Player Queen: So many journeys may the sun and moon
    Make us again count o'er ere love be done!
    But, woe is me, you are so sick of late,
    So far from cheer, and from your former state,   160
    That I distrust you. Yet, though I distrust,
    Discomfort you, my lord, it nothing must:
    For women's fear and love holds quantity;
    In neither aught, or in extremity.
    Now, what my love is, proof hath made you know,   165
    And as my love is sized, my fear is so.
    Where love is great, the littlest doubts are fear;
    Where little fears grow great, great love grows there.
Player King: 'Faith, I must leave thee, love, and shortly
    too;
    My operant powers their functions leave to do: 170
    And thou shalt live in this fair world behind,
    Honour'd, beloved; and haply one as kind
    For husband shalt thou—
Player Queen: O, confound the rest!
    Such love must needs be treason in my breast:
    In second husband let me be accurst!   175
    None wed the second, but who kill'd the first.

Hamlet [Aside]: Wormwood, wormwood.
Player Queen: The instances that second marriage move
    Are base respects of thrift, but none of love.
    A second time I kill my husband dead   180
    When second husband kisses me in bed.
Player King: I do believe you think what now you speak,
    But what we do determine oft we break.
    Purpose is but the slave to memory,
    Of violent birth but poor validity: 185
    Which now, like fruit unripe, sticks on the tree,
    But fall unshaken when they mellow be.
    Most necessary 'tis that we forget
    To pay ourselves what to ourselves is debt:
    What to ourselves in passion we propose,   190
    The passion ending, doth the purpose lose.
    The violence of either grief or joy
    Their own enactures with themselves destroy:
    Where joy most revels, grief doth most lament;

196   *for aye:* static (the same forever)

202   *tend:* depend

205   *seasons:* matures (i.e., turns him into)

207-209 *Our wills . . . our own:* The plans we make for the future are very different from what fortune actually brings.

213   *Sport . . . night!:* May I have no enjoyment during the day nor rest at night.

215   *an anchor's cheer:* a hermit's (anchorite's) existence

216   *Each opposite . . . joy:* each unfortunate experience that changes joy to sorrow

223   *rock:* soothe

224   *twain:* two

226   *protests:* declares her feelings too strongly

228   *argument:* plot

Grief joys, joy grieves, on slender accident.   195
This world is not for aye, nor 'tis not strange,
That even our loves should with our fortunes change,
For 'tis a question left us yet to prove,
Whether love lead fortune, or else fortune love.
The great man down, you mark his favourite flies;   200
The poor advanced makes friends of enemies:
And hitherto doth love on fortune tend:
For who not needs shall never lack a friend,
And who in want a hollow friend doth try
Directly seasons him his enemy.   205
But, orderly to end where I begun,
Our wills and fates do so contrary run,
That our devices still are overthrown,
Our thoughts are ours, their ends none of our own;
So think thou wilt no second husband wed,   210
But die thy thoughts when thy first lord is dead.
Player Queen: Nor earth to me give food nor heaven light!
Sport and repose lock from me day and night!
To desperation turn my trust and hope!
An anchor's cheer in prison be my scope!   215
Each opposite, that blanks the face of joy,
Meet what I would have well and it destroy!
Both here and hence pursue me lasting strife,
If, once a widow, ever I be wife!
Hamlet: If she should break it now!   220
Player King: 'Tis deeply sworn. Sweet, leave me here
    awhile:
My spirits grow dull, and fain I would beguile
The tedious day with sleep.   *[Sleeps.]*
Player Queen: Sleep rock thy brain;
And never come mischance between us twain!
                [Exit.]
Hamlet: Madam, how like you this play?   225
Queen: The lady protests too much, methinks.
Hamlet: O, but she'll keep her word.
King: Have you heard the argument? Is there no offence
    in't?
Hamlet: No, no, they do but jest, poison in jest; no offence 230
    i' the world.

233   *Marry:* by Mary (a mild oath); *Tropically:* metaphorically

237   *free:* innocent

238   *galled jade:* a horse whose shoulders have been rubbed raw by the saddle; *withers:* ridge between a horse's shoulders

238-239 *let . . . unwrung:* Let the guilty ones flinch; the innocent ones feel nothing

241   *chorus:* A chorus would explain or comment on the play's action.

242   *interpret:* The person who interprets in a puppet show explains the puppet's actions.

244   *keen:* sharp-tongued

245   *It would cost . . . edge:* Hamlet is making a lewd comment.

251   *Confederate season:* suitable time

253   *Hecate's ban:* the curse of Hecate, goddess of witchcraft

254   *dire property:* dread power

262   *false fire:* blank cartridge (i.e., make-believe)

King: What do you call the play?

Hamlet: The Mouse-trap. Marry, how? Tropically. This
    play is the image of a murder done in Vienna: Gonzago
    is the duke's name; his wife, Baptista: you shall see   235
    anon: 'tis a knavish piece of work: but what o' that?
    your majesty, and we that have free souls, it touches
    us not: let the galled jade wince, our withers are
    unwrung.

    [*Enter Lucianus.*]

    This is one Lucianus, nephew to the king.   240

Ophelia: You are as good as a chorus, my lord.

Hamlet: I could interpret between you and your love, if I
    could see the puppets dallying.

Ophelia: You are keen, my lord, you are keen.

Hamlet: It would cost you a groaning to take off my edge.   245

Ophelia: Still better, and worse.

Hamlet: So you must take your husbands. Begin murderer;
    pox, leave thy damnable faces, and begin. Come: the
    croaking raven doth bellow for revenge.

Lucianus: Thoughts black, hands apt, drugs fit, and time
      agreeing;   250
    Confederate season, else no creature seeing;
    Thou mixture rank, of midnight weeds collected,
    With Hecate's ban thrice blasted, thrice infected,
    Thy natural magic and dire property,
    On wholesome life usurp immediately.   255
                [*Pours the poison in his ears.*]

Hamlet: He poisons him i' the garden for his estate. His
    name's Gonzago; the story is extant, and writ in choice
    Italian: you shall see anon how the murderer gets the
    love of Gonzago's wife.   260

Ophelia: The king rises.

Hamlet: What, frighted with false fire!

Queen: How fares my lord?

Polonius: Give o'er the play.

King: Give me some light. Away!

All: Lights, lights, lights!   265
            [*Exeunt all but Hamlet and Horatio.*]

Hamlet: Why, let the stricken deer go weep,

270   *a forest of feathers:* part of an actor's costume

271   *turn Turk with me:* turn against me

271-272 *Provincial roses:* roses from Provence (a region in southern France); *razed shoes:* shoes made of leather that has been cut to form a pattern; *cry:* troupe. The image is of a pack of hounds.

276   *Damon:* a loyal friend in mythology

279   *peacock:* The peacock was a symbol of negative qualities such as vanity, pride and lechery.

288   *perdy:* a mild oath, from "par Dieu"

294   *distempered:* upset, or drunk. Hamlet deliberately mistakes Guildenstern's meaning.

296   *choler:* anger. According to the theory of humours, a choleric person suffered from an excess of bile.

299   *purgation:* cleansing. Hamlet intends two meanings: to get rid of his bile and to get rid of his guilt.

301   *frame:* order

The hart ungalled play:
    For some must watch, while some must sleep;
    So runs the world away.
Would not this, sir, and a forest of feathers—if the rest   270
of my fortunes turn Turk with me—with two Provincial
roses on my razed shoes, get me a fellowship in a cry
of players, sir?
Horatio: Half a share.
Hamlet: A whole one, I.   275
    For thou dost know, O Damon dear,
      This realm dismantled was
    Of Jove himself; and now reigns here
      A very, very—peacock.
Horatio: You might have rhymed.   280
Hamlet: O good Horatio, I'll take the ghost's word for a
    thousand pound. Didst perceive?
Horatio: Very well, my lord.
Hamlet: Upon the talk of the poisoning?
Horatio: I did very well note him.   285
Hamlet: Ah, ha! Come, some music; come the recorders!
    For if the king like not the comedy,
    Why, then, belike, he likes it not, perdy.

[Re-enter Rosencrantz and Guildenstern.]

Come, some music.
Guildenstern: Good my lord, vouchsafe me a word with you.   290
Hamlet: Sir, a whole history.
Guildenstern: The king, sir,—
Hamlet: Ay, sir, what of him?
Guildenstern: Is in his retirement marvellous distempered.
Hamlet: With drink, sir?   295
Guildenstern: No, my lord, rather with choler.
Hamlet: Your wisdom should show itself more richer to
    signify this to his doctor; for, for me to put him to his
    purgation would perhaps plunge him into more choler.
Guildenstern: Good my lord, put your discourse into some   300
    frame, and start not so wildly from my affair.
Hamlet: I am tame, sir: pronounce.
Guildenstern: The queen, your mother, in most great affliction
    of spirit hath sent me to you.

309   *pardon:* permission to go

318   *admiration:* astonishment

325   *trade:* business

327   *pickers and stealers:* hands

331   *I lack advancement:* Hamlet knows that Rosencrantz and
        Guildenstern will report this to Claudius.

334   *"While the grass grows":* (a proverb) While the grass grows,
        the horse starves.

337-338 *why do you . . . toil?":* Why are you setting up a trap for me?
        The metaphor is taken from hunting. A hunter would get up-
        wind of the prey so that his scent would frighten the animal
        into running away and into his trap (toil).

339-340 *O . . . unmannerly:* I'm trying so hard to fulfill my duty (to the
        King) that I've been rude to you.

Hamlet: You are welcome. 305

Guildenstern: Nay, good my lord, this courtesy is not of the right breed. If it shall please you to make me a wholesome answer, I will do your mother's commandment: if not, your pardon and my return shall be the end of my business. 310

Hamlet: Sir, I cannot.

Guildenstern: What, my lord?

Hamlet: Make you a wholesome answer; my wit's diseased: but, sir, such answer as I can make, you shall command; or, rather, as you say, my mother: therefore, 315 no more, but to the matter: my mother, you say,—

Rosencrantz: Then thus she says: your behaviour hath struck her into amazement and admiration.

Hamlet: O wonderful son, that can so astonish a mother! But is there no sequel at the heels of this mother's 320 admiration? Impart.

Rosencrantz: She desires to speak with you in her closet, ere you go to bed.

Hamlet: We shall obey, were she ten times our mother. Have you any further trade with us? 325

Rosencrantz: My lord, you once did love me.

Hamlet: So I do still, by these pickers and stealers.

Rosencrantz: Good my lord, what is your cause of distemper? You do freely bar the door of your own liberty, if you deny your griefs to your friend. 330

Hamlet: Sir, I lack advancement.

Rosencrantz: How can that be, when you have the voice of the king himself for your succession in Denmark?

Hamlet: Ay, sir, but "While the grass grows,"—the proverb is something musty. 335

[*Re-enter Players with recorders.*]

O, the recorders! let me see one. To withdraw with you:—why do you go about to recover the wind of me, as if you would drive me into a toil?

Guildenstern: O, my lord, if my duty be too bold, my love is too unmannerly. 340

Hamlet: I do not well understand that. Will you play upon this pipe?

348 *ventages:* openings (on the recorder)

351 *stops:* openings

362 *fret:* annoy or equip with frets (the ridges on a stringed instrument which mark the positions for the finger). Hamlet is playing on the double meaning.

364-372 Hamlet is doing to Polonius what he has just criticized Guildenstern for doing: playing him like an instrument.

375 *to the top of my bent:* to my limit

Guildenstern: My lord, I cannot.

Hamlet: I pray you.

Guildenstern: Believe me, I cannot.   345

Hamlet: I do beseech you.

Guildenstern: I know no touch of it, my lord.

Hamlet: 'Tis as easy as lying: govern these ventages with
    your fingers and thumb, give it breath with your mouth,
    and it will discourse most excellent music. Look you,   350
    these are the stops.

Guildenstern: But these cannot I command to any utterance
    of harmony; I have not the skill.

Hamlet: Why, look you now, how unworthy a thing you
    make of me! You would play upon me; you would seem 355
    to know my stops; you would pluck out the heart of
    my mystery; you would sound me from my lowest note
    to the top of my compass: and there is much music,
    excellent voice, in this little organ; yet cannot you make
    it speak. 'Sblood, do you think that I am easier to   360
    be played on than a pipe? Call me what instrument you
    will, though you can fret me, yet you cannot play
    upon me.

   [*Re-enter Polonius.*]

    God bless you, sir!

Polonius: My lord, the queen would speak with you, and   365
    presently.

Hamlet: Do you see yonder cloud that's almost in shape of
    a camel?

Polonius: By the mass, and 'tis like a camel, indeed.

Hamlet: Methinks it is like a weasel.   370

Polonius: It is backed like a weasel.

Hamlet: Or like a whale?

Polonius: Very like a whale.

Hamlet: Then will I come to my mother by and by.
    They fool me to the top of my bent. I will come by   375
    and by.

Polonius: I will say so.   [*Exit Polonius.*]

Hamlet: "By and by" is easily said. Leave me, friends.
      [*Exeunt Rosencrantz, Guildenstern, Horatio, etc.*]
  'Tis now the very witching time of night,

381   *Contagion:* disease-bearing mists

385   *Nero:* Nero, the Roman emperor, was rumoured to have put his mother to death.

388   *My tongue and soul in this be hypocrites:* I will not express all the bitterness in my soul.

389   *shent:* put to shame, rebuked

390   *To give them seals:* confirm them (my words) by acting upon them

When churchyards yawn, and hell itself breathes out   380
Contagion to this world: now could I drink hot blood,
And do such bitter business as the day
Would quake to look on. Soft! now to my mother.
O, heart, lose not thy nature; let not ever
The soul of Nero enter this firm bosom: 385
Let me be cruel, not unnatural:
I will speak daggers to her, but use none;
My tongue and soul in this be hypocrites;
How in my words soever she be shent,
To give them seals never, my soul, consent!   [*Exit.*] 390

Act 3, Scene 2: Activities

1. In groups or as a class, make a list of "do's" and "don'ts" of good acting, according to Hamlet. If possible, view one of Hamlet's soliloquies a few times on videotape or film and discuss the acting in terms of Hamlet's own standards.

2. Hamlet states that the purpose of drama has always been "to hold, as 'twere, the mirror up to nature; to show virtue her own feature, scorn her own image, and the very age and body of the time his form and pressure" (lines 21 – 26). In groups, discuss the meaning of Hamlet's words. Do you think that serious drama on television or in movies today does "hold the mirror up to nature"? Write a short essay explaining your answer and giving examples to support your opinion.

3. Write a paraphrase of Hamlet's words to Horatio (lines 65 – 76). Compare your work with that of a partner. Then, in pairs, discuss why you think Hamlet is moved to praise Horatio just at this moment. What does Hamlet reveal about his own personality here?

4. Which "dozen or sixteen lines" of *The Mousetrap* do you think Hamlet had a hand in writing? Explain your ideas.

5. Whose ideas do you think would form a better basis for a marriage—those expressed by the Player King or those of the Player Queen? Discuss this question in groups.

6. To Hamlet, Claudius' behaviour is conclusive proof of his guilt. However, other people in the *Mousetrap* audience may have had different interpretations of what happened. Divide the class into five groups. Each group should write a diary entry about the performance from the point of view of a different character: Polonius, Ophelia, Gertrude, Rosencrantz and Lucianus (the actor).

7. As a man, whom would you prefer to have as a best friend—Hamlet or Horatio? As a woman, which of the two would you be more likely to fall in love with? In your journal, explain your answer by describing the qualities you admire and those you dislike in each character.

For the next scene . . .

In your journal, write about a time when telling one lie or doing one wrong thing put you in a situation where, to cover your first lie, you had to tell more. How did you finally break the cycle of lies? (If this hasn't happened to you, think of a time when it could have happened.)

Act 3, Scene 3

In this scene . . .

Claudius' plans are moving ahead quickly as he prepares Rosencrantz and Guildenstern to accompany
Hamlet to England. Then, alone on stage, Claudius
struggles with his conscience and tries to pray for forgiveness. He knows, however, that prayer alone will
not bring forgiveness if he continues to benefit from
his sin. Hamlet enters, sees the King at prayer and
debates with himself whether or not to kill him.

3   *I . . . dispatch:* I will quickly prepare your instructions.

5   *terms of our estate:* my position as king

7   *provide:* prepare

11   *single and peculiar life:* private life of an individual

13   *'noyance:* harm

14   *weal:* welfare

15   *cease of majesty:* death of a king

16   *gulf:* whirlpool

17   *massy:* huge, massive

20   *mortised:* joined (a carpenter's term)

21   *annexment:* addition

22   *Attends the boisterous ruin:* is included in its violent destruction

24   *Arm:* get ready

Scene 3

A room in the same.

*Enter King, Rosencrantz, and
Guildenstern.*

King: I like him not, nor stands it safe with us
  To let his madness range. Therefore prepare you;
  I your commission will forthwith dispatch,
  And he to England shall along with you:
  The terms of our estate may not endure   5
  Hazard so dangerous as doth hourly grow
  Out of his lunacies.
Guildenstern: We will ourselves provide:
  Most holy and religious fear it is
  To keep those many many bodies safe
  That live and feed upon your majesty.   10
Rosencrantz: The single and peculiar life is bound
  With all the strength and armour of the mind
  To keep itself from 'noyance; but much more
  That spirit upon whose weal depend and rest
  The lives of many. The cease of majesty   15
  Dies not alone, but like a gulf doth draw
  What's near it with it: it is a massy wheel,
  Fix'd on the summit of the highest mount,
  To whose huge spokes ten thousand lesser things
  Are mortised and adjoin'd; which, when it falls,   20
  Each small annexment, petty consequence,
  Attends the boisterous ruin. Never alone
  Did the king sigh, but with a general groan.
King: Arm you, I pray you, to this speedy voyage,
  For we will fetters put upon this fear,   25
  Which now goes too free-footed.
Rosencrantz, Guildenstern: We will haste us.
                    [*Exeunt Rosencrantz and Guildenstern.*]

30   *To hear the process:* to hear what happens; *tax him home:* scold him thoroughly

32   *meet:* appropriate

34   *of vantage:* from an advantageous position, or, in addition

37   *rank:* disgusting

38   *the primal eldest curse:* In the Bible, God cursed Cain for murdering his brother Abel.

43   *in pause:* in doubt

46   *rain:* Rain is traditionally associated with mercy.

47-48   *Whereto serves . . . offence?:* How can mercy act except on a sinner?

49-51   The two purposes of prayer are to prevent sin before it happens or to pardon it afterwards.

57   *offence:* benefits of the crime.

58   *currents:* courses of events

59   *Offence's gilded hand:* the gold-filled hand of the guilty person; *shove by:* push aside

60-61   *the wicked . . . law:* The illegally acquired money can be used to bribe officers of law.

62   *shuffling:* evasion by trickery; *lies:* is exposed

[*Enter Polonius.*]

Polonius: My lord, he's going to his mother's closet:
Behind the arras I'll convey myself,
To hear the process; I'll warrant she'll tax him home: 30
And, as you said, and wisely was it said,
'Tis meet that some more audience than a mother,
Since nature makes them partial, should o'erhear
The speech, of vantage. Fare you well, my liege:
I'll call upon you ere you go to bed,   35
And tell you what I know.
  King: Thanks, dear my lord.

                          [*Exit Polonius.*]

O, my offence is rank, it smells to heaven; It hath the
  primal eldest curse upon't,
A brother's murder. Pray can I not,
Though inclination be as sharp as will: 40
My stronger guilt defeats my strong intent,
And like a man to double business bound,
I stand in pause where I shall first begin,
And both neglect. What if this cursed hand
Were thicker than itself with brother's blood,   45
Is there not rain enough in the sweet heavens
To wash it white as snow? Whereto serves mercy
But to confront the visage of offence?
And what's in prayer but this two-fold force,
To be forestalled ere we come to fall,   50
Or pardon'd being down? Then I'll look up;
My fault is past. But, O, what form of prayer
Can serve my turn? "Forgive me my foul murder"?
That cannot be, since I am still possess'd
Of those effects for which I did the murder,   55
My crown, mine own ambition and my queen.
May one be pardon'd and retain the offence?
In the corrupted currents of this world
Offence's gilded hand may shove by justice,
And oft 'tis seen the wicked prize itself   60
Buys out the law: but 'tis not so above:
There is no shuffling, there the action lies
In his true nature, and we ourselves compell'd

64   *to the teeth and forehead:* to the fullest extent

65   *what rests?:* what remains?

69   *limed soul:* Birds were trapped with birdlime, a sticky substance that was smeared on twigs.

70   *engaged:* entangled; *assay:* an attempt

74   *pat:* easily

76   *That would be scann'd:* That should be considered carefully.

80   *hire and salary:* acting like a hired killer. The implication is that it would not be real revenge.

81   *grossly:* when his sins were unrepented; *full of bread:* not having fasted (in penance)

82   *broad blown:* in full bloom; *flush:* blooming

83   *audit:* account. (The credits and debits would be good and evil deeds.)

84   *in our circumstances . . . thought:* as far as we humans understand

87   *season'd:* prepared

89   *hent:* opportunity

92   *gaming:* gambling

93   *relish:* trace

96   *stays:* waits

97   *physic:* medicine (referring to Claudius' prayers)

Even to the teeth and forehead of our faults
To give in evidence. What then? what rests? 65
Try what repentance can: what can it not?
Yet what can it when one can not repent!
O wretched state! O bosom black as death!
O limed soul, that struggling to be free
Art more engaged! Help, angels! make assay! 70
Bow stubborn knees, and, heart with strings of steel,
Be soft as sinews of the new-born babe!
All may be well!   [*Retires and kneels.*]

[*Enter Hamlet.*]

Hamlet: Now might I do it pat, now he is praying;
  And now I'll do't: and so he goes to heaven: 75
  And so am I revenged. That would be scann'd:
  A villain kills my father; and, for that,
  I, his sole son, do this same villain send
  To heaven.
  O, this is hire and salary, not revenge. 80
  He took my father grossly, full of bread,
  With all his crimes broad blown, as flush as May;
  And how his audit stands who knows save heaven?
  But in our circumstance and course of thought,
  'Tis heavy with him: and am I then revenged, 85
  To take him in the purging of his soul,
  When he is fit and season'd for his passage?
  No.
  Up, sword; and know thou a more horrid hent:
  When he is drunk asleep, or in his rage, 90
  Or in the incestuous pleasure of his bed,
  At gaming, swearing, or about some act
  That has no relish of salvation in't:
  Then trip him, that his heels may kick at heaven
  And that his soul may be as damn'd and black 95
  As hell, whereto it goes. My mother stays:
  This physic but prolongs thy sickly days.   [*Exit.*]
King [*Rising*]: My words fly up, my thoughts remain below:
  Words without thoughts never to heaven go.   [*Exit.*]

Act 3, Scene 3: Activities

1. Write a short news report informing the public that Hamlet is being sent to England. The report could take different forms:
   - an international news release by the palace press corps. This is intended for an audience in Norway. The readers of this report might be looking for signs of weakness in Denmark's political life.
   - a "tabloid-type" article emphasizing the sensational aspects of recent events in the palace. This article should arouse curiosity, appeal to the emotions, and perhaps exaggerate the facts.
   - a local press release from the palace, to be read aloud outside the palace gates. It should boost allegiance to Claudius, and calm down the people who support Hamlet.

2. In your journal, summarize the conflict that Claudius expresses in his prayer. What were your feelings toward Claudius while you were reading his prayer? Do you feel sympathy for him or identify with his predicament because you have experienced a similar conflict yourself? Explain your response in your journal.

3. As a class, make point-form notes about Hamlet's reasons for not killing Claudius. Then, in groups, rank the reasons, from strongest to weakest. Be prepared to explain your ranking to the class.

For the next scene . . .

Most of us have had, or will have, reason to confront another person and express a lot of anger that we have been storing up. In your journal, make a list of "do's" and "don'ts" about this type of confrontation. Then think of a confrontation you have already experienced. How many of your "do's" and "don'ts" did you follow? If a similar situation were to occur, how would you handle it this time?

Act 3, Scene 4

In this scene . . .

Polonius hides behind a tapestry in the Queen's room just as Hamlet is arriving. When Hamlet speaks harshly to Gertrude, she fears that he might hurt her and she cries out. When Polonius also cries out, Hamlet thinks he has caught Claudius spying and thrusts his sword through the tapestry, killing Polonius. As Hamlet is shaming his mother for marrying Claudius, the Ghost appears to Hamlet. Gertrude, however, cannot see the Ghost and thinks Hamlet must be insane. After Hamlet convinces Gertrude of his own sanity and of her immorality in marrying Claudius, she promises to lie to the King by telling him that Hamlet is indeed mad.

1 *straight:* right away

2 *broad:* unrestrained, extreme

4 *heat:* anger

5 *round:* direct

12 *idle:* silly

15 *rood:* cross

20 *glass:* mirror

25 *for a ducat:* I'll bet a ducat (a gold coin)

Stage direction

(following line 25): *pass:* sword thrust

Scene 4

The Queen's closet.

Enter Queen and Polonius.

Polonius: He will come straight. Look you lay home to him:
Tell him his pranks have been too broad to bear with,
And that your grace hath screen'd and stood between
Much heat and him. I'll silence me e'en here.
Pray you, be round with him.   5
Hamlet [Without]: Mother! mother! mother!
Queen: I'll warrant you; fear me not.
Withdraw, I hear him coming.
                        [*Polonius hides behind the arras.*]

[*Enter Hamlet.*]

Hamlet: Now, mother; what's the matter?
Queen: Hamlet, thou hast thy father much offended.   10
Hamlet: Mother, you have my father much offended.
Queen: Come, come, you answer with an idle tongue.
Hamlet: Go, go, you question with a wicked tongue.
Queen: Why, how now, Hamlet?
Hamlet: What's the matter now?
Queen: Have you forgot me?
Hamlet: No, by the rood, not so: 15
You are the queen, your husband's brother's wife;
And—would it were not so!—you are my mother.
Queen: Nay, then, I'll set those to you that can speak.
Hamlet: Come, come, and sit you down; you shall not budge:
You go not, till I set you up a glass   20
Where you may see the inmost part of you.
Queen: What wilt thou do? thou wilt not murder me?
Help, help, ho!
Polonius [Behind]: What, ho! help! help! help!
Hamlet [Drawing]: How now! a rat? Dead, for a ducat, dead! 25
                [*Hamlet makes a pass through the arras.*]

30-32   Hamlet is probably not accusing Gertrude of murder. He is combining the two acts of murder and marriage into one, in which Gertrude is implicated. Gertrude, by her response, shows her innocence.

39   *damned custom:* sinful habits; *brass'd it:* covered it (Gertrude's heart) with brass

40   *proof and bulwark:* impenetrable

44   *rose:* symbol of perfection

46   *sets a blister there:* Hamlet is referring to the practice of branding the foreheads of prostitutes.

48   *contraction:* marriage contract

50   *rhapsody of words:* a string of meaningless words

51-53   *this solidity . . . at the act:* Even the earth is sorrowful, as if it were Doomsday.

54   *That roars . . . index?:* that deserves such a violent introduction; *index:* preface

56   *counterfeit presentment:* representation

58   *Hyperion:* sun-god; *front:* forehead

60   *station:* pose, bearing; *Mercury:* messenger of the gods. Mercury represented grace and beauty.

61   *heaven-kissing hill:* Mount Olympus, home of the gods

Polonius [Behind]: O, I am slain.   *[Falls and dies.]*
Queen: O me, what hast thou done?
Hamlet: Nay, I know not: is it the king?
Queen: O, what a rash and bloody deed is this!
Hamlet: A bloody deed; almost as bad, good mother,   30
  As kill a king, and marry with his brother.
Queen: "As kill a king!"
Hamlet: Ay, lady, 'twas my word.
          [Lifts up the arras and sees Polonius.]
  Thou wretched, rash, intruding food, farewell!
  I took thee for thy better; take thy fortune:
  Thou find'st to be too busy is some danger.   35
  Leave wringing of your hands: peace! sit you down,
  And let me wring your heart: for so I shall,
  If it be made of penetrable stuff:
  If damned custom have not brass'd it so,
  That it is proof and bulwark against sense.   40
Queen: What have I done, that thou darest wag thy tongue
  In noise so rude against me?
Hamlet: Such an act
  That blurs the grace and blush of modesty,
  Calls virtue hypocrite, takes off the rose
  From the fair forehead of an innocent love,   45
  And sets a blister there; makes marriage vows
  As false as dicers' oaths: O, such a deed
  As from the body of contraction plucks
  The very soul, and sweet religion makes
  A rhapsody of words: heaven's face doth glow;   50
  Yea, this solidity and compound mass,
  With tristful visage, as against the doom,
  Is thought-sick at the act.
Queen: Ay me, what act,
  That roars so loud and thunders in the index?
Hamlet: Look here, upon this picture, and on this,   55
  The counterfeit presentment of two brothers.
  See what a grace was seated on this brow:
  Hyperion's curls; the front of Jove himself,
  An eye like Mars, to threaten and command;
  A station like the herald Mercury   60
  New-lighted on a heaven-kissing hill;

66   *mildew'd ear:* a rotting ear of corn

67   *Blasting:* infecting

68   *leave:* cease

69   *batten:* eat gluttonously

71   *hey-day:* youthful wild spirits; *blood:* Blood was considered the source of sexual desire.

75   *apoplex'd:* paralysed

76-78 *Nor sense . . . difference:* Perception (sense) was never so enslaved (thrall'd) to madness (ecstasy) that it lost all ability to distinguish between things.

79   *cozen'd:* cheated; *hoodman-blind:* blindman's bluff

83   *so mope:* be so dull and stupid

84-87 *Rebellious hell . . . fire:* If middle-aged people can be so given to passion, young people should not be expected to show any self-control.

90   *panders:* caters to, acts as a pimp for

92   *grained:* permanently stained

93   *leave their tinct:* lose their colour

94   *enseamed:* filthy, disgusting

A combination and a form, indeed,
Where every god did seem to set his seal
To give the world assurance of a man:
This was your husband. Look you now, what follows: 65
Here is your husband; like a mildew'd ear,
Blasting his wholesome brother. Have you eyes?
Could you on this fair mountain leave to feed,
And batten on this moor? Ha! have you eyes?
You cannot call it love, for at your age   70
The hey-day in the blood is tame, it's humble,
And waits upon the judgment: and what judgment
Would step from this to this? Sense sure you have,
Else could you not have motion: but sure that sense
Is apoplex'd: for madness would not err,   75
Nor sense to ecstasy was ne'er so thrall'd
But it reserved some quantity of choice,
To serve in such a difference. What devil was't
That thus hath cozen'd you at hoodman-blind?
Eyes without feeling, feeling without sight,   80
Ears without hands or eyes, smelling sans all,
Or but a sickly part of one true sense
Could not so mope.
O shame! where is thy blush? Rebellious hell,
If thou canst mutine in a matron's bones,   85
To flaming youth let virtue be as wax
And melt in her own fire: proclaim no shame
When the compulsive ardour gives the charge,
Since frost itself as actively doth burn,
And reason panders will.
Queen: O Hamlet, speak no more: 90
Thou turn'st mine eyes into my very soul,
And there I see such black and grained spots
As will not leave their tinct.
Hamlet: Nay, but to live
In the rank sweat of an enseamed bed,
Stew'd in corruption, honeying and making love   95
Over the nasty sty—
Queen: O, speak to me no more;
These words like daggers enter in my ears.
No more, sweet Hamlet!

99   *not twentieth part the tithe:* not even a small fraction (a twentieth of one-tenth)

100   *a vice of kings:* an actor playing a king, who combines the qualities of a villain and a clown

101   *cutpurse:* thief

102   *diadem:* crown

104   *A king of shreds and patches:* Multi-coloured rags (shreds and patches) were the costume worn by a professional clown.

107   *he's mad:* The Ghost is not visible to Gertrude, who thinks it is one of Hamlet's hallucinations.

109   *lapsed in time and passion:* having let both time and passion slip away

113   *whet:* sharpen

116   *Conceit:* imagination

120   *incorporal:* without substance

122   *in the alarm:* when the alarm is raised

123   *like life in excrements:* as if your hair were alive ("excrements" means "outgrowths" such as hair and fingernails)

128-129 *His form . . . capable:* His appearance and grievances would even make stones responsive.

130-131 *Lest . . . effects:* for fear that by your look you turn me away from accomplishing my grim purpose

132   *want true colour:* lack courage

Hamlet: A murderer and a villain;
A slave that is not twentieth part the tithe
Of your precedent lord: a vice of kings;   100
A cutpurse of the empire and the rule,
That from a shelf the precious diadem stole
And put it in his pocket!
Queen: No more!
Hamlet: A king of shreds and patches!—

[*Enter Ghost.*]

Save me, and hover o'er me with your wings,   105
You heavenly guards! What would you, gracious figure?
Queen: Alas! he's mad.
Hamlet: Do you not come your tardy son to chide,
That, lapsed in time and passion, lets go by
The important acting of your dread command?   110
O, say!
Ghost: Do not forget: this visitation
Is but to whet thy almost blunted purpose.
But, look! amazement on thy mother sits:
O, step between her and her fighting soul: 115
Conceit in weakest bodies strongest works:
Speak to her, Hamlet.
Hamlet: How is it with you, lady?
Queen: Alas, how is't with you,
That you do bend your eye on vacancy,
And with the incorporal air do hold discourse?   120
Forth at your eyes your spirits wildly peep;
And, as the sleeping soldiers in the alarm,
Your bedded hair, like life in excrements,
Starts up, and stands on end. O gentle son,
Upon the heat and flame of thy distemper   125
Sprinkle cool patience. Whereon do you look?
Hamlet: On him, on him! Look you how pale he glares!
His form and cause conjoin'd, preaching to stones,
Would make them capable. Do not look upon me,
Lest with this piteous action you convert   130
My stern effects: then what I have to do
Will want true colour; tears perchance for blood.
Queen: To whom do you speak this?

139   *coinage:* invention

140-141   *This bodiless . . . in:* Madness can easily create such hallucinations.

145   *And I . . . re-word:* I will repeat my ideas in the same words; or, I will repeat my ideas in different words. Either way would be proof of Hamlet's sanity.

147   *Lay not . . . soul:* don't console yourself by thinking; *unction:* ointment

149-151   *It will but . . . unseen:* It will form a scab over the infected area, while the infection continues spreading underneath.

153   *compost:* manure (which will cause the evil weeds to grow even more)

154   *virtue:* adopting a virtuous or self-righteous tone

155   *pursy:* pudgy, fat

156-157   *Virtue . . . good:* Goodness must bend and beg in order to change evil.

158   *cleft my heart in twin:* broken my heart, or, divided my loyalties

162   *Assume:* pretend

163-167   *That monster . . . put on:* Custom (habitual action) is like a monster in that it destroys our good sense and strengthens our bad behaviour. But custom can also be an angel in that it strengthens good behaviour, just as frequent wearing makes clothes comfortable.

Hamlet: Do you see nothing there?
Queen: Nothing at all; yet all that is I see.
Hamlet: Nor did you nothing hear?
Queen: No, nothing but ourselves. 135
Hamlet: Why, look you there! look, how it steals away!
  My father, in his habit as he lived!
  Look, where he goes, even now, out at the portal!
                                  [*Exit Ghost.*]
Queen: This is the very coinage of your brain:
  This bodiless creation ecstasy   140
  Is very cunning in.
Hamlet: Ecstasy!
  My pulse, as yours, does temperately keep time,
  And makes as healthful music: it is not madness
  That I have utter'd: bring me to the test,
  And I the matter will re-word, which madness   145
  Would gambol from. Mother, for love of grace,
  Lay not that flattering unction to your soul,
  That not your trespass but my madness speaks:
  It will but skin and film the ulcerous place,
  While rank corruption, mining all within,   150
  Infects unseen. Confess yourself to heaven;
  Repent what's past, avoid what is to come,
  And do not spread the compost on the weeds,
  To make them ranker. Forgive me this my virtue,
  For in the fatness of these pursy times   155
  Virtue itself of vice must pardon beg,
  Yea, curb and woo for leave to do him good.
Queen: O Hamlet! thou hast cleft my heart in twain.
Hamlet: O throw away the worser part of it,
  And live the purer with the other half.   160
  Good night: But go not to my uncle's bed.
  Assume a virtue, if you have it not.
  That monster, custom, who all sense doth eat,
  Oft habit's devil, is angel yet in this,
  That to the use of actions fair and good   165
  He likewise gives a frock or livery,
  That aptly is put on. Refrain to-night,
  And that shall lend a kind of easiness
  To the next abstinence: the next more easy;

170   *For use . . . nature:* Forming a new habit can change an ingrained quality.

177   *their scourge and minister:* the instrument and the agent of heaven's punishment (i.e., both the lash and the wielder of the lash)

178   *bestow: dispose of*

185   *wanton:* lewdly

188   *ravel:* unravel, explain

192   *paddock:* toad; *gib:* tomcat. The toad, bat and tomcat were associated with witchcraft.

193   *dear concernings:* important matters

195-196 *Unpeg the basket . . . fly:* give away secrets

197   *To try conclusions:* to repeat the experiment

206   *sweep my way:* clear my path

For use almost can change the stamp of nature,   170
And either master the devil, or throw him out
With wondrous potency. Once more, good night:
And when you are desirous to be blest,
I'll blessing beg of you. For this same lord,
                          [*Pointing to Polonius.*]
I do repent: but heaven hath pleased it so,   175
To punish me with this, and this with me,
That I must be their scourge and minister.
I will bestow him, and will answer well
The death I gave him. So, again, good night.
I must be cruel, only to be kind: 180
Thus bad begins, and worse remains behind.
One more word, good lady.
Queen: What shall I do?
Hamlet: Not this, by no means, that I bid you do:
  Let the bloat king tempt you again to bed;
  Pinch wanton on your cheek; call you his mouse;   185
  And let him, for a pair of reechy kisses,
  Or paddling in your neck with his damn'd fingers,
  Make you to ravel all this matter out,
  That I essentially am not in madness,
  But mad in craft. 'Twere good you let him know;   190
  For who, that's but a queen, fair, sober, wise,
  Would from a paddock, from a bat, a gib,
  Such dear concernings hide? who would do so?
  No, in despite of sense and secrecy,
  Unpeg the basket on the house's top,   195
  Let the birds fly, and, like the famous ape,
  To try conclusions, in the basket creep,
  And break your own neck down.
Queen: Be thou assured if words be made of breath,
  And breath of life, I have no life to breathe   200
  What thou hast said to me.
Hamlet: I must to England; you know that?
Queen: Alack,
  I had forgot: 'tis so concluded on.
Hamlet: There's letters sealed: and my two schoolfellows,
  Whom I will trust as I will adders fang'd,   205
  They bear the mandate; they must sweep my way,

207   *marshal me to knavery:* make me suffer from their foolishness, or lead me on to evil

208   *engineer:* maker of engines (bombs)

209   *Hoist with his own petar:* blown up by his own bomb

212   *When in one . . . meet:* when two schemes collide

213   *This man:* i.e., Polonius; *set me packing:* hasten by departure

216   *grave:* another pun

217   *prating:* foolish

218   *to draw toward an end:* to finish my business. There is a play on "draw," which also means "drag."

And marshal me to knavery. Let it work,
For 'tis the sport to have the engineer
Hoist with his own petar: and't shall go hard
But I will delve one yard below their mines,   210
And blow them at the moon: O, 'tis most sweet,
When in one line two crafts directly meet.
This man shall set me packing.
I'll lug the guts into the neighbour room.
Mother, good night. Indeed, this counsellor   215
Is now most still, most secret and most grave,
Who was in life a foolish prating knave.
Come, sir, to draw toward an end with you.
Good night, mother.

> [*Exeunt severally: Hamlet dragging out the
> body of Polonius.*]

Act 3, Scene 4: Activities

1. If there had been a radio talk show on family problems, what question might Gertrude have asked while waiting for Hamlet to arrive? If you were the host of the program, what advice would you have given Gertrude?

2. In groups of three (representing Hamlet, Gertrude and an acting coach), prepare lines 6 – 23 for dramatic reading to the class. The class should decide which readings were most effective and discuss what made them effective.

3. In small groups, complete all the questions below:
   - Why does Gertrude not . . . ?
   - After Hamlet kills Polonius, why . . . ?
   - Why does the Ghost . . . ?
   - Why didn't Shakespeare . . . ?
   - How does this scene . . . ?
   - Why . . . ?

   Each group should submit its three most interesting questions to a moderator. The moderator will choose one question for each group to answer, making sure there are no duplications. Each group will then have three minutes to prepare an answer for the class.

4. Do you think the Ghost should have spoken more directly and at length to both Hamlet and Gertrude? If so, what might he have said?

5. Make a list of Hamlet's comments about Polonius throughout the scene. Do you see a pattern to what he says?

6. Write a soliloquy reflecting Gertrude's emotions and thoughts about the future as Act 3 ends. You could use contemporary English prose, or, if you like, poetry.

7. Write a letter to Hamlet, commenting on his behaviour in this scene.

8. Write an obituary for Polonius, to be carried by the Danish national newspaper.

Act 3: Consider the Whole Act

1. The class should divide into eight small groups, with each group assigned to a part of Act 3:
   - the "To be, or not to be" soliloquy (III, i: 57-89)
   - the nunnery scene (III, i: 90-151)
   - Hamlet's advice to the players (III, ii: 1-45)
   - Hamlet's speech to Horatio (III, ii: 55-86)
   - the *Mousetrap* scene (III, ii: 94-265)
   - the prayer scene (III, iii: 36-99)
   - the closet scene (III, iv: 1-35)
   - the portrait scene (III, iv: 36-219, excluding references to the murder of Polonius)

   Each group should review its scene and prepare a report about Hamlet's behaviour—both positive and negative qualities. Present the report to the class. While one group is reporting, others should take notes. Form new groups of five or six and discuss all the reports. Decide whether Act 3 generally presents Hamlet in a positive or a negative light. Be ready to support your opinions. Report your conclusions to the class.

2. The "dumb show" (Act 3, Scene 2, lines 134 – 265) provides an opportunity for a director to display his or her creativity and to entertain an audience. In a group, prepare your version of the dumb show. Before you present your show, decide whether you want to include features such as costuming, music, choreography and make-up in your performance.

3. Choose one of the following characters: Hamlet, Gertrude, Claudius, Polonius, Ophelia. Suppose you are acting this role, and your director has asked you to choose one prop or piece of clothing to use during rehearsals in order to either look or feel the part. What would you choose, and why?

4. When Hamlet first heard about his father's murder, he said, "Haste me to know't; that I, with wings as swift,/As meditation or the thoughts of love,/May sweep to my revenge" (I, v: 29-31). What do you think has stopped Hamlet from "sweeping" to his revenge? In graphic form, show what has prevented Hamlet from acting. For example, you could develop a flow chart to show how and when Hamlet has been diverted from his purpose. Or you could create a visual symbol or group of symbols to represent the obstacles in Hamlet's way.

5. *Make a video*
In your group, choose a segment of a scene in this act that is about fifty to seventy-five lines long. The segment should contain one complete event or dialogue. Decide who will act each part and whether the segment requires "walk-ons" (actors who are present but do not speak any lines). Rehearse the segment several times to work out the movements and gestures of all the characters and to practise delivering the lines effectively. Decide whether or not to use costumes and/or props. Before you shoot the segment,
   • Consider the kind of camera shot that you want to use for each frame of your segment: close-up, medium close-up, or distanced.
   • Write a description of exactly what it is that you are going to shoot in precise shooting frames.
   • Decide what the audio portion, other than dialogue, will be.
   • Think about the beginning and ending of your segment. Do they have dramatic impact?

Practise using the camera and then shoot the segment. Share your video.

6. For hundreds of years, scholars have written about problems of interpreting this play. Complete one or more of the following statements yourself and develop your thoughts in a paragraph.
   - What puzzles me most about Hamlet's behaviour is . . .
   - I don't understand why Shakespeare included (didn't include) . . .
   - My first impression of _____ has changed because . . .
   - I'm not sure whether . . .
   - There seems to be a contradiction . . .

7. Find a personality description for each sign of the zodiac (horoscope), and decide which sign suits each of the main characters in the play.

8. Choose three images that you found most effective in this act. Paraphrase each image you have chosen and list everything the image suggests to you. Make a note of any situations or experiences in your life that could be described using the same or a similar image.

For the next scene . . .

In your journal, describe an occasion when something terrible has happened to someone close to you (a family member or a friend), but you have been too wrapped up in your own problems to think about that person's troubles. What was your first reaction to the other person's bad news? How did you behave toward him or her? In the future, would you try to deal with similar situations any differently? If so, how?

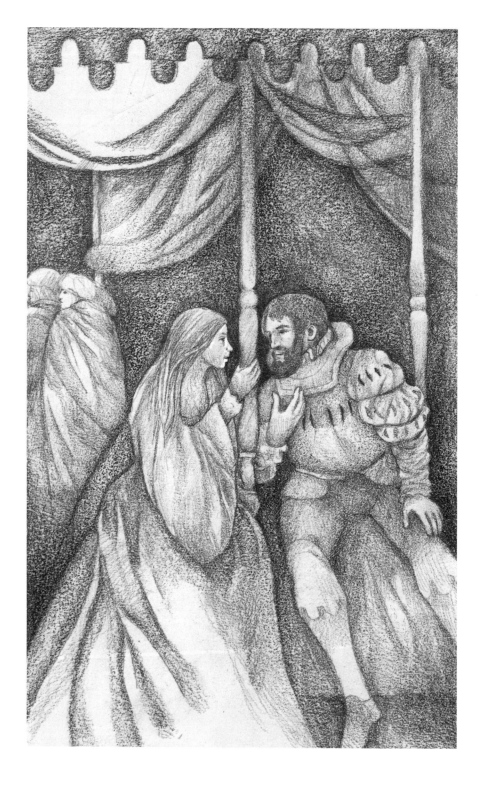

Act 4, Scene 1

In this scene . . .

Gertrude reports Polonius' death to Claudius. She also follows through on her promise to Hamlet and confirms that he is mad. Claudius resolves to send Hamlet away to England immediately. He sends Rosencrantz and Guildenstern to recover Polonius' body and then departs with Gertrude to meet with their advisors.

2   *translate:* interpret

11   *brainish apprehension:* brainsick state of mind

16   *answer'd:* explained

17   *providence:* foresight

18   *kept short:* kept under control; *out of haunt:* away from others

21-23   Note the disease imagery that Claudius is using.

22   *divulging:* becoming public knowledge

23   *pith:* vital substance

25   *ore:* precious metal, e.g., gold

26   *Among a mineral:* in a mine

27   *he weeps for what is done:* Is this the truth, or Gertrude's invention?

Act 4, Scene 1

The same.

*Enter King, Queen, Rosencrantz,
and Guildenstern.*

King: There's matter in these sighs, these profound heaves:
  You must translate: 'tis fit we understand them.
  Where is your son?
Queen: Bestow this place on us a little while.
              [*Exeunt Rosencrantz and Guildenstern.*]
  Ah, mine own lord, what have I seen to-night!   5
King: What, Gertrude? How does Hamlet?
Queen: Mad as the sea and wind, when both contend
  Which is the mightier: in his lawless fit,
  Behind the arras hearing something stir,
  He whips his rapier out, and cries, "A rat! a rat!"   10
  And in this brainish apprehension kills
  The unseen good old man.
King: O heavy deed!
  It had been so with us, had we been there.
  His liberty is full of threats to all,
  To you yourself, to us, to every one.   15
  Alas, how shall this bloody deed be answer'd?
  It will be laid to us, whose providence
  Should have kept short, restrain'd and out of haunt,
  This mad young man: but so much was our love,
  We would not understand what was most fit,   20
  But, like the owner of a foul disease,
  To keep it from divulging, let it feed
  Even on the pith of life. Where is he gone?
Queen: To draw apart the body he hath kill'd:
  O'er whom his very madness, like some ore   25
  Among a mineral of metals base,
  Shows itself pure; he weeps for what is done.

32   *countenance:* sanction, justify

33   *join you with some further aid:* get some help

36   *speak fair:* speak courteously (so as not to anger)

40   *haply:* perhaps

42   *level:* straight to the mark; *blank:* bull's eye

40-44   Claudius is expressing the hope that he will escape blame for Polonius' murder.

44   *woundless:* invulnerable

King: O, Gertrude, come away!
The sun no sooner shall the mountains touch,
But we will ship him hence: and this vile deed   30
We must, with all our majesty and skill,
Both countenance and excuse. Ho, Guildenstern!

[*Re-enter Rosencrantz and Guildenstern.*]

Friends both, go join you with some further aid:
Hamlet in madness hath Polonius slain,
And from his mother's closet hath he dragg'd him: 35
Go seek him out; speak fair, and bring the body
Into the chapel. I pray you, haste in this.
                    [*Exeunt Rosencrantz and Guildenstern.*]
Come, Gertrude, we'll call up our wisest friends;
And let them know, both what we mean to do,
And what's untimely done: so, haply, slander,   40
Whose whisper o'er the world's diameter
As level as the cannon to his blank
Transports his poisoned shot, may miss our name
And hit the woundless air. O come away!
My soul is full of discord and dismay.   [*Exeunt.*] 45

Act 4, Scene 1: Activities

1. In lines 1-32, both Gertrude and Claudius are pretending to some extent. After each of their speeches, write what you think their inner thoughts would be.

2. Claudius voices a number of fears in this scene. In groups, make a list of everything Claudius is afraid of. What do you think Claudius fears most? Discuss whether or not you agree with his priorities.

For the next scene . . .

If you were on a bus and overheard a conversation in which one person called the other a "sponge," what would you think it meant?

Act 4, Scene 2

In this scene . . .

Rosencrantz and Guildenstern try to find out from Hamlet where Polonius' body is hidden. Hamlet refuses to tell them. When they say he must go with them to Claudius, Hamlet leads them on a chase.

7   *Compounded:* mixed

12   *counsel:* secrets

13   *to be demanded of:* to be questioned by; *replication:* reply

16   *countenance:* favour

17   *authorities:* influence

24   *knavish:* wicked

28-29   *The body . . . body:* This statement could be taken as an expression of Hamlet's madness. As well, Hamlet could mean that Polonius' body is with old King Hamlet, but King Claudius is not (yet) dead.

29-31   *The king . . . Of nothing:* Is Hamlet warning Rosencrantz and Guildenstern about Claudius' fate?

31   *Hide fox . . . after:* Hamlet turns the search for Polonius' body into a game.

Scene 2

Another room in the castle.

Enter Hamlet.

Hamlet: Safely stowed—
Rosencrantz, etc. [*Without*]: Hamlet! lord Hamlet!
Hamlet: But soft, what noise? who calls on Hamlet?
  O, here they come.

[*Enter Rosencrantz and Guildenstern.*]

Rosencrantz: What have you done, my lord, with the dead   5
  body?
Hamlet: Compounded it with dust, whereto 'tis kin.
Rosencrantz: Tell us where 'tis, that we may take it thence
  And bear it to the chapel.
Hamlet: Do not believe it.   10
Rosencrantz: Believe what?
Hamlet: That I can keep your counsel and not mine own.
  Besides, to be demanded of a sponge! what replication
  should be made by the son of a king?
Rosencrantz: Take you me for a sponge, my lord?   15
Hamlet: Ay, sir; that soaks up the king's countenance, his
  rewards, his authorities: but such officers do the king
  best service in the end: he keeps them, like an ape
  doth nuts, in the corner of his jaw; first mouthed, to
  be last swallowed: when he needs what you have   20
  gleaned, it is but squeezing you, and, sponge, you shall
  be dry again.
Rosencrantz: I understand you not, my lord.
Hamlet: I am glad of it: a knavish speech sleeps in a foolish
  ear.   25
Rosencrantz: My lord, you must tell us where the body is,
  and go with us to the king.
Hamlet: The body is with the king, but the king is not with
  the body. The king is a thing—
Guildenstern: A thing, my lord?   30
Hamlet: Of nothing: bring me to him. Hide fox, and all
  after.   [*Exeunt.*]

Act 4, Scene 2: Activities

1. An analogy is an extended comparison of two things that are alike in some respects. In this scene, Hamlet uses the analogy of a sponge to describe Rosencrantz. Suggest other analogies that could be used to describe people like Rosencrantz and Guildenstern. What analogy could you use to describe Hamlet? Form groups and share your ideas.

2. Guildenstern is present throughout this scene, but he says very little. In your groups, discuss the following:
   • At this point, how do you think Guildenstern feels about Hamlet? about Rosencrantz? about their decision to spy on Hamlet for Gertrude and Claudius?
   • When he finally does speak (line 30), what tone of voice do you think he uses?

For the next scene . . .

Sometimes people find themselves laughing and/or joking in a situation where they are expected to be serious. How would you explain this unexpected response? Have you ever found yourself in this situation? If so, explain why you think you responded the way you did.

Act 4, Scene 3

In this scene . . .

Hamlet is brought before Claudius and eventually reveals where Polonius' body is hidden. Claudius informs Hamlet that he must go to England for his own safety. Once Claudius is alone, he reveals his plan to send the King of England a letter containing instructions to kill Hamlet as soon as he reaches England.

4   *of:* by; *distracted:* irrational

5   *Who like not . . . eyes:* who judge by appearances, not by
     reason

6   *scourge:* punishment

7   *To bear . . . even:* to make everything go smoothly

9   *Deliberate pause:* the result of careful consideration

10   *appliance:* remedy

20-23 These lines reveal Hamlet's new preoccupation with the grisly
       details of death and physical decay.

21   *convocation:* gathering; *politic:* shrewd, busy in statecraft

Scene 3

Another room in the castle.

Enter King, attended.

King: I have sent to seek him, and to find the body.
How dangerous is it that this man goes loose!
Yet must not we put the strong law on him:
He's loved of the distracted multitude,
Who like not in their judgment, but their eyes;   5
And where 'tis so, the offender's scourge is weigh'd,
But never the offence. To bear all smooth and even,
This sudden sending him away must seem
Deliberate pause: diseases desperate grown
By desperate appliance are relieved,   10
Or not at all.

[*Enter Rosencrantz.*]

               How now? what hath befall'n?
Rosencrantz: Where the dead body is bestow'd, my lord,
We cannot get from him.
King: But where is he?
Rosencrantz: Without, my lord, guarded, to know your
    pleasure.
King: Bring him before us.   15
Rosencrantz: Ho, Guildenstern! bring in my lord.

[*Enter Hamlet and Guildenstern.*]

King: Now, Hamlet, where's Polonius?
Hamlet: At supper.
King: At supper! Where?
Hamlet: Not where he eats, but where he is eaten: a certain   20
    convocation of politic worms are e'en at him. Your
    worm is your only emperor for diet: we fat all
    creatures else to fat us, and we fat ourselves for

25   *variable service:* different courses

32   *progress:* royal journey

34   *messenger:* Why would Claudius have to send a messenger to heaven?

42   *which we do tender:* which we are concerned about

45   *at help:* favourable

46   *tend:* are waiting; *bent:* ready

49   *I see . . . them:* There is a little angel who knows your plans and tells me of them.

55   *at foot:* closely

58   *leans on:* depends on

maggots: your fat king and your lean beggar is but
variable service, two dishes, but to one table: that's   25
the end.

King: Alas, alas!

Hamlet: A man may fish with the worm that hath eat of a
king, and eat of the fish that hath fed of that worm.

King: What dost thou mean by this?   30

Hamlet: Nothing but to show you how a king may go a
progress through the guts of a beggar.

King: Where is Polonius?

Hamlet: In heaven: send thither to see: if your messenger
find him not there, seek him i' the other place   35
yourself. But indeed, if you find him not within this
month, you shall nose him as you go up the stairs into
the lobby.

King: Go seek him there.   [*To some Attendants.*]

Hamlet: He will stay till you come.   40

[*Exeunt Attendants.*]

King: Hamlet, this deed, for thine especial safety,
Which we do tender, as we dearly grieve
For that which thou hast done, must send thee hence
With fiery quickness: therefore prepare thyself;
The bark is ready and the wind at help,   45
The associates tend, and everything is bent
For England.

Hamlet: For England?

King: Ay, Hamlet.

Hamlet: Good.

King: So is it, if thou knew'st our purposes.

Hamlet: I see a cherub that sees them. But, come; for
England! Farewell, dear mother.   50

King: Thy loving father, Hamlet.

Hamlet: My mother: father and mother is man and wife;
man and wife is one flesh, and so, my mother. Come,
for England!   [*Exit.*]

King: Follow him at foot; tempt him with speed aboard;   55
Delay it not; I'll have him hence to-night:
Away! for everything is seal'd and done
That else leans on the affair: pray you, make haste.

[*Exeunt Rosencrantz and Guildenstern.*]

59   *England:* King of England; *thou hold'st at aught:* you value at all

61   *cicatrice:* scar

62-63 *thy free . . . us:* Although England was not occupied by Danish troops, it still paid tribute to Denmark.

63   *coldly set:* view with indifference

64   *process:* plan

65   *conjuring:* urging, ordering

66   *present:* immediate

67   *hectic:* fever

69   *Howe'er my haps:* whatever happens to me

And England, if my love thou hold'st at aught—
As my great power thereof may give thee sense,   60
Since yet thy cicatrice looks raw and red
After the Danish sword, and thy free awe
Pays homage to us—thou may'st not coldly set
Our sovereign process; which imports at full,
By letters conjuring to that effect,   65
The present death of Hamlet. Do it, England;
For like the hectic in my blood he rages,
And thou must cure me: till I know 'tis done,
Howe'er my haps, my joys were ne'er begun.

                                                                [Exit.]

Act 4, Scene 3: Activities

1. Hamlet's references to Polonius' already-decaying body (lines 17 – 38) reflect a new mood—one in which he contemplates death in terms of rot and decay. Nevertheless, Hamlet expresses his thoughts humorously. Why have Hamlet's thoughts taken such a macabre turn at this point in the play? Is this change consistent with what we already know about Hamlet? The kind of humour Hamlet is using is often called "black humour." Most people have heard many jokes of this type. Discuss how these jokes make you feel. Why do you find them funny (or not funny)? Share your ideas with classmates, explaining why you think these jokes are popular.

2. Scenes 1, 2, and 3 have given us an opportunity to see Claudius' actions under stress. In the role of a psychologist, write an article about how different people react to stress, using Hamlet and Claudius as examples.

For the next scene . . .

In your journal, reflect on a situation where you took a strong stand on principle about an issue that other people did not think was important. What did you gain or lose by doing this?

Act 4, Scene 4

In this scene . . .

This outdoor scene takes place as Hamlet and Rosencrantz and Guildenstern are about to embark for England. On a plain near the seashore, Fortinbras and his army walk by. One of Fortinbras' captains tells Hamlet about their military campaign, in which thousands of soldiers have died to protect Norway's honour. Hamlet is deeply moved and, in a soliloquy, he criticizes his own inaction by comparing himself to Fortinbras.

3   *conveyance:* carrying out

6   *express . . . eye:* pay our respects in his presence

8   *softly:* slowly

9   *powers:* troops

10   *How purposed?:* What is their destination?

14   *the main of Poland:* all of Poland

16   *with no addition:* without exaggeration

19   *five ducats:* a small sum of money; *farm:* rent

21   *ranker rate:* higher value; *sold in fee:* sold outright (rather
        than leased)

25   *Will not debate . . . straw:* will not be enough to settle the
        argument over this thing of little value

26   *impostume:* abscess (a sore full of pus)

Scene 4

A plain in Denmark.

*Enter Fortinbras, and Forces
marching.*

Fortinbras: Go, captain, from me greet the Danish king;
 Tell him, that by his licence Fortinbras
 Claims the conveyance of a promised march
 Over his kingdom. You know the rendezvous.
 If that his majesty would aught with us,   5
 We shall express our duty in his eye:
 And let him know so.
Captain: I will do't, my lord.
Fortinbras: Go softly on.   [*Exeunt Fortinbras and Forces.*]

[*Enter Hamlet, Rosencrantz, Guildenstern, and others.*]

Hamlet: Good sir, whose powers are these?
Captain: They are of Norway, sir.
Hamlet: How purposed, sir, I pray you?   10
Captain: Against some part of Poland.
Hamlet: Who commands them, sir?
Captain: The nephew to old Norway, Fortinbras.
Hamlet: Goes it against the main of Poland, sir,
 Or for some frontier?   15
Captain: Truly to speak, and with no addition,
 We go to gain a little patch of ground
 That hath in it no profit but the name.
 To pay five ducats, five, I would not farm it;
 Nor will it yield to Norway or the Pole   20
 A ranker rate, should it be sold in fee.
Hamlet: Why, then the Polack never will defend it.
Captain: Yes, it is already garrison'd.
Hamlet: Two thousand souls and twenty thousand ducats
 Will not debate the question of this straw: 25
 This is the imposthume of much wealth and peace,
 That inward breaks, and shows no cause without
 Why the man dies. I humbly thank you, sir.

31   *occasions:* happenings; *inform against me:* accuse me

33   *market:* employment, use

35   *discourse:* intelligence

36   *Looking before and after:* able to think about both past and future

38   *fust:* become musty, full of mould

39   *Bestial oblivion:* animal-like forgetfulness; *craven scruple:* cowardly hesitation

40   *event:* outcome

41   *quarter'd:* divided into four, analyzed

44   *Sith:* since

46   *charge:* cost

47   *delicate:* not robust; *tender:* young

49   *Makes mouths at:* mocks; *invisible event:* unknown outcome

52-55   *Rightly to be great . . . stake:* True greatness is *not* fighting over unimportant things; it *is* being ready to fight, even over a small issue, if it is a question of honour.

53   *argument:* cause

57   *blood:* emotions

60   *trick:* trifle (small amount)

62   *Whereon . . . the cause:* not big enough to hold all those who fight for it

63   *continent:* container

Captain: God be wi' you, sir.   [*Exit Captain.*]
Rosencrantz: Will't please you go, my lord?
Hamlet: I'll be with you straight. Go a little before.   30
                    [*Exeunt all but Hamlet.*]
How all occasions do inform against me,
And spur my dull revenge! What is a man,
If his chief good and market of his time
Be but to sleep and feed? a beast, no more.
Sure, he that made us with such large discourse,   35
Looking before and after, gave us not
That capability and godlike reason
To fust in us unused. Now, whether it be
Bestial oblivion, or some craven scruple
Of thinking too precisely on the event,—   40
A thought which, quarter'd, hath but one part wisdom,
And ever three parts coward,—I do not know
Why yet I live to say, "this thing's to do,"
Sith I have cause, and will, and strength, and means,
To do't. Examples gross as earth exhort me: 45
Witness this army, of such mass and charge,
Led by a delicate and tender prince,
Whose spirit, with divine ambition puff'd
Makes mouths at the invisible event,
Exposing what is mortal and unsure   50
To all that fortune, death, and danger dare,
Even for an egg-shell. Rightly to be great
Is not to stir without great argument,
But greatly to find quarrel in a straw
When honour's at the stake. How stand I then,   55
That have a father kill'd, a mother stain'd,
Excitements of my reason and my blood,
And let all sleep, while to my shame I see
The imminent death of twenty thousand men,
That for a fantasy and trick of fame   60
Go to their graves like beds, fight for a plot
Whereon the numbers cannot try the cause,
Which is not tomb enough and continent
To hide the slain? O, from this time forth,
My thoughts be bloody, or be nothing worth!   65
                    [*Exit.*]

Act 4, Scene 4: Activities

1. In pairs, write the dialogue for a brief conversation between Hamlet and Horatio that could be inserted before this scene. What would Hamlet want to tell Horatio? What advice might Horatio give?

2. In Act 3, Scene 2 (lines 381 – 383), Hamlet says, "now could I drink hot blood,/And do such bitter business as the day/Would quake to look on." At the end of this scene, Hamlet says, "O, from this time forth,/My thoughts be bloody, or be nothing worth!" In groups, consider the events that prompted each statement, Hamlet's state of mind in each case, and the changes that have taken place in his situation between these two occasions. Discuss whether you find either of these statements convincing. Do you find one of them more convincing than the other? Practise reading these two passages. Convey your sense of the differences between them through tone of voice, emphasis, loudness and so on. When you are happy with your interpretations, tape them. Play your tape for your class and discuss their response to your interpretations.

3. Hamlet admires Fortinbras because he is willing to fight heroically for a small issue when his country's honour is at stake. Discuss whether you think Fortinbras' behaviour would still be considered heroic nowadays. In your journal, complete the following statement: "A hero is someone . . . "

4. In groups, discuss how you would stage this scene so that it provides a contrast in mood and setting to the intensity of the past few scenes. Decide what kind of stage you would be working with, and consider lighting, backdrop, costuming and movement.

For the next scene . . .

Suppose you are writing a screenplay about someone your age who has a mental breakdown as a result of a traumatic experience. Make notes in your journal on what that person's appearance, conversation and actions would be like.

Act 4, Scene 5

In this scene . . .

Hamlet's murder of Polonius has driven Ophelia out of her mind and stirred up Laertes and his followers to take revenge. At the beginning of the scene, Ophelia appears, singing songs and making allusions which seem to make no sense, but which, in fact, do tell her story. Not yet aware of his sister's madness, Laertes storms into the palace demanding vengeance on Claudius, whom he thinks was responsible for Polonius' murder. The King no sooner calms Laertes than Ophelia re-enters, and Laertes is overwhelmed with grief over her madness. Claudius leads him away to talk in private about the circumstances of his father's death. The King hints that he will help Laertes avenge his father.

1   *her:* Ophelia

2   *importunate:* insistent; *distract:* out of her mind

6   *Spurns enviously at straws:* gets upset over small things

7   *nothing:* without meaning

8-9   *Yet . . . collection:* Yet its incoherence encourages listeners to draw their own conclusions.

9   *aim at it:* make suggestions as to what it means

10   *And botch . . . thoughts:* clumsily attempt to interpret (Ophelia's) words according to their own ideas

11   *Which:* refers to "words"; *yield:* reveal

11-13   *Which . . . unhappily:* Her words and gestures give the impression that she has experienced some great misfortune.

15   *ill-breeding:* mischief-making

18   *toy:* small event; *amiss:* disaster

19-20   *So full . . . spilt:* A guilty person can be so afraid of revealing his guilt that he does reveal it in the same way that a person who is nervous about spilling the contents of a glass will spill them.

23-66   Ophelia, whose mind has become disoriented, sings songs about death and lost love.

25   *cockle hat:* A cockle hat represents a pilgrim. A lover might describe himself as a pilgrim worshipping his lady.

26   *shoon:* shoes

Scene 5

Elsinore. A room in the castle.

*Enter Queen, Horatio, and a
Gentleman.*

Queen: I will not speak with her.
Horatio: She is importunate, indeed distract:
  Her mood will needs be pitied.
Queen: What would she have?
Horatio: She speaks much of her father, says, she hears
  There's tricks i' the world, and hems and beats her heart,   5
  Spurns enviously at straws; speaks things in doubt,
  That carry but half sense: her speech is nothing,
  Yet the unshaped use of it doth move
  The hearers to collection; they aim at it,
  And botch the words up fit to their own thoughts;   10
  Which, as her winks and nods and gestures yield them,
  Indeed would make one think there would be thought,
  Though nothing sure, yet much unhappily.
  'Twere good she were spoken with, for she may strew
  Dangerous conjectures in ill-breeding minds.   15
Queen: Let her come in.   *[Exit Gentleman.]*
  [Aside.] To my sick soul, as sin's true nature is,
  Each toy seems prologue to some great amiss:
  So full of artless jealousy is guilt,
  It spills itself in fearing to be spilt.   20

[Re-enter Gentleman with Ophelia.]

Ophelia: Where is the beauteous majesty of Denmark?
Queen: How now, Ophelia?

Ophelia [Sings]:   How should I your true love know
                From another one?
                By his cockle hat and staff,   25
                And his sandal shoon.

27   *imports:* is the meaning of

31   *turf:* clump of earth

37   *Larded:* decorated

39   *showers:* tears

41   *God 'ield you!:* May God reward you.

41-42   *They say . . . daughter:* An old legend told of a baker's
        daughter who was changed into an owl when she scolded
        her mother for giving bread to Jesus.

44   *Conceit:* imaginative thoughts

47   *Saint Valentine's day:* According to tradition, the first person
        seen on St. Valentine's day would be a true love.

52   *dupp'd:* opened

57   *By Gis:* By Jesus

59   *Young men will do't:* Young men will seduce maidens.

60   *By cock:* By God

Queen: Alas, sweet lady, what imports this song?
Ophelia: Say you? nay, pray you, mark.

      [*Sings*]: He is dead and gone, lady,
            He is dead and gone;   30
            At his head a grass-green turf,
            At his heels a stone.
  Oh, oh!
Queen: Nay, but Ophelia,—
Ophelia: Pray you, mark.

      [*Sings*]: White his shroud as the mountain snow.   35

  [*Enter King.*]

Queen: Alas, look here, my lord.
Ophelia [*Sings*]: Larded with sweet flowers;
            Which bewept to the grave did go
            With true-love showers.
King: How do you, pretty lady?   40
Ophelia: Well, God'ield you! They say the owl was a baker's
    daughter. Lord, we know what we are, but know not
    what we may be. God be at your table!
King: Conceit upon her father.
Ophelia: Pray you, let us have no words of this; but when   45
    they ask you what it means, say you this:

      [*Sings*]: To-morrow is Saint Valentine's day,
            All in the morning betime,
            And I a maid at your window,
            To be your Valentine.   50

            Then up he rose, and donn'd his clothes,
            And dupp'd the chamber-door;
            Let in the maid, that out a maid
            Never departed more.

King: Pretty Ophelia!   55
Ophelia: Indeed, la, without an oath, I'll make an end on't:

      [*Sings*]: By Gis, and by Saint Charity,
            Alack, and fie for shame!
            Young men will do't if they come to't,
            By cock, they are to blame.   60

61   *tumbled me:* made love to me

65   *An:* if

76-77 *they come not . . . battalias:* The image is of an army of sorrows. An equivalent modern expression would be, "It never rains but it pours."

79   *muddied:* confused. The image is of a pond whose muddy bottom has been stirred up.

80   *Thick:* confused, unclear

81   *greenly:* foolishly, like an unskilled youth

82   *In hugger-mugger:* secretly

84   *pictures:* outward forms (without souls)

87   *Feeds . . . clouds:* is filled with bewilderment and keeps his intentions secret

88   *wants not buzzers:* does not lack gossipers

89   *pestilent:* poisonous

90-92 *Wherein necessity . . . ear:* Because the gossipers have no definite information about Polonius' death, they will accuse Claudius.

92   *this:* i.e., all these problems

93   *murdering-piece:* a cannon that scatters its shot, hitting many targets at once

94   *superfluous death:* more than one death

95   *Switzers:* Swiss mercenary soldiers who were used as palace guards

> Quoth she, before you tumbled me,
> You promised me to wed.

He answers:

> So would I ha' done, by yonder sun,
> And thou hadst not come to my bed.   65

King: How long has she been thus?
Ophelia: I hope all will be well. We must be patient: but I
    cannot choose but weep, to think they should lay him
    i' the cold ground. My brother shall know of it, and
    so I thank you for your good counsel. Come, my   70
    coach! Good night, ladies; good night, sweet ladies;
    good night, good night.   [*Exit.*]
King: Follow her close; give her good watch, I pray you.
                       [*Exit Horatio.*]
O, this is the poison of deep grief; it springs
All from her father's death. O Gertrude, Gertrude,   75
When sorrows come, they come not single spies,
But in battalias! First, her father slain;
Next, your son gone; and he most violent author
Of his own just remove; the people muddied,
Thick and unwholesome in their thoughts and whispers,   80
For good Polonius' death; and we have done but greenly,
In hugger-mugger to inter him; poor Ophelia,
Divided from herself and her fair judgment,
Without the which we are pictures, or mere beasts:
Last, and as much containing as all these,   85
Her brother is in secret come from France,
Feeds on his wonder, keeps himself in clouds,
And wants not buzzers to infect his ear
With pestilent speeches of his father's death;
Wherein necessity, of matter beggar'd,   90
Will nothing stick our person to arraign
In ear and ear. O my dear Gertrude, this,
Like to a murdering-piece, in many places
Gives me superfluous death.   [*A noise without.*]
Queen: Alack! what noise is this?
King: Where are my Switzers? Let them guard the door.   95

[*Enter a Gentleman.*]

97-100 *The ocean . . . officers:* The rebellious people, under Laertes' leadership, overwhelm your guards just as an overflowing ocean floods the land.

99 *head:* armed force

101 *as:* as if

102-103 *Antiquity forgot . . . word:* History and established order, which are the sources of authority, have been forgotten.

108 *counter:* The image is of hounds following the wrong scent, i.e., wrongly accusing Claudius.

116 *cuckold:* a man whose wife has betrayed him; *brands the harlot:* burns a mark onto the forehead of a prostitute

117 *unsmirch'd:* unstained, pure

120 *fear our person:* fear for my safety

121 *There's such . . . king:* This is a reference to a belief in the divine right of kings, which held that God would establish and protect the monarch.

122-123 *That treason . . . will:* Treason cannot accomplish its aims.

What is the matter?
Gentleman: Save yourself, my lord:
  The ocean, overpeering of his list,
  Eats not the flats with more impetuous haste
  Than young Laertes, in a riotous head,
  O'erbears your officers. The rabble call him lord;   100
  And, as the world were now but to begin,
  Antiquity forgot, custom not known,
  The ratifiers and props of every word,
  They cry, "Choose we! Laertes shall be king!"
  Caps, hands and tongues applaud it to the clouds,   105
  "Laertes shall be king, Laertes king!"
Queen: How cheerfully on the false trail they cry!
  O, this is counter, you false Danish dogs!
King: The doors are broke.   [*Noise within.*]

[Enter Laertes, armed; Danes following.]

Laertes: Where is this king? Sirs, stand you all without.   110
Danes: No, let's come in.
Laertes: I pray you, give me leave.
Danes: We will, we will.   [*They retire without the door.*]
Laertes: I thank you: keep the door. O thou vile king,
  Give me my father!
Queen: Calmly, good Laertes.
Laertes: That drop of blood that's calm proclaims me bastard, 115
  Cries cuckold to my father, brands the harlot
  Even here, between the chaste unsmirch'd brows
  Of my true mother.
King: What is the cause, Laertes,
  That thy rebellion looks so giant-like?
  Let him go, Gertrude; do not fear our person: 120
  There's such divinity doth hedge a king,
  That treason can but peep to what it would,
  Acts little of his will. Tell me, Laertes,
  Why thou art thus incensed. Let him go, Gertrude:
  Speak man.   125
Laertes: Where is my father?
King: Dead.
Queen: But not by him.
King: Let him demand his fill.

128-134   Laertes is ready to take revenge at any cost.

130   *grace:* divine forgiveness

133   *both the worlds:* i.e., this world and the next; *I give to negli-gence:* I care nothing about

136   *husband:* manage

139-141   *is't writ . . . loser?:* Is it your intention to destroy both friends and enemies?; *swoopstake:* sweepstake, a game in which "winner takes all"

144   *pelican:* From the way she feeds her offspring, the pelican appears to be letting them eat her flesh; therefore, the pelican was a symbol of self-sacrifice.

145   *Repast:* feed

148   *sensibly:* feeling

149   *level:* directly

152-153   *O heat . . . eye!:* Laertes wishes he could lose his reason (brain) and eyesight.

154-155   *thy madness . . . beam:* The revenge I take on those who caused your madness will be so heavy it will tilt the scale of justice.

158   *mortal:* vulnerable, easily killed

159-161   *Nature is fine . . . loves:* Ophelia's love for her father was so strong that she has sent part of herself—her sanity—with him to the grave.

Laertes: How came he dead? I'll not be juggled with;
   To hell, allegiance! vows, to the blackest devil!
   Conscience and grace, to the profoundest pit!   130
   I dare damnation: to this point I stand,
   That both the worlds I give to negligence,
   Let come what comes; only I'll be revenged
   Most thoroughly for my father.
King: Who shall stay you?
Laertes: My will, not all the world: 135
   And for my means, I'll husband them so well,
   They shall go far with little.
King: Good Laertes.
   If you desire to know the certainty
   Of your dear father's death, is't writ in your revenge
   That, swoopstake, you will draw both friend and foe,   140
   Winner and loser?
Laertes: None but his enemies.
King: Will you know them then?
Laertes: To his good friends thus wide I'll ope my arms;
   And, like the kind life-rendering pelican,
   Repast them with my blood.
King: Why, now you speak   145
   Like a good child and a true gentleman.
   That I am guiltless of your father's death,
   And am most sensibly in grief for it,
   It shall as level to your judgment pierce
   As day does to your eye.
Danes [Within]:   Let her come in.   150
Laertes: How now! what noise is that?

   [*Re-enter Ophelia, fantastically dressed with straws and*
     flowers.]

   O heat, dry up my brains! tears seven times salt,
   Burn out the sense and virtue of mine eye!
   By heaven, thy madness shall be paid by weight,
   Till our scale turns the beam. O rose of May!   155
   Dear maid, kind sister, sweet Ophelia!
   O heavens! is't possible a young maid's wits
   Should be as mortal as an old man's life?
   Nature is fine in love, and where 'tis fine

172   *This nothing's more than matter:* This nonsense has more meaning than rational speech does.

173-182 Each of the flowers Ophelia mentions has symbolic meaning. Considering their symbolism, who might receive each one.

174   *pansies:* from the French word "pensées." Pansies are a symbol of thoughts of love.

176   *document:* lesson

178   *fennel:* symbol of flattery; *columbines:* symbol of infidelity in marriage

179   *rue:* symbol of repentance

180   *herb-grace:* herb of repentance

181   *with a difference:* with a different meaning; *daisy:* symbol of false promises of love

182   *violets:* symbol of faithfulness

193   *flaxen:* yellowish-brown (like flax); *poll:* part of the head on which hair grows

It sends some precious instance of itself 160
After the thing it loves.

Ophelia [*Sings*]: They bore him barefaced on the bier;
Hey non nonny, nonny, hey nonny;
And on his grave rains many a tear,—

Fare you well, my dove! 165
Laertes: Hadst thou thy wits, and didst persuade revenge,
It could not move thus.
Ophelia [*Sings*]: You must sing down-a-down
An you call him a-down-a.
O, how the wheel becomes it! It is the false steward, 170
that stole his master's daughter.
Laertes: This nothing's more than matter.
Ophelia: There's rosemary, that's for remembrance, pray,
love, remember: and there is pansies, that's for
thoughts. 175
Laertes: A document in madness; thoughts and remembrance
fitted.
Ophelia: There's fennel for you, and columbines: there's
rue for you; and here's some for me: we may call it
herb-grace o' Sundays: O, you must wear your rue 180
with a difference. There's a daisy: I would give you
some violets, but they withered all when my father died:
they say he made a good end,—

[*Sings*]: For bonny sweet Robin is all my joy.

Laertes: Thought and affliction, passion, hell itself, 185
She turns to favour and to prettiness.

Ophelia [*Sings*]: And will a'not come again?
And will a'not come again?
No, no, he is dead,
Go to thy death-bed, 190
He never will come again.

His beard as white as snow,
All flaxen was his poll:
He is gone, he is gone,
And we cast away moan: 195
God ha' mercy on his soul!

199   *commune with:* share

203   *collateral:* indirect

204   *They find us touch'd:* they find me guilty

210   *obscure:* lowly, degrading

211   *hatchment:* a stone tablet displaying the coat of arms of the dead person

212   *formal ostentation:* official ceremony

214   *call't in question:* find an explanation

215   *the great axe:* the executioner's axe

And of all Christian souls, I pray God. God be wi' you!

[*Exit Ophelia.*]

Laertes: Do you see this, O God?

King: Laertes, I must commune with your grief

Or you deny me right. Go but apart,   200

Make choice of whom your wisest friends you will,

And they shall hear and judge 'twixt you and me:

If by direct or by collateral hand

They find us touch'd, we will our kingdom give,

Our crown, our life, and all that we call ours,   205

To you in satisfaction; but if not,

Be you content to lend your patience to us,

And we shall jointly labour with your soul

To give it due content.

Laertes: Let this be so;

His means of death, his obscure burial,   210

No trophy, sword, nor hatchment o'er his bones,

No noble rite, nor formal ostentation,

Cry to be heard, as 'twere from heaven to earth,

That I must call't in question.

King: So you shall;

And where the offence is let the great axe fall.   215

I pray you, go with me.   [*Exeunt.*]

Act 4, Scene 5: Activities

1. In the role of Queen Gertrude, write a diary entry in which you reflect on the events in this scene. Among your reflections, include your true feelings about Ophelia's madness, and your feelings toward Claudius and Laertes. Do you think you will be able to keep your promise to Hamlet for much longer?

2. In lines 4 – 5, Horatio suggests that people will draw dangerous conclusions from Ophelia's incoherent words. With a partner, create a "gossipy" conversation between two court attendants in which they speculate about the meaning behind Ophelia's words. Read some of these conversations aloud to the class.

3. The part of the mad Ophelia is considered to be a very demanding one for both the director and the actress. In groups of five, take the roles of director, costume designer, composer or music director, choreographer, and the actress who plays Ophelia. Conduct a brainstorming session and then report to the class on how this scene would be performed. If you prefer, you could design a modern production of the scene.

4. Laertes describes Ophelia's behaviour as a "document in madness" (line 176). In the role of a court psychiatrist, write a commentary about Ophelia's behaviour. Document the behaviour first before commenting on it. You may want to make some comparisons with Hamlet's "antic disposition."

5. Create a dialogue between Claudius and an advisor friend after the events of this scene. In the dialogue, have Claudius reflect about the way in which he handled Laertes. The advisor could make observations about Claudius' actions. Role-play the dialogue for the others.

6. *Make a video*

In groups, choose a segment of this scene to produce as a video that reveals the emotional state of a character. As you plan your production, consider the following:

- What is the main emotion of the central character?
- How is that emotion expressed? (Consider both speech and body language.)
- How are the other characters responding to the emotional state of the central character?

Rehearse the scene segment, and then prepare a video script. As you plan each shot, try to think of ways of conveying the emotional emphases of the scene. Remember that different camera angles will create different moods. Similarly, light and colour can alter moods and convey particular feelings. Changing the distance between the camera and the subject will change the focus and balance of a shot. As you prepare your shooting script, keep in mind that the audio portion is as important as the video portion. Plan sound effects to support your visual images. Also, remember that silence can be very effective in conveying emotion. Consider using music to lead into and out of the scene, and, possibly, as background. Now you are ready to shoot. Share your finished video with the rest of your class.

For the next scene . . .

In your journal, write about a time when, under pressure, you acted in a way that surprised you.

Act 4, Scene 6

In this scene . . .

Sailors have brought letters from Hamlet to Horatio and the King. From the letter to Horatio we learn that Hamlet has escaped from the ship bound for England, and has returned to Denmark. Rosencrantz and Guildenstern have continued the voyage to England.

9   *the ambassador:* i.e., Hamlet

12-30   Notice the condensed, restrained style of Hamlet's letter.

12   *overlooked this:* looked this over

13   *means:* access

15   *appointment:* equipment

17   *compelled valour:* courage that was forced on us by the situation

20   *thieves of mercy:* merciful thieves

22   *repair:* come

25-26   *yet are . . . matter:* My words cannot convey the importance of the event. Hamlet is comparing his words to ammunition that is too small for the gun barrel (bore).

Scene 6

Another room in the castle.

Enter Horatio and a Servant.

Horatio: What are they that would speak with me?
Servant: Sea-faring men, sir; they say they have letters for
    you.
Horatio: Let them come in.   [*Exit Servant.*]
    I do not know from what part of the world
    I should be greeted, if not from lord Hamlet.   5

    [*Enter Sailors.*]

First Sailor: God bless you, sir.
Horatio: Let him bless thee too.
First Sailor: He shall, sir, an't please him. There's a letter
    for you, sir; it comes from the ambassador that was
    bound for England; if your name be Horatio, as I am   10
    let to know it is.
Horatio [*Reads*]: Horatio, when thou shalt have overlooked
    this, give these fellows some means to the king; they
    have letters for him. Ere we were two days old at
    sea, a pirate of very warlike appointment gave us   15
    chase. Finding ourselves too slow of sail, we put on
    a compelled valour, and in the grapple I boarded
    them: on the instant, they got clear of our ship; so I
    alone became their prisoner. They have dealt with
    me like thieves of mercy; but they knew what they   20
    did; I am to do a good turn for them. Let the king
    have the letters I have sent; and repair thou to me
    with as much speed as thou woulds't fly death. I
    have words to speak in thine ear will make thee
    dumb: yet are they much too light for the bore of   25

31   *way for:* a way to deliver

the matter. These good fellows will bring thee
where I am. Rosencrantz and Guildenstern hold their
course for England: of them I have much to tell
thee. Farewell.
He that thou knowest thine.—*Hamlet.*   30

Come, I will give you way for these your letters;
And do't the speedier, that you may direct me
    To him from whom you brought them.

                                        [*Exeunt.*]

Act 4, Scene 6: Activities

1. Hamlet's short letter leaves many questions unanswered. If you were Horatio, what questions would you want to ask Hamlet?

2. Do you think Hamlet's letter reveals or suggests that any changes have taken place in him? In the role of Horatio, write a diary entry in which you analyze Hamlet's letter and consider the changes that might have happened once Hamlet left the environment of the palace.

3. Since we do not yet know the contents of Hamlet's letter to Claudius, try composing a twenty-word message Hamlet might have sent. Announce your return and hint that you have uncovered Claudius' scheme to have you killed. Several people could read their messages to members of their group, and discuss the implication of each message.

For the next scene . . .

In your journal, write about a time when someone used flattery to manipulate you into doing something. Have you ever tried to manipulate someone else through flattery? What were the results?

Act 4, Scene 7

In this scene . . .

This scene introduces a strong counterplot against Hamlet. It begins with Claudius convincing Laertes that Hamlet was responsible for Polonius' murder. The letter from Hamlet is delivered, announcing his return to Denmark. Claudius manipulates Laertes into a plan to kill Hamlet in a duelling match. Laertes adds to the plan by offering to put a deadly poison on the end of his sword. Claudius suggests a cup of poisoned wine for Hamlet, if the first plan fails. The conversation is interrupted by Gertrude, who announces that Ophelia is dead.

1   *Now must . . . seal:* Now that you know the facts, you will confirm my innocence.

3   *Sith:* since

6   *feats:* actions

7   *capital:* punishable by death

9   *mainly:* very greatly

10   *unsinew'd:* weak

13   *be it either which:* whichever of the two it might be

14   *conjunctive:* closely linked

17   *count:* trial

18   *general gender:* common people

21   *Convert his gyves to graces:* change his fetters to adornments, i.e., make a martyr of him

21-24   *so that my arrows . . . aim'd them:* The public's affection for Hamlet is so strong that my plan for dealing with him would be turned against me, just as an arrow that is too light would be turned back by a strong wind, missing its mark.

26   *terms:* circumstances

27   *go back again:* refer to her as she used to be

28   *Stood challenger . . . age:* was unequalled in her time

Scene 7

Another room in the castle.

Enter King and Laertes.

King: Now must your conscience my acquittance seal.
And you must put me in your heart for friend,
Sith you have heard, and with a knowing ear,
That he which hath your noble father slain,
Pursued my life.
Laertes: It well appears: but tell me   5
Why you proceeded not against these feats,
So crimeful and so capital in nature,
As by your safety, wisdom, all things else,
You mainly were stirr'd up.
King: O, for two special reasons,
Which may to you perhaps seem much unsinew'd,   10
And yet to me they're strong. The queen his mother
Lives almost by his looks; and for myself—
My virtue or my plague, be it either which—
She's so conjunctive to my life and soul,
That, as the star moves not but in his sphere,   15
I could not but by her. The other motive,
Why to a public count I might not go,
Is the great love the general gender bear him;
Who, dipping all his faults in their affection,
Would, like the spring that turneth wood to stone,   20
Convert his gyves to graces; so that my arrows,
Too slightly timber'd for so loud a wind,
Would have reverted to my bow again
And not where I had aim'd them.
Laertes: And so have I a noble father lost;   25
A sister driven into desperate terms,
Whose worth, if praises may go back again,
Stood challenger on mount of all the age
For her perfections: but my revenge will come.

33   *You shortly shall hear more:* Claudius is expecting news of Hamlet's death in England.

50   *abuse:* deception

52   *character:* handwriting

59   *it:* i.e., Hamlet's return

63   *checking at:* turning back from. The image is taken from falconry. Sometimes the hawk would swerve away from (check at) its prey to chase some other bird.

King: Break not your sleeps for that: you must not think   30
  That we are made of stuff so flat and dull
  That we can let our beard be shook with danger
  And think it pastime. You shortly shall hear more:
  I loved your father, and we love ourself;
  And that, I hope, will teach you to imagine—   35

[*Enter a Messenger with letters.*]

  How now! what news?
Messenger: Letters, my lord, from Hamlet:
  This to your majesty; this to the queen.
King: From Hamlet! Who brought them?
Messenger: Sailors, my lord, they say: I saw them not:
  They were given to me by Claudio; he received them   40
  Of him that brought them.
King: Laertes, you shall hear them.
  Leave us.   [*Exit Messenger.*]
  [*Reads*]: High and mighty, You shall know, I am set
    naked on your kingdom. To-morrow shall I beg leave   45
    to see your kingly eyes: when I shall, first asking
    your pardon thereunto, recount the occasions of my
    sudden and more strange return.—*Hamlet.*
  What should this mean? Are all the rest come back?
  Or is it some abuse, and no such thing?   50
Laertes: Know you the hand?
King: 'Tis Hamlet's character. "Naked!"
  And in a postscript here, he says "alone."
  Can you advise me?
Laertes: I am lost in it, my lord. But let him come: 55
  It warms the very sickness in my heart,
  That I shall live and tell him to his teeth,
  "Thus diddest thou!"
King: If it be so, Laertes,—
  As how should it be so? how otherwise?—
  Will you be ruled by me?
Laertes: Ay, my lord;   60
  If so you'll not o'errule me to a peace.
King: To thine own peace. If he be now return'd,
  As checking at his voyage, and that he means
  No more to undertake it, I will work him

65   *device:* contrivance, plotting

68   *uncharge the practice:* not accuse us

71   *organ:* instrument (for killing Hamlet)

74   *your sum of parts:* all your qualities

77   *unworthiest siege:* least worth

78   *riband:* ribbon

80, 81 *livery, weeds:* clothing

85   *can:* are skillful

88-89 *As he . . . beast:* as if he and the horse were one being (like the centaurs of classical mythology)

89-91 *so far . . . did:* His actions surpassed anything I expected or could even imagine.

94   *brooch:* main ornament

96   *made confession of you:* acknowledged your skill

97   *masterly report:* report of your mastery

98   *defence:* fencing (means of defence)

99   *rapier:* a two-edged sword, popular in fencing

To an exploit now ripe in my device,   65
Under the which he shall not choose but fall,
And for his death no wind of blame shall breathe;
But even his mother shall uncharge the practice,
And call it accident.

Laertes: My lord, I will be ruled:
The rather, if you could devise it so   70
That I might be the organ.

King: It falls right.
You have been talk'd of since your travel much,
And that in Hamlet's hearing, for a quality
Wherein, they say, you shine: your sum of parts
Did not together pluck such envy from him,   75
As did that one, and that, in my regard,
Of the unworthiest siege.

Laertes: What part is that, my lord?

King: A very riband in the cap of youth,
Yet needful too; for youth no less becomes
The light and careless livery that it wears   80
Than settled age his sables and his weeds,
Importing health and graveness. Two months since
Here was a gentleman of Normandy:—
I've seen myself, and served against, the French,
And they can well on horseback: but this gallant   85
Had witchcraft in't; he grew into his seat,
And to such wondrous doing brought his horse
As he had been incorpsed and demi-natured
With the brave beast: so far he topp'd my thought
That I, in forgery of shapes and tricks   90
Come short of what he did.

Laertes: A Norman was't?

King: A Norman.

Laertes: Upon my life, Lamond.

King: The very same.

Laertes: I know him well: he is the brooch indeed
And gem of all the nation.   95

King: He made confession of you,
And gave you such a masterly report,
For art and exercise in your defence,
And for your rapier most especial,

101   *scrimers:* fencers

102   *motion:* the movements that fencers are trained in

106   *play:* to engage in a fencing match

112-114 *love is . . . it:* Time brings love into being and also causes it
        to die.

115-116 *There lives . . . abate it:* The snuff is the charred wick of a
        candle which causes the flame to dim. The idea is that love
        carries within it the cause of its own destruction.

117   *And nothing . . . still:* Nothing remains at the same level of
        goodness forever.

118   *plurisy:* excess

118-124 Ironically, Claudius is commenting on the weaknesses in
        Hamlet that have prevented him from killing Claudius.

121   *abatements:* a lessening in intensity

123   *spendthrift sigh:* It was believed that each sigh drew blood
        from the heart. A sigh gave temporary relief, but it harmed
        the person by carelessly wasting lifeblood.

124   *the quick o' the ulcer:* the heart of the trouble

128   *sanctuarize:* provide safety, refuge. In mediaeval times,
        murderers could seek sanctuary in a church.

132   *put on:* appoint

134   *in fine:* finally

135   *remiss:* carelessly trustful

That he cried out, 'twould be a sight indeed   100
If one could match you: the scrimers of their nation,
He swore, had neither motion, guard, nor eye,
If you opposed them. Sir, this report of his
Did Hamlet so envenom with his envy
That he could nothing do but wish and beg   105
Your sudden coming o'er, to play with him.
Now, out of this,——
Laertes: What out of this, my lord?
King: Laertes, was your father dear to you?
  Or are you like the painting of a sorrow,
  A face without a heart?
Laertes: Why ask you this?   110
King: Not that I think you did not love your father,
  But that I know love is begun by time,
  And that I see, in passages of proof,
  Time qualifies the spark and fire of it.
  There lives within the very flame of love   115
  A kind of wick or snuff that will abate it;
  And nothing is at a like goodness still,
  For goodness, growing to a plurisy,
  Dies in his own too-much: that we would do
  We should do when we would; for this "would" changes 120
  And hath abatements and delays as many
  As there are tongues, are hands, are accidents,
  And then this "should" is like a spendthrift sigh,
  That hurts by easing. But, to the quick o' the ulcer:
  Hamlet comes back: what would you undertake,   125
  To show yourself your father's son in deed
  More than in words?
Laertes: To cut his throat i' the church.
King: No place indeed should murder sanctuarize;
  Revenge should have no bounds. But, good Laertes,
  Will you do this, keep close within your chamber.   130
  Hamlet return'd shall know you are come home:
  We'll put on those shall praise your excellence
  And set a double varnish on the fame
  The Frenchman gave you; bring you in fine together
  And wager on your heads: he, being remiss,   135
  Most generous, and free from all contriving,

137 *peruse:* examine

139 *unabated:* unprotected, with the point exposed; *pass of practice:* practice round, or well-rehearsed (treacherous) thrust

140 *Requite:* repay

142 *unction:* ointment; *mountebank:* a travelling quack doctor

143 *mortal:* deadly

144 *cataplasm:* poultice, bandage

145 *simples:* medicinal herbs; *virtue:* power

146 *Under the moon:* Herbs collected by moonlight were thought to be especially powerful.

148 *contagion:* poison; *gall:* graze his skin

150-151 *Weigh . . . shape:* Consider the best time and action to achieve our purpose.

152-153 *And that . . . assay'd:* If our scheme becomes obvious because we didn't carry it out well, it would be better not to attempt it at all.

154 *back:* backup plan

155 *blast in proof:* fail (be destroyed in the attempt)

156 *your cunnings:* your respective skills

161 *chalice:* a wine goblet; *nonce:* occasion

162 *stuck:* sword thrust

168 *willow:* The willow tree is a symbol of lost love.

169 *hoar:* The underside of a willow leaf is white like frost (hoar).

172 *liberal:* free of speech; here, lewd

Will not peruse the foils, so that with ease,
Or with a little shuffling, you may choose
A sword unbated, and, in a pass of practice
Requite him for your father.
Laertes: I will do't: 140
   And for that purpose I'll anoint my sword.
   I bought an unction of a mountebank,
   So mortal, that but dip a knife in it,
   Where it draws blood no cataplasm so rare,
   Collected from all simples that have virtue   145
   Under the moon, can save the thing from death
   That is but scratch'd withal: I'll touch my point
   With this contagion, that, if I gall him slightly,
   It may be death.
King: Let's further think of this;
   Weigh what convenience both of time and means   150
   May fit us to our shape: if this should fail,
   And that our drift look through our bad performance,
   'Twere better not assay'd; therefore this project
   Should have a back or second, that might hold
   If this should blast in proof. Soft!—let me see: 155
   We'll make a solemn wager on your cunnings:
   I ha't!
   When in your motion you are hot and dry—
   As make your bouts more violent to that end—
   And that he calls for drink, I'll have prepared him   160
   A chalice for the nonce; whereon but sipping,
   If he by chance escape your venom'd stuck,
   Our purpose may hold there. But stay, what noise?

[*Enter Queen.*]

How now, sweet queen?
Queen: One woe doth tread upon another's heel,   165
   So fast they follow: your sister's drown'd, Laertes.
Laertes: Drown'd! O, where?
Queen: There is a willow grows aslant a brook,
   That shows his hoar leaves in the glassy stream;
   There, with fantastic garlands did she come   170
   Of crow-flowers, nettles, daisies, and long purples,
   That liberal shepherds give a grosser name,

173   *cold:* chaste

174   *pendent:* overhanging; *coronet weeds:* flowers woven into a crown

175   *envious:* spiteful; *sliver:* small branch

180   *incapable:* unaware

181-182 *a creature . . . element:* a creature that lives in water

189   *trick:* human nature

191   *The woman will be out:* These tears will be the last signs of womanly behaviour in me.

193   *douts:* extinguishes

But our cold maids do dead-men's-fingers call them;
There, on the pendent boughs her coronet weeds
Clambering to hang, an envious sliver broke; 175
When down the weedy trophies and herself
Fell in the weeping brook. Her clothes spread wide,
And mermaid-like a while they bore her up:
Which time she chanted snatches of old tunes,
As one incapable of her own distress, 180
Or like a creature native and indued
Unto that element: but long it could not be,
Till that her garments, heavy with their drink,
Pull'd the poor wretch from her melodious lay
To muddy death.
Laertes: Alas! then, she is drown'd! 185
Queen: Drown'd, drown'd.
Laertes: Too much of water hast thou, poor Ophelia,
And therefore I forbid my tears: but yet
It is our trick; nature her custom holds,
Let shame say what it will: when these are gone, 190
The woman will be out. Adieu, my lord:
I have a speech of fire that fain would blaze,
But that this folly doubts it.   *[Exit.]*
King: Let's follow, Gertrude:
How much I had to do to calm his rage!
Now fear I this will give it start again; 195
Therefore let's follow.   *[Exeunt.]*

Act 4, Scene 7: Activities

1. Claudius singles out two words from Hamlet's letter: "naked" and "alone." Brainstorm and decide what these words might mean to Claudius. Suggest other phrases in the letter that might worry him.

2. Write diary entries that Claudius and Laertes each might have written after their conversation in this scene. The diary entries should reveal their personalities and their motivations, as well as their opinions of each other.

3. Do you think Ophelia's death could be considered suicide? What effect did the details of her death create on you? What effect do you think Shakespeare wanted to create? Was Ophelia an innocent victim? Discuss your ideas in groups.

4. Imagine that you are a reporter for a nightly television newscast. You have been sent with a camera crew to do a story on the death of Ophelia. Whom would you try to interview? What questions would you ask them? What locations would you try to shoot? What setting would you use to deliver your report? Write the story you would present on the news. It should be two minutes long.

Act 4: Consider the Whole Act

1. Beginning with the death of Polonius at the end of Act 3, create a flow chart showing the main plot events up until the end of Act 4. Extend the flow chart with your own predictions about:
   - how Hamlet will behave when he returns to the castle
   - Hamlet's reaction to news of Ophelia's death
   - Laertes' response when he comes face to face with Hamlet
   - other developments.

2. Considering the behaviour of Gertrude and Ophelia in this act, debate Hamlet's earlier statement that "Frailty, thy name is woman!"

3. Although Claudius is clearly an unscrupulous character, he has some qualities that could be considered admirable. Make a list of his admirable qualities, with references as to where in Act 4 they are best demonstrated. Considering Claudius' qualities, what role or profession might he succeed at in modern life?

4. After considering how you respond to Claudius' character, think about villains or antagonists in contemporary popular culture (consider novels, movies and television). What seems to motivate them? Why are we interested in them? Interview a range of people on this subject, and then write an essay or make a presentation to the class about people's attitudes toward villains in modern media.

5. Think about Hamlet's definition of greatness:

   > . . . Rightly to be great
   > Is not to stir without great argument,
   > But greatly to find quarrel in a straw
   > When honour's at the stake . . .
   >
   > (Act 4, Scene 4, lines 52 – 55)

   With Hamlet's idea in mind, consider a recent newsworthy event in which someone took a strong stand because honour was at stake. (You will have to define "honour.") Do you agree with the stand that was taken? Write an editorial about this event, using some of Hamlet's words and/or ideas.

6. Hamlet, Laertes and Fortinbras are three very different young men, but they are all involved in conflicts in which their honour is at stake. Divide a page in three columns vertically, one column for each character. Then divide the page horizontally using the following headings:
   • The Problem
   • The Plan of Action
   • Personal Qualities Likely to Help Plan
   • Personal Qualities Likely to Hinder Plan

   Once you have filled in this chart, predict how well each character will carry out his plan. Discuss your predictions in groups or with the class.

7. In Scene 4 (lines 38 – 40), Hamlet suggests reasons for his procrastination. Write a fable in which procrastination affects the outcome. Do not state the moral of your story. Read your fable to your classmates and ask them to write their own versions of the moral. The class could then decide on the best version. If possible, you might want to try reading your fable to Grade 7 or 8 students and asking them to write the moral.

8. Images of disease and decay occur frequently in this act. What kinds of disease images do people use today? In examples you consider, what is being compared to each disease? In your opinion, are the images effective? Why or why not?

For the next scene . . .

In your journal, write about a time when a friend or relative returned from an absence and seemed to have a very different personality. Did you believe that the change was real? What circumstances might cause a person to change greatly in a short period of time?

Act 5, Scene 1

In this scene . . .

Two gravediggers (played by clowns) are preparing Ophelia's grave. As they pass the time joking about their work, Hamlet and Horatio approach and join in their conversation. Hamlet comes upon the skull of Yorick, a court jester who entertained Hamlet in his childhood. Ophelia's funeral procession approaches and Hamlet learns that Ophelia is dead. When Laertes expresses his grief by leaping into Ophelia's grave, Hamlet also leaps in and fights with him. As the scene ends, Claudius reminds Laertes of their plan to murder Hamlet.

Stage direction

Enter two clowns: The first and second clowns are gravediggers. They are simple, rough people.

1   *Christian burial:* This question arises because suicides were denied Christian funeral rites.

4   *straight:* right away. *The crowner hath sat on her:* The coroner has considered her case; *finds:* has given a verdict

9   *"se offendendo":* a mistaken attempt at the legal term "se defendendo" (in self-defence)

9-13   The gravedigger creates humour by confusing legal terminology and by attempting to construct a legal argument.

12   *argal:* a corruption of "ergo" (therefore)

17   *will he, nill he:* willy-nilly, i.e., willingly or not

22   *marry:* indeed; *crowner's quest law:* coroner's inquest law

25   *out o' Christian burial:* without Christian ceremony

26   *there thou say'st:* that's right

27   *countenance:* permission

28-29   *even Christian:* fellow Christians. *Come, my spade:* Hand me my spade.

31   *hold up:* follow

Act 5, Scene 1

A churchyard.

Enter two Clowns, with
spades, etc.

First Clown: Is she to be buried in Christian burial that
   wilfully seeks her own salvation?
Second Clown: I tell thee she is; and therefore make her
   grave straight: the crowner hath sat on her, and finds
   it Christian burial.   5
First Clown: How can that be, unless she drowned herself
   in her own defence?
Second Clown: Why, 'tis found so.
First Clown: It must be "se offendendo"; it cannot be else.
   For here lies the point: if I drown myself wittingly,   10
   it argues an act: and an act hath three branches; it is,
   to act, to do, and to perform: argal, she drowned
   herself wittingly.
Second Clown: Nay, but hear you, goodman delver.
First Clown: Give me leave. Here lies the water; good: here   15
   stands the man; good: if the man go to this water, and
   drown himself, it is, will he, nill he, he goes; mark
   you that; but if the water come to him and drown him,
   he drowns not himself: argal, he that is not guilty of
   his own death, shortens not his own life.   20
Second Clown: But is this law?
First Clown: Ay, marry is't; crowner's quest law.
Second Clown: Will you ha' the truth on't? If this had not
   been a gentlewoman, she should have been buried
   out o'Christian burial.   25
First Clown: Why, there thou say'st: and the more pity that
   great folk should have countenance in this world to
   drown or hang themselves, more than their even
   Christian. Come, my spade. There is no ancient
   gentlemen but gardeners, ditchers, and gravemakers;   30
   they hold up Adam's profession.

33   *bore arms:* a pun—had arms or had weapons

38-39   *confess thyself:* The rest of this saying was "and be hanged."

40   *Go to:* Nonsense.

42   *mason:* a worker in stone; *shipwright:* a shipbuilder

52   *unyoke:* take a rest (as when oxen were unyoked)

55   *Mass:* by the Mass

60   *Yaughan:* Possibly Yaughan was a tavern-keeper near the Globe Theatre; *stoup:* large drinking cup

Second Clown: Was he a gentleman?

First Clown: A' was the first that ever bore arms.

Second Clown: Why, he had none.

First Clown: What, art a heathen? How dost thou understand   35
the Scripture? The Scripture says, Adam digged: could
he dig without arms? I'll put another question to thee:
if thou answerest me not to the purpose, confess
thyself—

Second Clown: Go to.   40

First Clown: What is he, that builds stronger than either
the mason, the shipwright, or the carpenter?

Second Clown: The gallows-maker; for that frame outlives
a thousand tenants.

First Clown: I like thy wit well, in good faith; the gallows   45
does well: but how does it well? it does well to those
that do ill: now, thou dost ill to say the gallows is built
stronger than the church; argal, the gallows may do
well to thee. To't again; come.

Second Clown: Who builds stronger than a mason, a   50
shipwright, or a carpenter?

First Clown: Ay, tell me that, and unyoke.

Second Clown: Marry, now I can tell.

First Clown: To't.

Second Clown: Mass, I cannot tell.   55

[*Enter Hamlet and Horatio at a distance.*]

First Clown: Cudgel thy brains no more about it, for your
dull ass will not mend his pace with beating, and
when you are asked this question next, say "a grave-
maker": the houses that he makes last till doomsday.
Go, get thee to Yaughan; fetch me a stoup of liquor.   60
                                [*Exit Second Clown.*]

[*First Clown digs, and sings.*]

In youth, when I did love, did love,
    Methought it was very sweet,
To contract, O, the time, for—a my behove,
    O, methought there—a was nothing—a meet.

Hamlet: Hath this fellow no feeling of his business, that he   65
sings at grave-making!

67-68   *Custom . . . easiness:* Because he is accustomed to this (gruesome) work, he's at ease with it.

69-70   *the hand . . . sense:* The hand that isn't accustomed to work is more sensitive.

73   *intill:* into

76   *jowls:* knocks

77   *Cain's jaw-bone:* Cain is said to have killed his brother Abel with the jaw-bone of an ass.

78   *pate of a politician:* head of a crafty schemer; *o'er-reaches: gets the better of*

79   *circumvent:* outsmart

81   *courtier:* Courtiers were known for flattery.

86   *chapless:* jawless

87   *mazzard:* head; *sexton:* a person who takes care of church property

88   *revolution:* turn of the Wheel of Fortune; *trick:* skill

90   *loggats:* a game in which sticks are thrown at the ground

95-109 Hamlet is pointing out the uselessness of all the fine points of the law, since everything ends in the grave anyway.

96, 97 *quiddities, quillets:* arguments and fine points of the law

97   *tenures:* rights to property

99   *sconce:* head

100   *action of battery:* a pun—the gravedigger's act of banging the skull about the lawyer's charge (legal action) against the gravedigger for assault (battery)

Horatio: Custom hath made it in him a property of
    easiness.

Hamlet: 'Tis e'en so: the hand of little employment hath
    the daintier sense.   70

   First Clown [*Sings*]:

       But age, with his stealing steps,
          Hath claw'd me in his clutch,
       And hath shipped me intill the land,
          As if I had never been such.

                [*Throws up a skull.*]

Hamlet: That skull had a tongue in it, and could sing once: 75
    how the knave jowls it to the ground, as if it were
    Cain's jaw-bone, that did the first murder! It might be
    the pate of a politician which this ass now o'er-reaches;
    one that would circumvent God, might it not?

Horatio: It might, my lord   80

Hamlet: Or of a courtier; which could say, "Good-morrow,
    sweet lord! How dost thou, good lord?" This might
    be my lord such-a-one, that praised my lord such-a-one's
    horse, when he meant to beg it, might it not?

Horatio: Ay, my lord.   85

Hamlet: Why, e'en so: and now my lady Worm's: chapless,
    and knocked about the mazzard with a sexton's spade:
    here's a fine revolution, if we had the trick to see't. Did
    these bones cost no more the breeding, but to play
    at loggats with them? mine ache to think on't.   90

   First Clown [*Sings*]:

       A pickaxe, and a spade, a spade,
          For and a shrouding sheet:
       O, a pit of clay for to be made
          For such a guest is meet.

            [*Throws up another skull.*]

Hamlet: There's another! Why might not that be the skull 95
    of a lawyer? Where be his quiddities, now, his
    quillets, his cases, his tenures, and his tricks? why does
    he suffer this rude knave now to knock him about the
    sconce with a dirty shovel, and will not tell him of his
    action of battery? Hum! This fellow might be in's time 100

101,103   *statutes, recoveries:* legal terms to do with land rights

103-109   *is this . . . more:* is the end of all this man's complicated efforts that the land he finally possesses (i.e., his grave) is so small it would hardly hold all his paperwork?

  107   *conveyances:* deeds

  108   *box:* coffin

  119   *liest:* used in a double sense—to reside and to tell a lie

  123   *the quick:* the living

  124   *quick:* swift (another pun; see line 123)

  133   *absolute:* exact with words

133-134   *by the card:* precisely; *equivocation:* ambiguity

135-137   *the age . . . kibe:* Hamlet is commenting on peasants who imitate the manners of courtiers. The image is of one man following another so closely that he chafes (galls) the chilblains (kibe) of the man ahead.

  136   *picked:* refined, fussy

a great buyer of land, with his statutes, his
recognizances, his fines, his double vouchers, his
recoveries: is this the fine of his fines and the recovery
of his recoveries, to have his fine pate full of fine dirt?
will his vouchers vouch him no more of his purchases, 105
and double ones too, than the length and breadth of
a pair of indentures? The very conveyances of his
lands will hardly lie in this box, and must the inheritor
himself have no more, ha?

Horatio: Not a jot more, my lord. 110

Hamlet: Is not parchment made of sheep-skins?

Horatio: Ay, my lord, and of calf-skins too.

Hamlet: They are sheep and calves that seek out assurance
in that. I will speak to this fellow. Whose grave's this,
sir? 115

First Clown: Mine, sir.

> [*Sings*]: O, a pit of clay for to be made
>   For such a guest is meet.

Hamlet: I think it be thine, indeed, for thou liest in't.

First Clown: You lie out on't, sir, and therefore 'tis not 120
yours: for my part, I do not lie in't, and yet it is mine.

Hamlet: Thou dost lie in't, to be in't, and say it is thine:
'tis for the dead, not for the quick; therefore thou liest.

First Clown: 'Tis a quick lie, sir; 'twill away again, from
me to you. 125

Hamlet: What man dost thou dig it for?

First Clown: For no man, sir.

Hamlet: What woman, then?

First Clown: For none, neither.

Hamlet: Who is to be buried in't? 130

First Clown: One that was a woman, sir; but, rest her soul,
she's dead.

Hamlet: How absolute the knave is! we must speak by the
card, or equivocation will undo us. By the lord,
Horatio, these three years I have taken note of it: the 135
age is grown so picked that the toe of the peasant
comes so near the heel of the courtier, he galls his kibe.
How long has thou been a grave-maker?

First Clown: Of all the days i' the year, I came to't that

159   *How long . . . rot?:* Notice again Hamlet's preoccupation with death and decay.

160   *pocky:* diseased, infected with the pox

161   *laying in:* burial

170   *whoreson:* a casual expression of contempt

174   *flagon of Rhenish:* bottle of Rhine wine

day that our last king Hamlet o'ercame Fortinbras.   140
Hamlet: How long is that since?
First Clown: Cannot you tell that? every fool can tell that.
    It was the very day that young Hamlet was born; he
    that was mad, and sent into England.
Hamlet: Ay, marry, why was he sent into England?   145
First Clown: Why, because a' was mad: a' shall recover his
    wits there: or, if a' do not, it's no great matter there.
Hamlet: Why?
First Clown: 'Twill not be seen in him there; there the men
    are as mad as he.   150
Hamlet: How came he mad?
First Clown: Very strangely, they say.
Hamlet: How "strangely"?
First Clown: 'Faith, e'en with losing his wits.
Hamlet: Upon what ground?   155
First Clown: Why, here in Denmark. I have been sexton
    here, man and boy, thirty years.
Hamlet: How long will a man lie i' the earth ere he rot?
First Clown: 'Faith, if a' be not rotten before a' die—as we
    have many pocky corses nowadays, that will scarce   160
    hold the laying in—he will last you some eight year or
    nine year: a tanner will last you nine year.
Hamlet: Why he more than another?
First Clown: Why, sir his hide is so tanned with his trade,
    that a' will keep out water a great while; and your   165
    water is a sore decayer of your dead body. Here's a skull
    now: this skull has lain in the earth three-and-twenty
    years.
Hamlet: Whose was it?
First Clown: A whoreson mad fellow's it was: whose do you   170
    think it was?
Hamlet: Nay, I know not.
First Clown: A pestilence on him for a mad rogue! a' poured
    a flagon of Rhenish on my head once. This same skull,
    sir, was Yorick's skull, the King's jester.   175
Hamlet: This?
First Clown: E'en that.
Hamlet: Let me see. [*Takes the skull.*] Alas, poor Yorick! I
    knew him, Horatio; a fellow of infinite jest, of most

182 *my gorge rises at it:* It turns my stomach. Hamlet is not sickened by the skull itself, but by the fact that it once belonged to someone he knew.

184 *gibes:* jokes; *gambols:* jumping around, dancing

185-186 *that were wont . . . roar:* that used to make the people at the table roar with laughter

187 *chap-fallen:* with a hanging jaw, dejected

188 *paint:* put on makeup; *favour:* appearance

192 *Alexander:* Alexander the Great

199 *bung-hole:* a hole in a barrel

200 *curiously:* minutely, strangely

201-202 *with modesty . . . it:* without exaggeration and following probability

207 *Imperious:* imperial

210 *flaw:* a sudden gust of wind

213 *maimed rites:* shortened (mutilated) ceremony; *betoken:* suggest

215 *Fordo:* destroy; *estate:* rank

excellent fancy: he hath borne me on his back a   180
thousand times; and now how abhorred in my
imagination it is! my gorge rises at it. Here hung those
lips that I have kissed I know not how oft. Where be
your gibes now? your gambols? your songs? your
flashes of merriment, that were wont to set the table   185
on a roar: Not one now, to mock your own grinning?
quite chap-fallen? Now get you to my lady's chamber,
and tell her, let her paint an inch thick, to this favour
she must come; make her laugh at that. Prithee,
Horatio, tell me one thing.   190

Horatio: What's that, my lord?

Hamlet: Dost thou think Alexander looked o' this fashion
i' the earth?

Horatio: E'en so.

Hamlet: And smelt so? pah!   *[Throws down the skull.]* 195

Horatio: E'en so, my lord.

Hamlet: To what base uses we may return, Horatio!
Why may not imagination trace the noble dust of
Alexander, till he find it stopping a bung-hole?

Horatio: 'Twere to consider too curiously, to consider so.   200

Hamlet: No, faith, not a jot; but to follow him thither with
modesty enough and likelihood to lead it; as thus:
Alexander died, Alexander was buried, Alexander
returned into dust; the dust is earth; of earth we make
loam: and why of that loam, whereto he was converted,   205
might they not stop a beer-barrel?

　　Imperious Cæsar, dead, and turn'd to clay,
　　Might stop a hole to keep the wind away:
　　O, that that earth which kept the world in awe,
　　Should patch a wall to expel the winter's flaw!   210
But soft, but soft! aside: here comes the king.

[Enter Priests, etc., in procession; the corpse of
Ophelia, Laertes and Mourners following; King, Queen,
their Trains, etc.]

The queen, the courtiers: who is that they follow?
And with such maimed rites! This doth betoken,
The corse they follow did with desperate hand
Fordo its own life: 'twas of some estate.   215

·216   *Couch we:* Let's hide

220-221 *Her obsequies . . . warranty:* She has had as much of a funeral as the authorities permit.

221   *her death was doubtful:* It is not clear whether or not she committed suicide.

222   *great command:* the King's command; *order:* regular church practice

223   *in ground unsanctified:* Suicides could not be buried in a churchyard, i.e., in holy ground.

224   *for:* instead of

225   *Shards:* pieces of broken pottery

226   *virgin crants:* It was customary to hang flower wreaths (crants) in the church at a maiden's funeral.

227   *strewments:* flowers strewn on the grave

227-228 *the bringing home of:* bringing her to her final home with

231   *requiem:* music for the dead

232   *peace-parted souls:* souls who died in peace

234   *churlish:* rude

236   *howling:* i.e., in hell

240-248 Laertes' exaggerated expression of grief, which Hamlet will soon try to match, is called "ranting."

242   *ingenious sense:* lively intelligence

244   *Till I . . . arms:* Ophelia was buried in an open coffin.

247,248 *Pelion, Olympus:* high mountains in Greece. Olympus was the home of the gods.

247   *skyish:* reaching the sky

249   *Bears such an emphasis:* expresses itself with such force

Couch we awhile, and mark. [*Retiring with Horatio.*]
Laertes: What ceremony else?
Hamlet: That is Laertes, a very noble youth: mark.
Laertes: What ceremony else?
First Priest: Her obsequies have been as far enlarged   220
  As we have warranty: her death was doubtful;
  And, but that great command o'ersways the order,
  She should in ground unsanctified have lodged
  Till the last trumpet; for charitable prayers,
  Shards, flints and pebbles should be thrown on her: 225
  Yet here she is allow'd her virgin crants,
  Her maiden strewments and the bringing home
  Of bell and burial.
Laertes: Must there no more be done?
First Priest: No more be done!
  We should profane the service of the dead,   230
  To sing a requiem and such rest to her
  As to peace-parted souls.
Laertes: Lay her i' the earth;
  And from her fair and unpolluted flesh
  May violets spring! I tell thee, churlish priest,
  A minist'ring angel shall my sister be,   235
  When thou liest howling.
Hamlet: What, the fair Ophelia!
Queen [*Scattering flowers*]: Sweets to the sweet: fare well!
  I hoped thou shouldst have been my Hamlet's wife;
  I thought thy bride-bed to have deck'd, sweet maid,
  And not t' have strew'd thy grave.
Laertes: O, treble woe   240
  Fall ten times treble on that cursed head
  Whose wicked deed thy most ingenious sense
  Deprived thee of! Hold off the earth a while,
  Till I have caught her once more in mine arms:
                               [*Leaps into the grave.*]
  Now pile your dust upon the quick and dead,   245
  Till of this flat a mountain you have made
  To o'ertop old Pelion or the skyish head
  Of blue Olympus.
Hamlet [*Advancing*]: What is he whose grief
  Bears such an emphasis? whose phrase of sorrow

250 *Conjures the wandering stars:* charms the planets. The planets change their position in relation to the stars and were throught of, therefore, as "wandering."

251 *wonder-wounded:* struck by astonishment

255 *splenitive:* hot-headed. The spleen was considered the source of rage in the body.

261 *wag:* move

267 *forbear him:* leave him alone

269 *woul't:* wilt thou; *tear thyself:* rend your clothing

270 *eisel:* vinegar

272 *outface:* outdo

273 *quick:* alive

274-277 *And, if . . . wart!:* Hamlet is outdoing Laertes' references to mountains (247 – 248) by saying that Ossa, another Greek mountain, will look as small as a wart in comparison to the "millions of acres" of earth they will be buried under.

276 *Singeing . . . zone:* burning its head in the sun's region

277 *an thou'lt mouth:* if you rant

278 *mere:* complete, utter

280 *Anon:* soon

281 *When . . . are disclosed:* when her (the dove's) two fledglings, covered with yellow down, are hatched

Conjures the wandering stars, and makes them stand   250
Like wonder-wounded hearers? This is I,
Hamlet the Dane!   *[Leaps into the grave.]*
Laertes: The devil take thy soul!   *[Grappling with him.]*
Hamlet: Thou pray'st not well.
  I prithee, take thy fingers from my throat;
  For, though I am not splenitive and rash,   255
  Yet have I something in me dangerous,
  Which let thy wisdom fear. Hold off thy hand!
King: Pluck them asunder.
Queen: Hamlet, Hamlet!
All: Gentlemen,—
Horatio: Good my lord, be quiet.
  [The Attendants part them, and they come out of the grave.]
Hamlet: Why, I will fight with him upon this theme   260
  Until my eyelids will no longer wag.
Queen: O my son, what theme?
Hamlet: I loved Ophelia; forty thousand brothers
  Could not, with all their quantity of love,
  Make up my sum. What wilt thou do for her?   265
King: O he is mad, Laertes.
Queen: For love of God, forbear him.
Hamlet: 'Swounds, show me what thou'lt do:
  Woul't weep? woul't fight? woul't fast? woul't tear thyself?
  Woul't drink up eisel? eat a crocodile?   270
  I'll do't. Dost thou come here to whine?
  To outface me with leaping in her grave?
  Be buried quick with her, and so will I;
  And, if thou prate of mountains, let them throw
  Millions of acres on us, till our ground,   275
  Singeing his pate against the burning Zone,
  Make Ossa like a wart! Nay, an thou'lt mouth,
  I'll rant as well as thou.
Queen: This is mere madness:
  And thus a while the fit will work on him;
  Anon, as patient as the female dove   280
  When that her golden couplets are disclosed,
  His silence will sit drooping.
Hamlet: Hear you, sir;
  What is the reason that you use me thus?

288   *Strengthen . . . speech:* Remember what we planned last night and be patient.

289   *present push:* immediate action

I loved you ever: but it is no matter;
Let Hercules himself do what he may,   285
The cat will mew, and dog will have his day.

                                                   [Exit.]

King: I pray you, good Horatio, wait upon him.—
                                       [Exit Horatio.]
[To Laertes]: Strengthen your patience in our last night's
    speech;
We'll put the matter to the present push.
Good Gertrude, set some watch over your son.   290
This grave shall have a living monument:
An hour of quiet shortly shall we see;
Till then, in patience our proceeding be.   *[Exeunt.]*

Act 5, Scene 1: Activities

1. The gravediggers' work is quite grim, yet their conversation is humorous. In groups, discuss why you think Shakespeare used humour at this point in the play. Are there any jobs in modern society in which people would be likely to use this kind of humour? Why do you think they might joke about their work in this way? You might also consider how other members of society react to people who do these jobs. Share your ideas with the class.

2. In line 200, Horatio answers Hamlet's musings by saying, " 'Twere to consider too curiously, to consider so." Write a continuation of Horatio's comment, to follow Hamlet's argument on the fate of emperors (lines 203 – 210).

3. Describe Hamlet's sudden appearance at Ophelia's grave and his struggle with Laertes from the point of view of three of the following characters: Claudius, one of Claudius' advisors, Gertrude, Ophelia's lady-in-waiting, a minor court attendant, the priest, Horatio, or one of the gravediggers. As you retell the story, explain:
   • why Hamlet says, "This is I, Hamlet the Dane!"
   • how you feel about Hamlet's return to Denmark
   • what you think will result from the struggle between Laertes and Hamlet.

4. Do you think Hamlet is sincere when he declares that he loved Ophelia? If Hamlet's life had not been transformed by the appearance of his father's ghost, do you think he and Ophelia would have been happy together?

5. If you have ever attended a funeral, describe your experience in your journal. How were you affected by the presence of the corpse? In what ways were your reactions similar to or different from Hamlet's reaction to finding Yorick's skull? How would you account for the differences?

For the next scene . . .

In your journal, write about a situation in which you might have said, "I've done what I could, whether right or wrong. Now the rest is up to Fate." How did you feel once you had decided you could not do anything more? Looking back, do you think you were right? What did you mean by "Fate"?

Act 5, Scene 2

In this scene . . .

Hamlet tells Horatio what took place on board the ship and what is in store for Rosencrantz and Guildenstern. Osric, an affected courtier, comes to tell Hamlet that Claudius has proposed a duel between Hamlet and Laertes. Hamlet satirizes Osric's artificial manners, but agrees to the proposal. In private, Hamlet confesses to Horatio that he has a sense of foreboding. Despite Horatio's advice, however, he decides to go ahead with the duel. Before the duel, Hamlet apologizes to Laertes. During the sword play, the King drops poison into a cup intended for Hamlet but instead, Gertrude drinks the poisoned wine as Claudius looks on. Laertes wounds Hamlet with a poisoned sword. Then, in a scuffle, the swords are mixed up, and Hamlet poisons Laertes with the same sword. The Queen dies, and then Laertes dies after telling Hamlet of all the treachery. Hamlet finally kills Claudius. As the play ends, Hamlet urges Horatio to live on and tell his story to the world. Fortinbras approaches with his army and, just before he dies, Hamlet chooses Fortinbras as the new king. Following Fortinbras' instructions, Hamlet is carried off the stage like a soldier. Peace is restored to Denmark.

1   *So much . . . the other:* Hamlet, who has just finished one subject of discussion, is now turning to the subject of his escape at sea.

6   *mutines in the bilboes:* rebellious sailors imprisoned in iron shackles

9   *pall:* fail

10-11   *There's a divinity . . . will:* Providence (destiny) controls our lives, regardless of the efforts we make.

11   *Rough-hew:* crudely shape (as in shaping timber with an axe)

13   *scarfed:* loosely wrapped

14   *them:* Rosencrantz and Guildenstern

15   *Finger'd:* took; *in fine:* in conclusion, finally

20   *Larded:* embellished; *several:* separate

21   *Importing:* concerning

22   *With, ho! . . . my life:* with such imagined dangers (bugbears and goblins) if I continued to live

23   *on the supervise . . . bated:* immediately on reading this, without hesitation

Scene 2

A hall in the castle.

Enter Hamlet and Horatio.

Hamlet: So much for this, sir; now let me see the other;
    You do remember all the circumstance?
Horatio: Remember it, my lord!
Hamlet: Sir, in my heart there was a kind of fighting,
    That would not let me sleep: methought I lay   5
    Worse than the mutines in the bilboes. Rashly,
    And praised be rashness for it, let us know,
    Our indiscretion sometimes serves us well,
    When our dear plots do pall: and that should teach us
    There's a divinity that shapes our ends,   10
    Rough-hew them how we will.
Horatio: That is most certain.
Hamlet: Up from my cabin,
    My sea-gown scarfed about me, in the dark
    Groped I to find out them: had my desire,
    Finger'd their packet and in fine withdrew   15
    To mine own room again: making so bold,
    My fears forgetting manners, to unseal
    Their grand commission; where I found, Horatio,—
    O royal knavery!—an exact command,
    Larded with many several sorts of reasons,   20
    Importing Denmark's health and England's too,
    With, ho! such bugs and goblins in my life,
    That, on the supervise, no leisure bated,
    No, not to stay the grinding of the axe,
    My head should be struck off.
Horatio: Is it possible?   25
Hamlet: Here's the commission; read it at more leisure.
    But wilt thou hear me how I did proceed?
Horatio: I beseech you.

29   *be-netted:* ensnared

30-31   *Ere I could . . . play:* Before I consciously had time to think, my brain took over and started the action.

33   *statists:* politicians

36   *yeoman's service:* loyal service

38   *conjuration:* appeal

42   *And stand . . . amities:* and serve as a link in their friendship

43   *"Ases":* This refers to the word "as," repeated in his letter. It also suggests "asses" carrying a burden (great charge); *charge:* significance

47   *shriving-time:* time for confessing sins and receiving absolution

48   *was heaven ordinant:* heaven was guiding matters (in my favour)

49   *signet:* official seal

50   *model:* exact replica

52   *Subscribed . . . impression:* signed and sealed it (with wax)

54   *what . . . sequent:* what happened after this

56   *go to't:* go to their deaths

58   *near:* on

58-59   *their defeat . . . grow:* Their deaths were caused by their own meddling.

61   *pass:* sword thrust; *fell incensed:* fiercely angry

62   *mighty opposites:* i.e., Claudius and himself

63   *Does it not . . . upon:* Is it not my responsibility?

Hamlet: Being thus be-netted round with villainies,—
 Ere I could make a prologue to my brains, 30
 They had begun the play,—I sat me down;
 Devised a new commission; wrote it fair:
 I once did hold it, as our statists do,
 A baseness to write fair, and labour'd much
 How to forget that learning; but, sir, now 35
 It did me yeoman's service: wilt thou know
 The effects of what I wrote?
Horatio: Ay, good my lord.
Hamlet: An earnest conjuration from the king,
 As England was his faithful tributary,
 As love between them as the palm should flourish, 40
 As peace should still her wheaten garland wear,
 And stand a comma 'tween their amities,
 And many such like "Ases" of great charge,
 That, on the view and know of these contents,
 Without debatement further, more or less, 45
 He should the bearers put to sudden death.
 Not shriving-time allow'd.
Horatio: How was this seal'd?
Hamlet: Why, even in that was heaven ordinant.
 I had my father's signet in my purse,
 Which was the model of that Danish seal: 50
 Folded the writ up in form of the other;
 Subscribed it; gave't the impression; placed it safely,
 The changeling never known. Now, the next day
 Was our sea-fight: and what to this was sequent
 Thou know'st already. 55
Horatio: So Guildenstern and Rosencrantz go to't.
Hamlet: Why, man, they did make love to this
   employment;
 They are not near my conscience; their defeat
 Does by their own insinuation grow:
 'Tis dangerous when the baser nature comes 60
 Between the pass and fell incensed points
 Of mighty opposites.
Horatio: Why, what a king is this!
Hamlet: Does it not, think'st thee, stand me now upon—
 He that hath kill'd my king, and whored my mother;

66 *Thrown out . . . life:* attempted to take my own (proper) life. The image is taken from fishing (angling).

67 *cozenage:* trickery

68 *quit:* repay

69 *canker:* a spreading sore. Note the disease imagery.

70 *In:* into

73 *It:* the time (before news reaches Denmark of the deaths of Rosencrantz and Guildenstern). Note Hamlet's new resolution and confidence.

74 *And a man's . . ."One":* A man's life is barely long enough for him to say "One."

77-78 *For by . . . his:* My own cause appears the same as his.

79 *bravery:* flamboyance, bravado

82-83 *water-fly:* The water-fly, flapping its wings and skipping up and down on the water's surface, symbolizes a busybody.

86-87 *let a . . . mess:* Any rough person who has money can now be admitted to the royal court and dine at the King's table; the King himself is too crude to notice.

88 *chough:* jackdaw, a bird noted for its chattering.

93 *bonnet:* hat; *to his right use:* Osric is likely making exaggerated, sweeping gestures with his hat.

92-104 Hamlet is mocking Osric's exaggeratedly polite behaviour.

Popp'd in between the election and my hopes; 65
Thrown out his angle for my proper life,
And with such cozenage,—is't not perfect conscience,
To quit him with this arm? and is't not to be damn'd,
To let this canker of our nature come
In further evil? 70
Horatio: It must be shortly known to him from England
What is the issue of the business there.
Hamlet: It will be short: the interim is mine;
And a man's life's no more than to say, "One."
But I am very sorry, good Horatio, 75
That to Laertes I forgot myself;
For by the image of my cause, I see
The portraiture of his: I'll court his favours:
But, sure, the bravery of his grief did put me
Into a towering passion.
Horatio: Peace! who comes here? 80

[*Enter Osric.*]

Osric: Your lordship is right welcome back to Denmark.
Hamlet: I humbly thank you, sir. Dost know this water-
fly?
Horatio: No, my good lord.
Hamlet: Thy state is the more gracious, for 'tis a vice to 85
know him. He hath much land, and fertile; let a beast
be lord of beasts, and his crib shall stand at the king's
mess: 'tis a chough, but, as I say, spacious in the
possession of dirt.
Osric: Sweet lord, if your lordship were at leisure, I should 90
impart a thing to you from his majesty.
Hamlet: I will receive it with all diligence of spirit.
Put your bonnet to his right use: 'tis for the head.
Osric: I thank your lordship, it is very hot.
Hamlet: No, believe me, 'tis very cold; the wind is 95
northerly.
Osric: It is indifferent cold, my lord, indeed.
Hamlet: Methinks it is very sultry and hot, for my
complexion—
Osric: Exceedingly, my lord; it is very sultry, as 'twere,—I 100
cannot tell how. But, my lord, his majesty bade me

107 *differences:* distinctive qualities

108 *soft society:* pleasing manners

109-110 *card . . . gentry:* model of a perfect gentleman

110 *continent:* epitome

112 *his definement . . . in you:* His reputation doesn't suffer from your account of it.

112-119 Hamlet is matching Osric's affected language in describing Laertes.

113-114 *to divide . . . memory:* to try to make a list (inventory) of all his good qualities would make the memory reel

114-115 *and yet . . . sail:* and still the attempt to describe them would be slow and awkward in comparison, just as a boat rolling about heavily is surpassed by one sailing quickly

115-116 *in the verity of extolment:* to praise him truly

116 *article:* importance

117-119 *his infusion . . . more:* His qualities are of such value and rarity that, to speak truly of him, nothing is like him except his own reflection; anyone who tries to imitate him is no better than his shadow.

121 *The concernancy, sir?:* What is the point, sir? Hamlet is wondering why they are discussing Laertes.

122 *more rawer breath:* cruder language

124-125 *Is't not possible . . . really:* Can you not understand your own language when someone else speaks it? You will be able to if you try.

126 *What imports . . . gentleman?:* Why are you mentioning this gentleman?

133 *approve:* commend

135-137 *I dare . . . himself:* I do not dare agree with that because I will seem to be comparing my excellence with his; yet, one can only know another person if one knows oneself well first.

138 *weapon:* style of fencing

138-139 *but in the imputation . . . unfellowed:* The people in his service say his reputation is unequalled.

signify to you that he has laid a great wager on your
head: sir, this is the matter—

Hamlet: I beseech you, remember—

                [*Hamlet moves him to put on his hat.*]

Osric: Nay, good my lord; for mine ease, in good faith, Sir,   105
here is newly come to court, Laertes: believe me, an
absolute gentleman, full of most excellent differences,
of very soft society and great showing: indeed, to
speak feelingly of him, he is the card or calendar of
gentry, for you shall find in him the continent of what   110
part a gentleman would see.

Hamlet: Sir, his definement suffers no perdition in you;
though, I know, to divide him inventorially would dizzy
the arithmetic of memory, and yet but yaw neither,
in respect of his quick sail. But in the verity of   115
extolment, I take him to be a soul of great article, and
his infusion of such dearth and rareness, as, to make
true diction of him, his semblable is his mirror, and who
else would trace him, his umbrage, nothing more.

Osric: Your lordship speaks most infallibly of him.   120

Hamlet: The concernancy, sir? why do we wrap the
gentleman in our more rawer breath?

Osric: Sir?

Horatio: Is't not possible to understand in another tongue?
You will do't, sir, really.   125

Hamlet: What imports the nomination of this gentleman?

Osric: Of Laertes?

Horatio: His purse is empty already; all his golden words
are spent.

Hamlet: Of him, sir.   130

Osric: I know you are not ignorant—

Hamlet: I would, you did, sir; yet, in faith, if you did, it
would not much approve me. Well, sir?

Osric: You are not ignorant of what excellence Laertes is—

Hamlet: I dare not confess that, lest I should compare with   135
him in excellence; but, to know a man well, were to
know himself.

Osric: I mean, sir, for his weapon; but in the imputation
laid on him by them, in his meed he's unfellowed.

Hamlet: What's his weapon?   140

143-144 *Barbary horses:* a North African breed, famous for their speed

144   *imponed:* bet, wagered

145   *poniards:* daggers; *assigns:* accessories

146   *girdle:* sword belt; *hanger:* the straps that held the sword to the girdle

148   *of very liberal conceit:* richly ornamented

150   *edified by the margent:* instructed by explanatory notes (receive an explanation from notes in the margin)

153   *germane:* relevant

160   *laid:* bet, wagered

160-162 *The king . . . nine:* The King is allowing Hamlet a handicap. Laertes must win three bouts more than Hamlet in a total of twelve bouts.

163-164 *vouchsafe the answer:* accept the challenge

169   *breathing time of day:* time for exercise

170   *foils:* blunted rapiers used for fencing

174   *re-deliver you:* deliver your message

180   *This lapwing . . . head:* The shell probably refers to Osric's ornate hat. According to a popular proverb, the lapwing represented a pretentious young person, since it leaves its nest a few hours after birth.

Osric: Rapier and dagger.

Hamlet: That's two of his weapons: but, well.

Osric: The king, sir, hath waged with him six Barbary
    horses: against the which he has imponed, as I take it,
    six French rapiers and poniards, with their assigns,   145
    as girdle, hanger, and so: three of the carriages, in faith,
    are very dear to fancy, very responsive to the hilts,
    most delicate carriages, and of very liberal conceit.

Hamlet: What call you the carriages?

Horatio: I knew you must be edified by the margent ere   150
    you had done.

Osric: The carriages, sir, are the hangers.

Hamlet: The phrase would be more germane to the matter
    if we could carry cannon by our sides: I would it
    might be hangers till then. But on: six Barbary horses 155
    against six French swords, their assigns, and three
    liberal-conceited carriages: that's the French bet
    against the Danish. Why is this "imponed," as you
    call it?

Osric: The king, sir, hath laid, that in a dozen passes between 160
    you and him, he shall not exceed you three hits; he
    hath laid on twelve for nine; and it would come to
    immediate trial, if your lordship would vouchsafe
    the answer.

Hamlet: How if I answer "No"?   165

Osric: I mean, my lord, the opposition of your person in
    trial.

Hamlet: Sir, I will walk here in the hall; if it please his
    majesty, it is the breathing time of day with me: let
    the foils be brought, the gentleman willing, and the   170
    king hold his purpose, I will win for him an I can; if
    not, I will gain nothing but my shame and the odd
    hits.

Osric: Shall I re-deliver you e'en so?

Hamlet: To this effect, sir, after what flourish your nature 175
    will.

Osric: I commend my duty to your lordship.

Hamlet: Yours, yours. [*Exit Osric.*] He does well to commend
    it himself: there are no tongues else for's turn.

Horatio: This lapwing runs away with the shell on his head. 180

181   *He did comply . . . it:* He observed the formalities of polite social behaviour before he would suckle.

183   *drossy:* silly

183-184   *tune of the time:* superficial fashion; *outward habit of encounter:* the outward style of conversation

184-187   *a kind . . . are out:* Hamlet is using an image from breweries. Ultimately, these courtiers, are as empty as beer bubbles.

185   *yesty:* frothy

186   *fond:* foolish; *winnowed:* flimsy

188   *commended:* sent his respects

189   *attend:* wait for

193-194   *if his fitness . . . ready:* If he (Laertes) is ready, so am I.

196   *In happy time:* at an appropriate time

197-198   *use some . . . Laertes:* show some politeness

203   *how ill . . . heart:* Hamlet has a feeling something will go wrong.

206   *gain giving:* feeling of anxiety, misgiving

208-209   *forestall their repair:* prevent them from coming

210   *we defy augury:* I don't pay attention to superstitious prophecies.

210-211   *there's a special . . . sparrow:* This is a reference to the Bible (Matthew 10:29). "Are not two sparrows sold for a copper coin? And not one of them falls to the ground without your Father's will." Belief in fate and predestination was popular in Shakespeare's time.

211   *it:* death

213   *the readiness:* i.e., the readiness to accept one's fate, to die

213-215   *Since no man . . . betimes?:* Hamlet seems to be accepting the idea that he will never gain complete understanding of life.

214   *aught:* anything

215   *betimes:* early

Hamlet: He did comply with his dug before he sucked it.
Thus has he—and many more of the same breed that
I know the drossy age dotes on—only got the tune of
the time, and outward habit of encounter; a kind of
yesty collection, which carries them through and   185
through the most fond and winnowed opinions; and
do but blow them to their trial, the bubbles are out.

[*Enter a Lord.*]

Lord: My lord, his majesty commended him to you by young
Osric, who brings back to him, that you attend him
in the hall: he sends to know if your pleasure hold to   190
play with Laertes, or that you will take longer time.
Hamlet: I am constant to my purposes; they follow the king's
pleasure: if his fitness speaks, mine is ready; now or
whensoever, provided I be so able as now.
Lord: The king and queen and all are coming down.   195
Hamlet: In happy time.
Lord: The queen desires you to use some gentle
entertainment to Laertes before you fall to play.
Hamlet: She well instructs me.   [*Exit Lord.*]
Horatio: You will lose this wager, my lord.   200
Hamlet: I do not think so; since he went into France, I have
been in continual practice; I shall win at the odds. But
thou wouldst not think how ill all's here about my heart:
but it is no matter.
Horatio: Nay, good my lord—   205
Hamlet: It is but foolery; but it is such a kind of gain giving,
as would perhaps trouble a woman.
Horatio: If your mind dislike anything, obey it. I will forestall
their repair hither, and say you are not fit.
Hamlet: Not a whit; we defy augury: there's a special   210
providence in the fall of a sparrow. If it be now, 'tis
not to come; if it be not to come, it will be now; if it
be not now, yet it will come: the readiness is all: since
no man has aught of what he leaves, what is't to leave
betimes? Let be.   215

[*Enter King, Queen, Laertes, and Lords, Osric, and
Attendants with foils. A table with flagons of wine on it.*]

219   *This presence:* those who are present

222   *nature:* your natural feelings (as a son whose father has been killed); *exception:* your sense of being wronged

223-230   *I here proclaim madness . . . enemy:* Hamlet seems to be admitting that he really *was* mad. He admits that there were times when he temporarily lost control of his mind.

225   *If Hamlet from himself be ta'en away:* This idea reflects modern descriptions of madness: "He's beside himself." "She's not all there."

232   *purposed:* deliberate

235   *in nature:* with regard to my duty as a son

237   *in my terms of honour:* in matters affecting my honour

237-240   Even if Laertes forgives Hamlet personally, he is still obliged to defend his honour officially.

240   *a voice . . . peace:* an authoritative judgment as grounds for making peace

241   *name ungored:* reputation undamaged

246   *foil:* the setting of a jewel, which shows the stone at its best; also, a sword

248   *Stick fiery off:* stand out in brilliant contrast

King: Come, Hamlet, come, and take this hand from me.
    [*The King puts the hand of Laertes into that of Hamlet.*]
Hamlet: Give me your pardon, sir; I have done you wrong;
    But pardon't, as you are a gentleman.
    This presence knows, and you must needs have heard,
    How I am punish'd with a sore distraction.   220
    What I have done,
    That might your nature, honour, and exception
    Roughly awake, I here proclaim was madness.
    Was't Hamlet wrong'd Laertes? Never Hamlet:
    If Hamlet from himself be ta'en away,   225
    And when he's not himself does wrong Laertes,
    Then Hamlet does it not, Hamlet denies it.
    Who does it then? His madness: if't be so,
    Hamlet is of the faction that is wrong'd;
    His madness is poor Hamlet's enemy.   230
    Sir, in this audience,
    Let my disclaiming from a purposed evil
    Free me so far in your most generous thoughts,
    That I have shot mine arrow o'er the house,
    And hurt my brother.
Laertes: I am satisfied in nature,   235
    Whose motive, in this case, should stir me most
    To my revenge: but in my terms of honour
    I stand aloof, and will no reconcilement,
    Till by some elder masters, of known honour,
    I have a voice and precedent of peace,   240
    To keep my name ungored. But till that time,
    I do receive your offer'd love like love
    And will not wrong it.
Hamlet: I embrace it freely,
    And will this brother's wager frankly play.
    Give us the foils. Come on.
Laertes: Come, one for me.   245
Hamlet: I'll be your foil, Laertes; in mine ignorance
    Your skill shall, like a star i' the darkest night,
    Stick fiery off indeed.
Laertes: You mock me, sir.
Hamlet: No, by this hand.
King: Give them the foils, young Osric. Cousin Hamlet,   250

254   *since he's better'd:* since Laertes is considered the better swordsman

256   *This likes me well:* This pleases me.

260   *quit . . . exchange:* reach a tie in the third bout

261   *ordnance:* cannon

262   *better breath:* improved strength

263   *union:* a pearl

266   *kettle:* kettledrum

273   *this pearl is thine:* Claudius drops the pearl (and, thus, the poison) into Hamlet's wine cup.

280   *napkin:* handkerchief

281   *carouses to thy fortune:* drinks to your health

You know the wager?
Hamlet: Very well, my lord;
  Your grace hath laid the odds o' the weaker side.
King: I do not fear it; I have seen you both:
  But since he's better'd, we have therefore odds.
Laertes: This is too heavy, let me see another.   255
Hamlet: This likes me well: these foils have all a length?
                              [*They prepare to play.*]
Osric: Ay, my good lord.
King: Set me the stoups of wine upon that table.
  If Hamlet give the first or second hit,
  Or quit in answer of the third exchange,   260
  Let all the battlements their ordnance fire;
  The king shall drink to Hamlet's better breath;
  And in the cup an union shall he throw,
  Richer than that which four successive kings
  In Denmark's crown have worn. Give me the cups;   265
  And let the kettle to the trumpet speak,
  The trumpet to the cannonier without,
  The cannons to the heavens, the heaven to earth,
  Now the king drinks to Hamlet. Come, begin;
  And you, the judges, bear a wary eye.   270
Hamlet: Come on, sir.
Laertes: Come, my lord.   [*They play.*]
Hamlet: One.
Laertes: No.
Hamlet: Judgment.
Osric: A hit, a very palpable hit.
Laertes: Well; again.
King: Stay; give me drink. Hamlet, this pearl is thine;
  Here's to thy health.
          [*Trumpets sound; and cannons shot off within.*]
  Give him the cup.   275
Hamlet: I'll play this bout first; set it by awhile.
  Come. [*They play.*] Another hit; what say you?
Laertes: A touch, a touch, I do confess.
King: Our son shall win.
Queen: He's fat, and scant of breath.
  Here, Hamlet, take my napkin, rub thy brows: 280
  The queen carouses to thy fortune, Hamlet.

291   *you make a wanton of me:* you are not taking me seriously

297   *They bleed on both sides!:* They have both been wounded.

299   *as a woodcock to mine own springe:* like a bird caught in
        my own trap

301   *swounds:* faints

310   *practice:* scheme

Hamlet: Good, madam!
King: Gertrude, do not drink.
Queen: I will, my lord; I pray you pardon me.
King [Aside]: It is the poison'd cup: it is too late.
Hamlet: I dare not drink yet, madam; by and by. 285
Queen: Come, let me wipe thy face.
Laertes: My lord, I'll hit him now.
King: I do not think't.
Laertes [Aside]: And yet it is almost against my conscience.
Hamlet: Come, for the third, Laertes: you but dally;
 I pray you, pass with your best violence; 290
 I am afeard you make a wanton of me.
Laertes: Say you so? come on.   *[They play.]*
Osric: Nothing, neither way.
Laertes: Have at you now.
   [Laertes wounds Hamlet; then, in scuffling, they change
      rapiers, and Hamlet wounds Laertes.]
King: Part them; they are incensed. 295
Hamlet: Nay, come again.   *[The Queen falls.]*
Osric: Look to the queen there, ho!
Horatio: They bleed on both sides! How is it, my lord?
Osric: How is't Laertes?
Laertes: Why, as a woodcock to mine own springe, Osric:
 I am justly kill'd with mine own treachery. 300
Hamlet: How does the queen?
King: She swounds to see them bleed.
Queen: No, no, the drink, the drink!—O my dear
 Hamlet!—
 The drink, the drink! I am poison'd! *[Dies.]*
Hamlet: O villainy! Ho! let the door be lock'd:
 Treachery! seek it out. *[Laertes falls.]* 305
Laertes: It is here, Hamlet: Hamlet, thou art slain:
 No medicine in the world can do thee good,
 In thee there is not half an hour of life;
 The treacherous instrument is in thy hand,
 Unbated and envenom'd: the foul practice 310
 Hath turn'd itself on me; lo, here I lie,
 Never to rise again: thy mother's poison'd:
 I can no more: the king, the king's to blame.
Hamlet: The point envenom'd too!

319   *union:* a pun. Hamlet is referring to the pearl Claudius put in the cup and to the fact that now Claudius will join Gertrude in death.

321   *temper'd:* prepared

326   *I am dead:* I am certain to die.

327   *chance:* event

328   *mutes:* actors without speaking parts

329   *fell:* cruel; *sergeant:* Death is personified as an officer summoning Hamlet into his custody.

332-333 *report . . . unsatisfied:* Clear my name with those who do not understand why I behaved as I did.

334   *I am more . . . Dane:* Famous Romans committed suicide instead of accepting defeat.

340   *Absent thee from felicity awhile:* Forgo that happiness for a while.

346   *o'ercrows:* triumphs over (as a cock crows in triumph)

Then, venom, to thy work.   [*Stabs the King.*] 315
All: Treason! treason!
King: O, yet defend me, friends: I am but hurt.
Hamlet: Here, thou incestuous, murderous, damned
    Dane, Drink off this potion. Is thy union here?
    Follow my mother.   [*King dies.*]
Laertes: He is justly served;   320
    It is a poison temper'd by himself.
    Exchange forgiveness with me, noble Hamlet:
    Mine and my father's death come not upon thee.
    Nor thine on me!   [*Dies.*]
Hamlet: Heaven make thee free of it! I follow thee.   325
    I am dead, Horatio. Wretched queen, adieu!
    You that look pale and tremble at this chance,
    That are but mutes or audience to this act,
    Had I but time—as this fell sergeant, death,
    Is strict in his arrest—O, I could tell you,—   330
    But let it be. Horatio, I am dead;
    Thou livest; report me and my cause aright
    To the unsatisfied.
Horatio: Never believe it:
    I am more an antique Roman than a Dane:
    Here's yet some liquor left.
Hamlet: As thou'rt a man,   335
    Give me the cup: let go; by heaven I'll have it.
    O good Horatio, what a wounded name,
    Things standing thus unknown, shall live behind me!
    If thou didst ever hold me in thy heart,
    Absent thee from felicity a while,   340
    And in this harsh world draw thy breath in pain,
    To tell my story.   [*March afar off, and shot without.*]
              What warlike noise is this?

Osric: Young Fortinbras, with conquest come from
    Poland,
    To the ambassadors of England gives
    This warlike volley.
Hamlet: O, I die, Horatio;   345
    The potent poison quite o'ercrows my spirit;
    I cannot live to hear the news from England;

348-349   *the election lights . . . voice:* Hamlet gives his approval to Fortinbras as Denmark's new king.

350-351   *the occurrents . . . solicited:* The events, great and small, that have led to this moment.

357   *This quarry cries on havoc:* This pile of dead bodies indicates a terrible slaughter.

357-360   *O proud . . . struck?:* Once again, death is personified. Here, death is compared to a hunter who will devour his prey (quarry).

358   *What feast . . . cell:* What feast is being prepared in the grave?

360   *dismal:* dreadful

365   *his:* Claudius'

368   *jump upon this bloody question:* at the precise moment of this bloody event

374   *carnal, bloody, and unnatural acts:* Claudius' sins

375   *accidental judgments:* Ophelia's death, and perhaps Gertrude's as well; *casual slaughters:* the murder of Polonius

376   *deaths put on by cunning:* Rosencrantz and Guildenstern's deaths, and perhaps Hamlet's death too

377-378   *purposes . . . heads:* the deaths of Laertes and Claudius

379   *deliver:* report

But I do prophesy the election lights
On Fortinbras; he has my dying voice;
So tell him, with the occurrents, more and less,   350
Which have solicited. The rest is silence.   [*Dies.*]
Horatio: Now cracks a noble heart. Good night, sweet
     prince,
And flights of angels sing thee to thy rest!

[*March within.*]

Why does the drum come hither?

[*Enter Fortinbras, the English Ambassadors and others.*]

Fortinbras: Where is this sight?
Horatio: What is it ye would see?   355
If aught of woe or wonder, cease your search.
Fortinbras: This quarry cries on havoc. O proud death,
What feast is toward in thine eternal cell,
That thou so many princes at a shot
So bloodily hast struck?
First Ambassador: The sight is dismal;   360
And our affairs from England come too late:
The ears are senseless that should give us hearing,
To tell him, his commandment is fulfill'd,
That Rosencrantz and Guildenstern are dead:
Where should we have our thanks?
Horatio: Not from his mouth 365
Had it the ability of life to thank you:
He never gave commandment for their death.
But since, so jump upon this bloody question,
You from the Polack wars, and you from England,
Are here arrived, give order that these bodies   370
High on a stage be placed to the view;
And let me speak, to the yet unknowing world
How these things came about: so shall you hear
Of carnal, bloody, and unnatural acts,
Of accidental judgments, casual slaughters,   375
Of deaths put on by cunning and forced cause,
And, in this upshot, purposes mistook
Fall'n on the inventors' heads: all this can I
Truly deliver.
Fortinbras: Let us haste to hear it,

And call the noblest to the audience.   380
For me, with sorrow I embrace my fortune;
I have some rights of memory in this kingdom,
Which now to claim my vantage doth invite me.
Horatio: Of that I shall have also cause to speak,
And from his mouth whose voice will draw on more: 385
But let this same be presently perform'd.
Even while men's minds are wild; lest more mischance
On plots and errors happen.
Fortinbras: Let four captains
Bear Hamlet, like a soldier, to the stage;
For he was likely, had he been put on,   390
To have proved most royally: and, for his passage,
The soldiers' music and the rites of war
Speak loudly for him.
Take up the bodies: such a sight as this
Becomes the field, but here shows much amiss.   395
Go, bid the soldiers shoot.

> [*A dead march. Exeunt, bearing off the bodies: after
> which a peal of ordnance is shot off.*]

Act 5, Scene 2: Activities

1. Do you think Rosencrantz and Guildenstern deserved to be put to death? In groups, discuss what alternative actions Hamlet might have taken. Examine Hamlet's reasoning (lines 57 – 62) and consider whether you think Hamlet was seeking justice or revenge.

2. Satire is the use of ridicule, sarcasm and irony to expose and make fun of people's foolishness and hypocrisy. The character of Osric is a satire of behaviour popular among members of the upper class in Shakespeare's time. In a production of Hamlet in modern dress, how would Osric be dressed? How would he talk? Name some similar character types in TV situation comedies.

3. In the role of Hamlet, who has already experienced a premonition of death (line 203), write a letter to your mother, expressing your final thoughts to her.

4. Throughout most of the play, Hamlet has seemed unwilling to do what he knows he must do. It is only in this final scene that Hamlet seems fully willing to accept his destiny (see lines 211 – 215). What do you think has caused this change in Hamlet? Write your ideas and share them with a partner.

5. Personification is a figure of speech in which a thing or an idea is represented as a person or as having human characteristics. In this scene, death is personified twice—first as a police officer by Hamlet (line 329), and then as a hunter by Fortinbras (lines 357 – 359). In groups, discuss why you think death is pictured as having these two particular occupations. What other jobs could death, as a person, perform? Choose one of the group's suggestions and draw a picture of death doing that job. You might choose to put together images cut from magazines and newspapers to represent death in that role.

6. Suppose that you are Fortinbras, taking over the kingdom of Denmark. Write a list of things you will do to restore order and win the confidence of the Danish people.

7. Just before Hamlet dies, he says to Horatio,

> If thou didst ever hold me in thy heart,
> Absent thee from felicity a while,
> And in this harsh world draw thy breath in pain,
> To tell my story. (Act 5, Scene 2, lines 339 – 342)

In about two hundred words, write a letter from Horatio to Hamlet's friends in Wittenberg, with the aim of helping them understand the shocking news of their friend Hamlet's death.

8. *Make a video*
In groups, design a video that expresses your feelings about Hamlet in this scene. You may choose to shoot one continuous segment of the scene (for example, Hamlet's account of what happened at sea, the sword fight between Hamlet and Laertes, or the death of Hamlet), or you may choose to shoot brief excerpts from several points in the scene. Decide how you want to portray Hamlet—what qualities you want to emphasize, what mood you want to create, what response you want to evoke in your audience. Rehearse your material and prepare a video script. Be sure to consider camera angles, distance, length of shots, lighting, sound effects and music. Show your video to your classmates. Have you made them feel the same way about Hamlet as you do?

Consider the Whole Play

1. Choosing three characters who die during the course of the play, write a monologue that each might deliver if they could come back from the dead. The characters should reflect on their lives, the manner of their deaths, and they should confess or reveal things that were not known during their lives (this could include things they did not realize themselves while they were still living). Present your monologues live or on videotape to your class.

2. Hamlet pretends to be insane for much of this play. It is even possible that he does lose his reason for a while. He also contemplates suicide on two different occasions. Ophelia, however, does go truly mad, and, as a result, she dies. If you were a member of the court who was an advisor to both Hamlet and Ophelia, how would your advice to Ophelia have differed from the advice you gave Hamlet? At what point would you have spoken to Hamlet? to Ophelia?

3. Prepare a radio news report (about four minutes long) covering the coronation of Fortinbras. Your report should include:
   - a description of the location
   - a description of the crowd—its size and its mood
   - an account of Fortinbras' background and personal qualities
   - highlights of Fortinbras' coronation speech (and the crowd's response)
   - a summary of the events in Elsinore, starting with the death of old King Hamlet, that led to Fortinbras' accession to the throne
   - a closing comment on the future of Denmark.

   Tape your report. If desired, include sound effects and excerpts from on-the-spot interviews or from Fortinbras' speech, but do not let these elements break up the flow of your report. Since you do not have much time in which to deliver your information, concentrate on being concise and on organizing the material so that it is easy to follow. You may wish to listen to some radio news reports as you plan your own report.

4. Actors often appear on television talk shows to attract a wider audience for a new play or film. Stage this type of talk show interview with one or two actors who will be playing major roles in an upcoming production of *Hamlet*. Your purpose is to arouse the interest of people who are not familiar with the play and who might shy away from a Shakespearean production. Videotape this interview for the class.

5. As an actress, you must choose to audition for the role of either Gertrude or Ophelia. As an actor, you must choose between the roles of Claudius, Polonius, Laertes and Horatio. Which role would you choose? Write a letter to the director, giving your concept of the character and telling why you would suit the role.

6. Design a program for a production of *Hamlet*. The program must provide all the information the audience need to prepare them for the play. The program must also be visually interesting—it should make use of graphic design and, possibly, illustrations. Furthermore, the program should emphasize the unique features of the particular production. Make a display of your finished programs.

7. Present Hamlet's complex mind as a collage. Demonstrate your own understanding of his character by your choice and positioning of images. (You might prefer to make a line drawing of Hamlet's mind map instead.)

8. Prepare a talk for the class about how women are presented in this play. From reviews of past productions of *Hamlet* in the library, find out about different ways these female roles have been interpreted. Make some suggestions about how the interpretation of Ophelia's and Gertrude's characters could be updated to be more in tune with women's roles today.

9. Disease and garden imagery appear often in *Hamlet*. Choose important images in the play and create a portfolio of drawings to accompany them. Your drawings should reflect your interpretation of the images. (Studies of imagery in *Hamlet* are available in the library.)

10. For the first half of the play, Hamlet seems to have the upper hand. Eventually, however, things turn against him. In groups, decide at what point you think Hamlet loses control of the situation. Is there something that Hamlet does or fails to do that tips the balance against him? What aspects of his character do you think make him behave this way? Compare your conclusions with those of other groups.

11. Using resource materials about Elizabethan England, investigate what Elizabethans in Shakespeare's time thought about the human mind and emotions. Research the theory of the elements and the theory of humours, as well as ideas about melancholy and insanity. Consult with your teacher as you do your research. Comment on the character of Hamlet in light of your discoveries. Present your ideas either in an essay or as a report to your class. Keep your notes and drafts in a separate folder.

12. Hamlet's advice to the players in Act 3, Scene 2 is a good starting point for investigating styles of acting in Elizabethan times. Using books about theatre history or the acting history of Shakespeare's plays, prepare a survey of different acting styles during Shakespeare's time. You might prefer to study the way different famous actors have interpreted Hamlet's character's during different eras. As you do your research, discuss your work with your teacher. Keep all your notes and rough drafts in a separate folder. Present your survey in an essay, a chart, or in an audio-visual format at the end of the time period specified for this activity.

13. You may have heard someone described as a "Renaissance man." With the help of your teacher and librarian, find out what the ideal man of the Renaissance would have been like. Then consider the following:
    • Do you think Hamlet fits the description of a Renaissance man?
    • How would you describe the ideal man or woman of our society? Do you think our values are very similar to those of the Renaissance?
    • Would Hamlet fit into our modern society?

    Explain your conclusions in an essay.

14. In groups, prepare a videotape or slide show which would preview *Hamlet* for next year's students. You should introduce the main characters and describe the plot (after deciding whether to tell the whole story or leave your audience in suspense). Explain briefly what you think is the significance of the play. This material could be read by a narrator as a voice-over on the videotape or as an accompaniment to the slides. Select a number of key incidents in the play and either video-tape performances of them or photograph moments in the action for a slide show. You could also choose background music that would tie all of these elements together. Your finished production should be about fifteen minutes long.